MY SIX CONVICTS

A psychologist's three years in Fort Leavenworth

MY SIX

A psychologist's three

CONVICTS

years in Fort Leavenworth

Donald Powell Wilson

RINEHART & COMPANY, Inc.

NEW YORK • TORONTO

Grateful acknowledgment is made to Thomas Y. Crowell Company for permission to reprint excerpts from *Criminology* by Ruth Shonle Cavan, Copyright, 1948 by Thomas Y. Crowell.

Grateful acknowledgment is also made to Prentice-Hall, Inc. for permission to reprint an excerpt from *New Horizons in Criminology* by Harry Elmer Barnes and Negley K. Teeters, Copyright, 1943, 1945 by Prentice-Hall, Inc., New York.

To co-authors and collaborators, without whom most books would not have been written—especially this one.

The first prison I ever saw had inscribed on it "Cease to Do Evil: Learn to Do Well"; but as the inscription was on the outside, the prisoners could not read it.

George Bernard Shaw

PREFACE

Recent events and the passage of time now make it possible to relate the human story that enlivened my research in drug addiction and criminality at Fort Leavenworth Penitentiary.

Out of deference to my administrators and colleagues whom I held in great respect, and to the prisoners themselves, six of whom comprised my regular staff of assistants, I have indulged literary license in the use of names, places and dates, and in the development of some of the episodes recorded. The dialogue passages do not represent total recall. While some of the conversations were of such a nature as to remain indelibly in my mind, in other instances I have attempted simply to recapture the mood and content of what was said as accurately as my memory—and decorum—allow.

This book is not a record of the research project. It is rather a reminiscent impression of the humors, whimsies and tragedies of my six convict assistants—my world as they saw it and their world as I saw it. Embarrassingly clever, they could have given me no end of trouble. Instead they bore me a real affection and did me a great service, which I now acknowledge in the writing of this book.

D. P. W.

MY SIX CONVICTS

A psychologist's three years in Fort Leavenworth

1

I WAS a professor of psychology when I reported for duty at Fort Leavenworth Penitentiary one fall day in the early thirties. I was a psychology professor when I left the penitentiary three years later, but not the same. Not at all the same.

When I arrived at the quiet little town of Leavenworth that morning in September, it was nine o'clock. The telegram in my pocket with the Washington date line instructed me to report at ten o'clock. An hour at the end of a thousand mile nonstop trip was cutting it pretty close.

So I took little notice that morning of the historic town that boasted the presence of Abraham Lincoln and General Sherman in its past; nor of colorful old Fort Leavenworth which flourished now in its outskirts as a tidy Army Post. Both time and inclination carried me quickly through them. I had a destination and a deadline. I drove on to where, at the edge of the Post, deeper into the self-effacing, protesting Kansas countryside pushing a promontory of the Missouri River, I came in view of the rocky shape which had drawn me abruptly out of my way of life.

Its wall rose unnaturally out of the friendly earth like a forbidding hand thrown up before the two thousand offenders behind it. From a distance I guessed it must have been two stories high across the front, and higher than that at points where the terrain dropped. It was gray and faceless.

It did not look much like the university campus I had just

left, whose buildings were shaking now with the promise and future of young life. A penitentiary, wherever it is found, looks like nothing in the world so much as a penitentiary. It is always a cold stoneheap from which every mark of normal life has been erased, a formidable mass of moral rectitude.

Nevertheless it was my destination and there was that deadline. My excitement mounted as I swung down the road to the point where it terminated in a broad angle in front of the penitentiary.

I was stopped first at the sentry box a good two hundred feet in front of the gate. It could have been a ticket box at the entrance to a county fair grounds, with a pleasant expanse of grass around it, except for the riot guns and mounted machine guns which commanded a full sweep of a circle around the box; and the guard who approached my car carried a rifle on his shoulder and sidearms on his hip.

He looked impressive in the blue uniform and cap of a Federal guard. He in no way encouraged small talk. He checked me out to the guard station at the main gate where I again stated my business, this time showing my papers. The guard gave them only a casual glance and phoned the warden's office, from where a uniformed assistant was detailed to escort me to the warden.

Nobody feels entirely innocent the first time he approaches a penitentiary, no matter what brings him there. I did not as I waited surrounded by so much law and order implemented by so much steel and concrete, while the assistant scanned my papers. But he apparently found everything in order, and we went through the inside gate opening on the courtyard, after a guard had unlocked it with a theatrical-looking key. He locked it noisily after us, and we were inside. We started across the corner of the courtyard to the warden's offices in a building which rose about the main gate wall.

It was then I noticed that the guns in three wall turrets were trained on me.

4

I knew they were on my side, but they seemed rather histrionic. I was a mild man. I hardly constituted a threat to anyone on the inside. No one could have "had" less on the inmates of a penitentiary than I. I was a man of peaceful intent, responding to a convergence of forces whose design in bringing me here both attracted and repelled me.

The warden's reception room was bare, perhaps traditionally so. No Nonsense Here, said the plain quarters, Crime Doesn't Pay in this office. The windows were barred, the fixtures steel, the walls and furniture battleship gray. The only pictures on the walls were a series of unsmiling staff photographs methodically nailed up side by side every few years.

As it turned out I had ample opportunity to cool my heels after my hurried trip. I waited over an hour for the warden, long enough to reflect with diminishing enthusiasm upon the urgent note of the telegram and the confusion it had created of my *status quo*.

I had been appointed to this unnatural world that summer by the United States Public Health Service to conduct a unit of research in the relationship between drug addiction and criminality in the new research hospital at Fort Leavenworth Penitentiary. I never quite understood the chain of events that led to my appointment. I had helped establish some psychological clinics and had delivered an unconscionable number of lectures in the past few years, but so had many other psychologists. And I had hardly had a penitentiary in view.

The Surgeon General's correspondence stated that I would be "duly notified" when to report to work, but I was totally unprepared for the telegram which followed a few weeks later. It gave me the usual forty-eight hours in which to terminate my professional activities and my consultation practice and travel half way across the country to Leavenworth. In response to my appeal to Washington I was allowed a few days' grace. But I still had to break up several years of living in a few hours and drive day and night to meet what I jokingly referred to as "a national crisis in narcotics." As I sat waiting I was relieved that an hour one way or the other was not serious in the crisis. . . .

In due time I was shown into the presence of the warden, sitting stiffly at a black metal desk, with my papers before him.

"Well, Wilson," he began in a quarterdeck voice that almost brought me out of my chair, "I've read your papers."

"Yes, sir?"

"And I must say that in spite of that telegram I didn't know you were coming. In fact—I didn't know about your appointment."

"You *didn't?*"

"Surprised?" He smiled. "You're in the army now, Doctor. Red tape. Your orders will be along in a few days, probably."

"Yes, probably." That took care of the national crisis. I relaxed.

"However," he went on in the same voice, "what I do or don't know about you isn't too important. In these circumstances you and I won't have much to do with each other. I'm only nominally your boss here. Your superior is Doctor Stevens, the chief medical officer."

That was logical, of course; but not nearly so logical as what he next pointed out. He had a very pertinent reason for saying hello and good-bye in the same breath.

"You see, Wilson, I'm a symbol of the Law to these convicts. Since that's what they're out to beat, you know how they feel about me. So the less you and I have to do with each other, the better your chances are of getting on with the men. I'm the Big Stick to them. I've got to maintain a certain authority among them. If they don't respect it, I have to do something about it. You're different. You're the Soft Voice, and you've got to have their good will to do your work. That's something you can't command, you've got to win it. And sometimes it isn't easy!"

He was a big graying blond Swede of sixty-five or so, full of

6

facts which he projected into this quarterdeck voice. I soon realized the noise was more a part of his job than his nature, an occupational front behind which a frequently bewildered, frustrated human being moved in a hard world.

He was an old school man by training, coming up through policeman's beat to guard, captain, warden's assistant. But he had kept an open mind through the years, and was proud that he had been given the Fort Leavenworth wardenship under the Federal penal reforms of 1930. Psychology and penology had joined hands for the first time in American history only within the past few years, and I was enormously relieved to find the warden giving more than lip service to the philosophy of the reform: rehabilitation instead of revenge.

I was amazed at his candor when he said: "I'm frank to say that after forty years of penitentiary work I still don't know much about the insides of a criminal. What's more, I'm suspicious of any cop who says he does. It's not much of a step from cop to con sometimes, you know."

My papers gave no indication of how the United States Public Health Service wanted me to proceed with my drug research, but he assured me he would give me what help and backing he could.

"There are a lot of new ideas about dope and crime these days—a lot of new ideas about criminals. I hope you can make some of them work. The old system says, Be firm. If that doesn't work, Get tough. If that doesn't work—" he shrugged.

When he, with his forty years of penitentiary experience, asked me how I meant to start my work, I felt a little like a flushed and dizzy high school valedictorian who is asked after graduating exercises, "And what do you plan to do *now?*" I didn't quite know. I said something about waiting until I knew my way around the place, doing something innocuous in the meantime, like some correlative studies between addicts and non-users. I named a battery of tests I would use: intelligence, per-

7

sonality, aptitude, the Rorschach Psychodiagnostic, the Willaughby Emotional Maturity Scale—

He raised his hand. "Never mind that! You go ahead and give your tests—I'll feed you the men."

He suggested that I begin the testing program with new prisoners as they arrived daily, and that I see them before he did. There would be less resistance if they didn't come from him to me. When they were admitted they would be deloused, scrubbed, photographed, fingerprinted, given a number, and a physical examination. Then they would be all mine. That sounded good and very decent.

"Now," he leaned intently over his desk toward me, "you have complete immunity professionally, of course. Otherwise the men would 'dummy up' on you."

Professional immunity meant in my case exactly what it meant in the case of chaplains and doctors, I was told: I was not expected to report anything irregular to the administration. It was not only unwise, it was *verboten*. I was not to be a stool pigeon unless I aspired to be a clay pigeon. To my surprise he said he did not use either convict or civilian stool pigeons. That kind of vision among wardens was a conspicuous statistical rarity.

"You know what happens to stool pigeons?" he asked.

"Yes, sir."

"Remember it!"

He admitted readily that if I were successful in getting next to the men I would hear things he would give his right arm to know.

"You may get wind of an impending break. Fine—just take care of your own neck. Maybe they're smuggling in hacksaws and machine guns, bribing a guard, masturbating in the warehouse. Maybe they're building an arsenal in the power house—we don't want to hear it from you. That's the captain's and my job. Is that clear?"

"Yes, sir!"

8

"Good. That's the only way we can keep you *alive,* not to mention working. The cons have got to believe you won't spill, or they won't spill and you won't learn anything about criminals. These cons have weird ideas of psychiatrists and psychologists, lots of suspicion and resistance about being 'bugged.' "

Then he asked me a question I had been expecting. "Have you ever worked with convicts before?"

I did not want to impose on his forbearance, so I didn't mention my occasional cases in jail and the youngsters in reform schools. I just said, "No, sir."

He smiled patiently. "At least you won't have any bad habits to unlearn. But watch the crackpot stuff. The boys will know it, and they'll get you. If they don't, I will. We want them to have a chance. And no blunders, Doctor. If you blunder in this place, only God can help you, I can't. Any questions?"

"Yes, sir—about a staff," I said. "I'll need some assistants."

The warden looked hard at me. "You have two thousand men to choose from," he said.

A convict staff! It had not occurred to me.

"And you better not make any mistakes there. What I mean is, you better be a bright guy, or you may be a dead one."

The warden detailed a guard to escort me to the captain's headquarters in the cell block which spread four hundred feet wide across the other end of the yard. Here I was to be finger-printed and photographed.

The captain's waiting room reminded me of the Third Precinct Police Station back home. It was big and barnlike, with a fifteen-foot ceiling from which four grueling light bulbs blazed at the end of four long chains. The room was full of yellow oak desks and benches, worn spittoons, old smoke, and convicts still smelling faintly of creosote. Like me, they were to be photographed and fingerprinted.

The captain being momentarily busy, his sergeant sent me with an orderly directly to the studio, which opened off the captain's record room. Out of a dark stall seven-by-nine, from the warped diaphragm of a convict-operated camera came a daily lode of opaque and lifeless photographs which served to identify —and intimidate—the subjects for the rest of their lives. They were enough to make one give up crime. Into this chamber I was led to face the candor of the lens.

And there I met Connie.

He was not in sight when we walked in.

"Hey, Connie—you got you some Brass!" And without looking at me, my orderly shuffled away.

From the next room a high tenor voice with more volume than resonance directed me to "Set down on that there stool." I obeyed, and the room lights went out.

As I sat impaled by the ghoulish headlights that Connie turned on me, my eyes began to follow his long blue denim behind the camera, flailing about in an orgy of motions. I could see little of him except his eyes, which occasionally loomed out of the black at me, and his large and mobile Adam's apple. Three years of close range observation did not dampen my admiration of that barometric organ of Connie's. Whatever his moods, they registered instantly upon his excitable larynx.

There were few laryngeal spasms that day, however. To Connie I was just some more dumb Brass. I knew exactly where his tongue was when he went through the charade of getting my picture. There was much moving of camera, minute attention to the contour of my head about which there had never been any question before in my life, much pursing of lips over precise measurements on a color meter for a black-and-white print. My interest was not in what he was doing, but in what he was saying as he worked. He had set me up to his satisfaction, and I was staring obediently into the eye of the camera, when he spoke into the darkness.

"You shouldda came by train, Doc. You didn't save yourself no time."

I may have started, but I kept on looking into the camera.

He ducked behind his sights. "You see Paducah, Kentucky on any o' them Highway 50 signs? I got sent up from Paducah onc't. Some jernt."

Highway 50 had been my route, all right!

"Hold it—"

I tried.

He stepped out and dropped the plate into the camera. "Last *psycho* we had here stayed six months. You sure got yourself some job!"

And quite in line with my thoughts he turned another floodlight on me. I blinked, and heard the click of the shutter.

"Okay, Doc!"

He turned on the room lights, and I took my first good look at the man who had just given me the recognition I had expected from the warden. What went on, that even a convict beat him to the news of my arrival? Under my curious eye Connie turned an ambivalent look on me which I soon found to be his constant expression. Can a man look both innocent and guilty? Connie came as near as anyone can to lending credibility to the illusion.

He was tall and rangy, fair-haired and slightly florid, perhaps forty. His exophthalmic eyes were blue. A small shred of toilet paper clung to his Adam's apple, covering what was probably a slip of his razor that morning. It bobbed as he spoke.

"Your print'll be right up, Doc. Takes no time at all for a perfect likeness!" And with a quick smile he ducked into his darkroom again.

His last words had particular point when I turned to an exhibit of his portraits on the wall of the studio. It was incredible that a device as simple and perfect as a lens and shutter could produce such mechanical atrocities. When I met the face of the warden in one of them, I guessed the exhibit was of the civilian

11

staff. In the right corner of each picture, scratched on the negative, was a blurred number, unmistakably a facsimile of the plates the convicts bore on their denims. The warden's picture was framed in a thin band of black, and beneath his and the captain's photographs, printed in a kindergartner's wobble, were the legends: "Our Warden" and "Our Captain." The warden's unrelenting frown was straight off the brow of Hosea the Prophet, and the captain had been caught in a sorrowful startle. *That,* I thought, could well be the *motif* of a conscientious prison captain. I laughed aloud.

I was still chuckling when the captain came out of his office and joined me.

He gave me his hand. "The warden just called me about you. Welcome to our happy little bivouac!"

He was a sturdy fifty, about my height, but I had the feeling that a small mountain had moved into my path. It was an ocular impossibility to miss his round belly across which the coat of his uniform met only fortuitously. It was also impossible to miss his native good cheer.

He pointed to the photographs, his blue eyes full of reproach.

"He asked us to sit for those damn things," he said accusingly. "He thinks they're wonderful. Y'know, I think he does this kind of thing on purpose, just to watch us squirm. What can you do with a man like that? And he calls himself a photographer!"

He's a photographer, all right, I thought.

Connie's long arm reaching out from behind me was the first knowledge the captain or I had that he had joined us. He moved as silently as an Indian. He was holding out my photograph still wet and dripping. With a quick glance at the captain he clipped it at the end of the row of staff members on the wall. I took a casual look, then a delighted one. My likeness was there, but not my prized expression of Olympian objectivity. I looked like the mask of a dead monk.

"It's wonderful!" I said.

The captain looked from the picture to me with precisely the startle Connie had caught in his photograph. Connie was watching me delightedly.

"Well—I mean it's the professorial look," I said. "I ought to know—I've seen enough of them!"

Connie's chest swelled and the approving gleam in his eye as he looked at me was unmistakable.

Seeing it, the captain sent Connie back to work and took me into his office.

His first question was, did Connie know who I was yet? I replied by asking him what did he mean *yet*? So far, I said, Connie had been the only man in the penitentiary who had expected me. What kind of scuttlebutt was this?

"The grapevine, Doctor, and you'll be hearing more of it." He sighed. "We think," he said, "the FBI uses it as a model of speed and secrecy. At least we think it should. It's really *very* generous the way the grapevine gives the administration a five-to-one handicap! Well—at least Connie liked you. And that's a happy coincidence around here, especially if you find yourself working with him."

Something in the way he was looking at me alarmed me. "*Who's* going to work with him?"

His speculation gave way to amusement. "Well, Mister Psychologist, you should have thought before you laughed at his pictures!"

"I'll watch myself!" I said. "But what makes you think he wants to work for me?"

"It was that look in his eye when you laughed at your photograph. He took quite a shine to you. He'll do something outrageous now, so that I'll be obliged to fire him."

The men, he said, wouldn't think of asking outright for a new job. They did everything the hard way. They would first foul things up so that they would be discharged. Then they would ask for a transfer to a new spot that looked like "an easy go." But not till they had been fired. That was a mark of distinction to them.

"Much as I admire his photography," I said, "I don't think Connie's my man, Captain."

That, he assured me, was a natural conclusion! Connie was a small-time criminal, a sideshow barker, a second-story man, a safe-cracker. He was in for robbery on a six-year sentence. He had served time in Sing Sing, Joliet, San Quentin and Atlanta. After several unsuccessful attempts to assimilate his exotic personality, the captain had given him the job of shooting and printing the new convicts as they arrived daily at the penitentiary. In five minutes Connie would know who their bosses were, what their sentences were, and whether they could be useful to him in his endless games in the penitentiary. He was always in and behind everything that happened, but he never knew "nothin' about nothin'."

I shook my head. He didn't sound like research temperament to me.

"Well, what would you like?" asked the captain. "Something a little more stable? You forget we don't specialize in stability around here. Besides," he chuckled, "I can't honestly say I'd be sorry to see him go. I only brought him into my office so I could keep my eye on him."

"Well, you better not count your chickens, Captain."

He shrugged. "Well, I will say that when Connie likes a man there's nothing he won't do for him."

What had the warden said? *You better not make any mistakes there.* The captain's look plainly said that I could do worse than Connie, much worse. And he ought to know.

"However—" he went on, "I wouldn't want you under any false notions. Connie may act like a clown a lot of the time, but odd things have been known to happen to people who cross him."

14

Then he added: "I don't know whether he does his own dirty work or whether he has it done. But it gets done, sir. And sometimes it's plenty dirty."

On the way from the cell block to the hospital with an orderly, I took a better look at the courtyard. Being an orderly-minded, habit-ridden professor, I had looked up some aerial photographs of the prison grounds in the library on campus. As I glanced around now, I tried to orient what I was seeing with the photographs. The laundry and dry cleaning shops were on my right, the shoe and brush factories across the yard. Behind the cell block, the power house and ice factory. Along the back wall, the warehouse, garage and machine shop, the railroad terminal. Over the back wall, the ball field. Far to the left across the river, the prison farm. And straight ahead on my right, the elegant little hospital. It was like a small homogeneous community.

Not quite. None of the buildings had exits and all of the windows were barred.

This was true even of the hospital. It conformed less than any of the buildings to the popular concept of prison architecture. Its brick was a rich deep red, the trim around the windows and doors was gray granite. It alone of all the buildings had its flat face broken by a porch. But recessed in its window frames were bars of toolproof steel. And across the entrance through which we now passed on our way to the chief medical officer's suite was a gate with a guard.

Inside, as we turned in the wide hall and went to the first door on the left, I crossed my fingers, wondering about that predecessor who had left at the end of six months.

In the chief's correct walnut-appointed reception room an administrative assistant took me over. He was very administrative. We shook hands, he relieved me of my papers and seated me on a bench under a large colored photograph of the *USS Missouri* which reminded me that as a USPHS appointee I would

15

soon be in a Navy uniform. Then he excused himself to summon the Assistant CMO.

I was looking up at the prow of the *Missouri* when I heard my name.

"Hello, Wilson."

On the other side of a counter was a big broad bulk of a man with unmanageable brown hair, an intense face and restless dark eyes, who was extending his hand to me.

"Name's Gordon." His handshake was cordial. "Sorry about your reception—" He patted the pockets of his white hospital coat. Not finding what he wanted, he reached into the pocket of the assistant's blue coat and extracted a cigarette which the assistant lighted for him as though he had done it before and expected to do it again. "Apparently no one knew you were coming."

"You should have consulted Connie," I said facetiously.

He raised his brows, then said: "I don't know why *I* show surprise—the cons run the joint, Wilson. How'd you fare with Connie?"

"Too well for my own good,.the captain said."

He laughed.

We went into his office, a light pleasant room in a mild state of disarray, like the man who worked in it, who at the moment was making an effort to look like an executive. My papers were on his desk.

"Awkward our not being notified when you were coming. Comes of not having the grapevine on our side. I remember the chief saying we'd have a psychologist some day, but whether it would be this year or next—? You had any experience with cons?"

There was that question again.

"Not in lots of two thousand," I said. "Am I going to be sorry?"

He waived the question with another. "Scared?"

"No. Should I be?"

"You will be. A little honest fear's a good thing around here as long as you don't show it. We've got a few boys who play for keeps. Hard to tell 'em sometimes from the roustabouts who wouldn't kill a house fly. You'll work out your own system of handling the men. No point in giving you a lot of advice. Either you've got what it takes or you haven't. I kid 'em a lot and they seem to like it. I don't have much trouble. The chief keeps 'em in their place, and they seem to like that, too. All depends on the man."

The executive relaxed, slumping into his chair until he was sitting on his lumbar spine.

He was pleased that my work was to be in addiction.

"Looks like you and I might find ourselves working together," he said. "The denarcotization ward is my baby. I'd like to get my teeth into something. By the way," he picked up my train of thought, "sorry the chief's not here today. He was O.D. last night, so he's sleeping in. Quite a guy, Stevens. He shouldn't have the Duty at all. Wouldn't have to lift his hand to hold his job—been with the USPHS for thirty years. But he works like an interne. Hell of a swell fellow. Runs a magnificent little hospital. Regular Prussian about it, but it pays off. He'll see you tomorrow, then we'll square away on some quarters and a staff for you."

He gave me a quick verbal description of the hospital with the pride and affection a good workman has for his shop and his tools.

He made a quick decision. "Take you through it."

It was a four-story structure built in the shape of a broad H, with two arms reaching into the courtyard and two stretching toward the wall. Its two hundred-fifty beds were the responsibility of about twenty regular staff members, exclusive of attendants and nursing care, for which a hundred convicts were kept in training.

It seemed probable that I would be quartered in the half-basement, a floor that was half below and half above ground level. The outside entrance was by way of stairs on either side of the front entrance. My suite would be on the front side of the H, overlooking the courtyard.

In this half-basement, in addition to my wing, were the pharmacy, the laboratory, treatment rooms for venereal disease, the Ear-Nose-Throat man, and admission rooms where the daily responses to Sick Call were given attention.

Three dentists were quartered here also. Their reception rooms were full.

"They're kept hopping," Gordon said, as we moved on. For one thing, an addict usually has poor teeth, and there were a thousand addicts at the penitentiary. The men did not have to be urged to consult a dentist, because a general anesthetic was rarely used. A convict fears anesthesia as he fears the Judgment. He's afraid he will talk when he's out.

"Another thing," Gordon said, "the convicts reason they might as well get their denture plates when they don't have to pay for them. That's their idea of a joke on the Government. Our dentists probably hold a record for extractions."

We stopped briefly to watch a long line of naked men in the hall who were receiving their syphilitic shots: salvarsan in the veins of their forearms and bismuth in the buttocks, the latter injected with wicked-looking three-inch needles. The groans from the gonorrheal ward across the hall were very real. There was little humor in having huge dilators inserted in the urethra to break down adhesions. But the syphilitics bellyached jovially about their injections.

"Hard-a-port there, Doc—hard-a-port! Starboard's already caved in!"

"Look, Doc. Would ya use the right side this time? I'm beginnin' to crawl like a crab!"

Underneath these occasional outbursts was a sustained undertone of bored talk. There were a hundred naked men in the line. The illusion was not one of charm and worldliness. The qualities of shyness and sensitivity were also conspicuously absent.

Both psychology and medicine repudiate the theory that a criminal can be recognized by body type any more than a pianist can. But there is much to be learned about a man's psychological thresholds from his mannerisms and reactions when he is stripped, thrown with a hundred naked men, and put under unusual tension.

I was attached to an army induction center in Los Angeles during a part of World War II, and viewed five hundred naked recruits daily as they passed my desk in the process of their physical and psychological examination. Such circumstances instantly exaggerate any behavior that deviates from normal, and in the case of the army a man with a psychoneurosis can be spared collapse and incapacity. Perhaps a recruit's heart examination will reveal severe palpitation; the laboratory may report this same man's inability to urinate under strain or in the presence of other men; his eye examination may show double vision or slow fusion; the psychologist will probably find that the man has a startle pattern, so that he jumps when a finger is pointed at him. Such a man is not good for the army and the army is not good for him.

Shyness itself is not necessarily an indication of psychoneurosis, of course. There were hale and hearty recruits who held their papers over their genitals all day long, and cowboys who could finally be persuaded to part with their clothes, but not with their hats and boots!

But the hundred naked convicts at whom I was now looking had risen above shyness to a more lofty emotion. They were very proud of having contracted a social disease. It established their sexual precocity. And sexual prowess is not at all typical of criminals; quite the opposite is true. Therefore venereal dis-

19

ease was a distinction. It meant that they had been in contact with a woman; *ergo,* they were "men." It would not occur to these convicts that syphilis proved neither their prowess nor their fertility, but simply their lack of hygiene. Fertility was another fetish with the criminal. The number of impregnations for which he may be responsible in his lifetime in order to keep his mind at rest about his potency is impressive. He wouldn't think of having a sperm test at the cost of five dollars. He does it the hard way.

So there stood the hundred waiting for the last indignity: the needle, right in the seat of their charm. There was little dash left among them, despite their recent philandering. Not even their pride was showing. They looked used up and blowzy.

"Wait until Sunday morning when they're shaved and dressed. You can't tell 'em from a Baptist Men's Sunday School class."

At Gordon's voice some of them turned around. Somewhere among them a sign had been given. The bored talk fell off, the listless motion froze. They were not looking at Gordon, but at me, in an explosive mural of suspicion and animosity. The shift was so sudden that even the doctors, busy with buttocks, craned their necks to see what had happened.

Gordon turned around and walked off, taking me with him. It was clear I was no stranger. It was also clear that everybody wasn't going to take to me as Connie had.

Gordon was absently pounding his pockets again, thinking. "Cigarette?" he asked.

That was the last time in three years that I was without a package. He was a smoker who began every day with his pockets well stocked with cigarettes which he regularly misplaced or gave away during the day. By noon he was bumming off everyone except the convicts, who had a hard time keeping themselves in tobacco and who for the most part smoked government issue cigarettes, for which even Gordon's expert vocabulary couldn't find a word. He finally pulled out a beaten pack from his hip pocket that looked as though it had been sat on for a month.

He lighted up. "Some psychologists haven't gotten along too well in a penitentiary," he began cautiously. He elaborated his statement by saying that they always started off with a big noise, but maybe it was the wrong kind of noise, because they usually ended up working only with the few parolees, giving them a battery of aptitude tests and writing cagey letters of recommendation to someone on the outside who might take a chance and give the convicts a job.

He glanced at me to see how I was taking it.

"A con isn't exactly waiting around for a chance to talk. So you can imagine what he thinks of someone who's 'gonna bug 'em.' They'd take to that like they would to a third degree."

"Maybe," I said, "I should set up a lab and get me some nice friendly white rats."

Gordon grinned. "You'd be surprised what a kind face will do in a place like this."

"Baby Face Pinero has a kind face," I reminded him. "By the way, is he still here?"

Gordon nodded. "Public Enemy Number Four, runs one of the ten largest cities in the country with all the usual rackets, and when the warden's office asked for his occupation, he said, 'Waiter.' Undertaker would have been nearer the truth. I guess he wanted to be near the commissary. He would have made some kind of a racket out of that in three weeks. The warden put him in the machine shop. He's probably turning out sawed-off machine guns by now."

On the second floor of the hospital I got a surprise. Thanks to the 71st Congress, the hospital was equipped with electrotherapy, hydrotherapy and physiotherapy: massage, mechanical exercise, autocondensation current, diathermy, lamps, tubs, baths, packs, nozzle guns, spray guns, steam. Gordon used these freely with his denarcotization patients, with notable success.

In the hydrotherapy ward I noticed two convicts sitting in sitz baths chinning like Park Avenue dowagers. They were not, however, discussing Mrs. Plushbottom's horse. They were commiserating hemorrhoidectomies and swollen prostates. The chattering stopped when we approached. They returned Gordon's greeting, but glared at me and muttered something unintelligible as I passed in doubtful review before them.

In Gordon's denarcotization ward the patients were newcomers, most of them having arrived within the last hundred hours. There was little opportunity for addiction after their arrival at the penitentiary. This would involve smuggling, not a very sure way of getting "the stuff" regularly. At Fort Leavenworth denarcotization was accomplished in an average of six days by immediate withdrawal of the drug. The same procedure was followed whether the addiction was to morphine, opium or heroin. Some of these denarcotization days were rough.

I wondered what would happen if hypnosis were used in that rough period from the second to the fourth day? If the patients were prepared through hypnosis to go through those days quietly, with the post-hypnotic suggestion that during that time they would be able to rest and sleep?

We stopped beside the bed of a wizened little Chinese who could have been a hundred years old from the appearance of his corroded yellow hide. Gordon told me he had been addicted at the age of eleven. He was now somewhere in the hell of the third day of denarcotization. His muscles were twitching, his pupils were dilated. He was sweating in spite of his dehydration. His tongue worked in and out of his dry mouth. Nevertheless he raised his hand in greeting and tried to smile at us. Here, I thought hopefully, is someone who doesn't know who I am. . . .

Gordon signaled an attendant and ordered a warm bath and massage for the stoic little patient who beamed at him, and nodded his thanks in quick bobs of his round bald head.

On the surgical floor Gordon turned to me. "You know,

Wilson, if you could arrange to go out and come in again, this time as a surgeon, you wouldn't meet any resistance. You can appreciate the fact that these shot-up bastards go for a good surgeon. Like our interne, Rodney Fellows. I sometimes think these guys trip on the catwalks deliberately so they can be sewed up by Fellows. They're crazy about him."

"He must be good," I said.

"He's good, all right. But what gets 'em is that he's a very devout Catholic—prays before a mean piece of surgery. These cons are a bunch of heathen, but they like their surgeon to know how to pray. He's an odd guy, but tops."

I asked Gordon how the prisoners felt about research—medical research. I knew how they felt about psychology. He said the anti-vivisection people would get quite a shock if they were around a penitentiary when a medical experiment failed in transition from animals to humans. Their response was a flood of requests, from the lifers especially, to be sacrificed to science.

" 'What the hell—who wants to live forever in this hole?' they say. 'You want me to pay my debt to society? Okay—so let 'em have me!' "

Another explanation of their interest in medical research was that a criminal is always looking for a scapegoat for his crimes.

"They don't like psychologists, but if you could prove there's a screw loose or one missing somewhere that explains their criminality—you're in," said Gordon.

I had one more question.

"You're ahead of me in this penitentiary game. What's your prognosis of a prison psychologist?"

He answered quickly. He didn't know, the field was too new, only a couple of years old. Ask him in ten years.

Then he qualified his words. "No, that's not true. Now or ten years from now, it'll always be how they feel about the particular man. Hell—I'm no psychologist, I don't know. But you can see there's a lot of resistance. And that can knock the hell out of your research. I'd say it's all up to you."

There's the word, I said to myself.

In the hospital dining room we had a late lunch, the best meal I had eaten in five days. Anything would have tasted good after the food I had snatched on my trip out. But apart from that the fare was as good as in any first class hospital outside.

When I left Gordon in his office, I felt sanguine about the next three years. It wouldn't be a picnic, but it would be all right.

I spent a couple of hours alone in the hospital library, checking books and catalogues, ordering collateral material I knew I would need, and left the penitentiary in the late afternoon.

I crossed the yard just before the four o'clock supper, when more prisoners were allowed in the courtyard than at any time in the day. A group of eight or ten convicts gathered around a handsome young Italian were watching me as I approached, and I caught the same verbal cadence I had heard when I had passed the sitz bath dowagers that morning. However, the cadence was louder this time, and the glances of the men were more direct. I was curious—but not so that I couldn't wait. With my eye on the main gate I walked past the young Italian and his satellites.

Suddenly one of them called out distinctly: "Hey, Pinero—ast him somethin'!"

Punch (Baby Face) Pinero, *waiter*. Notorious gangster-racketeer, lady-killer. Also a man killer in a less glamorous sense—with something like forty murders chalked up to him and his goons, as I remembered his case in the newspapers.

I don't know whether my pace quickened or slackened at the name, but I turned back and joined them. Pinero was eyeing me coolly, and nobody spoke.

24

"You the boss around here?" I finally asked him.

He said nothing, just eyed me insolently, with a faint trace of his devastating lady-killer smile.

"I'm curious," I said. "What are the men saying about me? I can't make it out."

I was not aware of movement in the ranks, I was watching my Italian, wondering what he would say. But when I glanced around the group again they had flanked him in a sullen semicircle. His smile broadened, but it didn't warm up.

"They're callin' you Squirrel Guy."

"Squirrel Guy?"

"Yeah. You know—" He tapped his head. "Nut Specialist."

"I see," I said, "the Bug."

I thought I was smiling to myself, but my amusement must have shown on my face because the Italian was staring at me suspiciously, and so were his men. My humor was apparently highly suspect in their minds.

"Well, thanks, men," I said. "Be seeing you."

I had gone only about five paces when one of them said, "Hey, Pinero—ask him is he gonna bug us?" The question was taken up by others in the group.

I turned around. Pinero was watching me with a smile that displayed all his white teeth but little humor.

"You hear the boys?" he asked through his smile. "They want to know are you gonna bug 'em?"

"Well—not all of them," I said, because it was the first thing that came to mind. It sounded stuffy, once it was out.

"Oh, I see! Just some of 'em, huh?" he mocked. "Well, would you mind tellin' us who's the lucky parties, Doc?"

"Well—just those who want to see me, I guess."

A roar of laughter went up from the crowd.

"*Shut up!*" The look on Pinero's face extinguished the laughter as a swift breath extinguishes a candle. Then his face became a mask of sweetness, and he looked around at the men.

"Anybody here wanna be bugged?"

At the moment I hoped there was not.

He turned to me with feigned regret. "Sorry, Doc—you see how it is: no volunteers."

I saw, all right. "Well, thanks anyway, Pinero," I said, "Nice try."

As I turned to go Pinero asked speculatively, "What's your racket, Doc?"

"Racket?"

"Yeah. What's your angle? They all got angles, these Squirrel Guys. Some of 'em ask us to fit square blocks in round holes, some of 'em want us to talk to 'em just like we would to our old mother—what you figger on doin'?"

I wasn't ready for this so soon, I was going to keep one step ahead of them. *I* was going to ask the questions. I would have liked nothing better than to tip my hat, smile ingratiatingly at the speaker and bow out. But of course I couldn't, not if I wanted to bow in again. The possible courses being very few, I quickly convinced myself to play it straight, tell Punch Pinero and the increasing crowd the truth. They would find it out anyway.

So I drew out my letter from the Surgeon General, my telegram, and a copy of my credentials and held them out to Punch. "Here—this will tell you what you want to know."

There was nothing rash about the move; it was only a matter of time until the grapevine made the contents of those papers common knowledge anyway.

Punch hesitated before taking the papers. Then he accepted them, looking hard at me, and the men crowded around while he scanned them in a thick mumble. I was glad he could read. Some of them obviously could not.

When he came to my vital statistics they looked me up and down professionally. Height: five-feet-nine. Weight: one-hundred-sixty. Age: thirty. Eyes: brown. Hair: brown. Race: Caucasian. Etc., etc.

Suddenly a voice rumbled out of a week's whiskers peering over Punch's shoulder.

"Three thousand dollars a year! He's a sucker! The guy's a sucker! Three thou—"

Punch's fist crashed into the speaker's face and the surprised man stood blinking at a broken denture plate. Pinero went calmly back to my papers, saying, "Who's a sucker? He's out, ain't he? An' you're in, ain't ya? Who's a sucker?"

The victim, assuring Punch that he, the speaker, was, turned away to spit blood. But his face appeared again a moment later happily peering over Punch's shoulder.

Punch came up with something else.

He read: " 'There will be a probationary period—' Hey, whatta ya know? Doc's on probation. Ha! Hey, Doc—" and this time his smile warmed up, "how come you're on probation? What did ya do? Steal a apple outta some kid's lunch?"

"Why wouldn't he," asked the toothless beard respectfully, "on *sree sousand* dollars a year?"

"Well, whatta ya know," said Punch again, "here's a guy gets sent up on six months' probation. Ha!"

He started to laugh. The men watched him until they were sure he was on the level. Then they joined in, until two guards strolled up, suspicious of the good humor.

When they had passed Punch reached in his jacket and pulled out my papers, which I had not seen him stuff away.

He slipped them to me with a glance at the guards. "So long, Doc. See you at tea tomorrow."

"So long, Punch," I said. "See you then."

There was a bustle of talk and exclamation as I walked away, and above it Punch's "Okay, knock off, you goons. Gimme some room! . . . . Awright—start movin'!"

Looking back over my shoulder I saw the men moving away

from Punch, and two or three of them picking themselves up off the cobblestones where he had scattered them. I was almost at the gate when I heard someone call out.

"Hey, Doc!"

I looked back. It was Punch, standing alone a half block away, his hands in his pockets, watching me.

"Don'tcha know you ain't supposed to cross the yard without a guard? Ya might get hurt!"

"It's like the man said, you might get hurt."

Gordon was standing at the guard station just outside the gate, shaking his head wonderingly. He had apparently watched the scene.

"Well, I said you'd work out your own way of handling them, didn't I?"

"Who do you suppose put Pinero on my tail?" I asked facetiously.

He grinned. "Not me! I may like my little joke, but I'm no sadist!"

He took me in tow then, got me a room in a pleasant old hotel whose bar had once provoked a visit from hatchet-wielding Carrie Nation. Then he showed me the town, which was, as he said, in all the history books.

It was an orderly little relic at the edge of what had been a colorful military fort in the Indian Wars, the last tie between the East and West on the Santa Fe Trail, where the covered wagons were outfitted for the rigors of the journey. Its main street was still the wide swathe which had been cut to accommodate the stage coaches as they rocked in and out of town in those lusty years. But its fate had changed since the West had subsided into respectability; it had lost its boom population.

Between 1863 and 1930 five penitentiaries, a disabled veterans hospital, and another handful of homes for the aged and the orphaned had blossomed in its tiny borders, all within a

. radius of three miles. The little town had prudently admitted its loss of color and accepted the influx of Army personnel and Government employees and their families. The latter had settled down to pursue the human husbandry of its 12,000 Government charges and the comforts of its Army personnel. This little community, which had sprung up in the path of expansion and war, had settled into the inertia of a prison center, the parasitic flora of the civilization it had once so brilliantly championed.

Ironically, life went placidly on for the 17,000 outside the institutions because life had stopped for the 12,000 inside them. Once in a while the town was thrown into excitement over a scandal in one of the prisons. Every few years the citizens quaked at the sound of gunfire accompanying a prison break. Occasionally the town readied itself to play host to a visiting Congressional committee investigating some claim made against one of the institutions. But on the whole life was quite uneventful for the 17,000 on the outside. It was even more uneventful for the 12,000 on the inside.

After a pleasant dinner on the Post with Gordon, I returned to my hotel room and went to bed early to catch up on the sleep I had lost on the trip. Stretched out on an emaciated bed I reflected on the turn my life had taken that day.

From classroom to prison was not a natural life progression, but it was one with an instant appeal to a psychologist. I was still oriented toward the ease of an authoritarian's life in a college town, the prefabricated social eminence of a professor's life and the wistful scholarship of students. It was an abrupt shift from that to the warden's immunity, the grapevine's "handicap," Connie's maneuvers and Punch's bravado, but it was exciting to ponder from a hotel bed.

Tomorrow I would get squared away with the chief medical officer. And with that thought I closed my mind on my first day at the penitentiary.

2

THE CHIEF medical officer was a large jovial prince of a veteran of thirty years of war, pestilence and Government service who was philosophical about red tape, tolerant of the frustrations and delays of his job, final and instant in his decisions.

He told me my orders had come that morning, that I was to get into a hospital coat and go the hell to work with his good wishes. But he said to take a couple of months getting the feel of the place, and when I was sure I was ready to begin seeing the new men as the warden had suggested, he would set up the machinery for it.

He asked me for a first blush requisition of office supplies which he would rush through so that I could set up my project. He stated that he would get me any apparatus I needed, but for me to remember that apparatus would never take the place of brains.

He said it seemed to him that nobody knew much yet about the causes of crime, drunkenness, drug addiction, or insanity, and that though he had an endowed, thoroughly modern hospital and a strong staff, he had not turned up any important evidence yet, in which connection he wished me a lot of luck. . . .

He advised me again to proceed slowly and use caution, and not to get the hospital or him in trouble by going off half-cocked.

He said I would be expected to attend the hospital staff

meetings on Tuesday afternoons, and that I would be issued a uniform which I was to wear whenever I represented the hospital, provided Washington got around to choosing an insignia for the new rank of psychologist; until that time I could work in mufti. And through a good-natured smile he told me not to ask him why the personnel of the USPHS, a civilian agency under the Treasury Department, was commissioned and wore a Navy uniform on an Army post in a Federal penitentiary administered by the Department of Justice.

At the end of the briefing he shook my hand cordially, took me to Gordon's office and deputized him to give me all possible assistance in getting my work under way. Then he excused himself: he was assisting Doctor Fellows—three stripes beneath him in rank—in surgery.

"A very fine man," I said, after Stevens had gone. "He told me to keep my nose and my quarters clean. And to pay a social call on the warden and his family within the next ten days."

Gordon laughed, probably at my expression.

"You only have to stay twenty minutes by the clock. Th warden doesn't like this teatime stuff either. You're in the army now, Wilson. Or is it the navy? You'll have to learn to crook that little finger around a tea cup as well as an ergograph. What now?"

I asked to go downstairs to the half-basement and see my quarters again, hoping I didn't sound too much like a small boy with a new set of carpenter tools waiting in the garage. I explained I would need some cubicles along one wall to use in giving tests.

That was easy, he said. There was a furniture factory, a carpenter shop, a paint shop and an upholstery shop inside the wall. "By any chance do you need any plumbing done?" he asked. "We have a plumbing detail here that is—well, I won't say they were plumbers on the outside, but they sure can go through a concrete wall in a hurry! . . . Let's go."

31

He rustled up a white coat for me and we went downstairs.

The windows of my suite were about shoulder height and a foot above the level of the courtyard. As Gordon and I stood looking out upon the yard I remarked on the small knots of men doing nothing, long files of men going nowhere. He assured me this illusion of apathy was sometimes misleading.

We were about to turn away from the window when one such file passed by and left behind it a huddled form. The file had gone several paces before anyone noticed the man. Then the yard was filled with guards and the air with screaming whistles.

I saw what he meant about illusion. This was violence right under our noses and in the presence of a dozen guards. Not a lost motion. The ranks just merged together, the poor devil was held up and passed down the line and by the time he collapsed, six men had stabbed him.

"A search is useless," Gordon said. "In the confusion that knife will just disappear. They'll herd the men into the cell block and take the place apart, but they won't find a thing. Do you want to watch Fellows sew him up, or would you rather watch the guards search the cell block?"

He assured me that trying to patch up a victim was generally a losing game. The men were masters at their craft and by the time their victim reached the hospital he would be dead. So I went to the cell block to watch the search.

I moved about unattended now, in my white coat. It was all the pass and protection I needed. No matter how the convicts might feel about me or my job, the hospital coat commanded respect.

The structure of the cell block at the penitentiary resembled a half wheel with two horizontal spokes—the first and seventh wings—reaching across the front of the block, and five additional wings between these two, radiating from the center hub of a rotunda. Around the rotunda and in the first wing were the captain's waiting room, his office and record room, the photographic studio and the guards' headquarters where the captain gave them their daily orders and where they played pinochle when they were off duty. The schoolrooms, library, social workers' offices, the Catholic chapel and the Protestant chaplain's office were on the floors above. The psychopathic cases and the solitary punishment cells occupied the basement of the seventh wing.

Three guards were locked at all times in a central control station, a steel cage approximately nine feet in diameter, in the center of the rotunda. Armed with riot guns and gas bombs, they covered the entrance to the cell block from the yard and the doors to all the wings. The doors were wide enough to accommodate only two men walking abreast, a precaution against riot. The only exception was the door to the fourth wing which accommodated six men at a time, this wing being given up entirely to the dining room, the kitchen with a refrigerator as large as a small apartment, and a storeroom the size of a five-room house. The dining room seated 1,500 men for meals, but 3,000 could view the weekly movies in the same room when the tables were stacked. The movie screen was at the back of a stage separating the kitchen and storeroom from the dining room, and the room demanded the longest movie beam in the country until the Radio City Music Hall was built.

The guards on duty when I entered the rotunda told me that the knife search was being conducted in the sixth wing, but that something perhaps more to my taste was in progress in the third wing. I thanked them and went through the door to the third wing, where I found a dozen guards racing up and down the five-tiered wing looking for something the presence of which one's nose confirmed, even if one's eye couldn't. I understood why the guards at the control station had said the third wing

33

might be more to my taste. Four baked hams were missing from the kitchen and the contraband goods had been traced to that wing.

As Gordon had said, they tore the place apart when they made a search. The men had been known to stuff contraband into the plumbing traps and waste lines. The guards were systematic and exasperated. It was entirely a game of wits. The place smelled to heaven of ham, there were grease spots on the balustrades, and the inmates looked well and recently fed. But the hams were nowhere to be found. The wing was half deserted, since most of the men were at work, and how those whole hams could elude a cordon of angry guards was something to contemplate.

The technique was maddeningly simple: where the guards were the hams weren't. Huge caches of contraband were frequently passed from one tier to another, up and down and back and forth, always under the noses but just out of range of the guards. A trusty pretending to have a hot clue would distract the guards momentarily while the contraband was transported up and down the catwalks, abetted by perhaps a pickpocket, a shoplifter or an ex-football player on a short run around left end.

The guards never did find the hams.

There are almost as many engineering plans for cell blocks as there are penitentiaries. The half wheel used at Fort Leavenworth seemed sound and efficient. The wings were built like a box within a box, crate-like, tier upon tier, toward the roof. Every wing had five tiers of cells. At no point did the individual cell lie closer than fifteen feet to the outside wall. Viewed from the side, the center unit of cells, of which there were two rows built back to back, reminded me of chickencoops piled on top of each other on an express wagon at the railroad station.

Each wing was a dead-end street, entrance and exit being made through the same door. The individual cells were walled on three sides and barred on the side opening on the catwalk.

34

Large windows in the outside walls of each wing, perhaps five feet wide and thirty feet high, gave outside light and ventilation to each cell. The cells were the largest in the country at that time, $4\frac{1}{2} \times 9 \times 7$. Those occupied by two prisoners were larger. Each cell contained a washbowl and a toilet. The men slept on bunks with clean mattress pads and bedding. They did their own housework, which had to pass daily inspection.

The prisoners were assigned to cells according to their work detail. The men from the paint shop slept on one tier, hospital men on another, kitchen men on another, so that work details could be handled as a unit. Furthermore, when anything suspicious occurred the quarters suspected could be searched for contraband without disturbing other units. If there was evidence of a gun being made in the machine shop, for instance, that unit of the cell block was inspected first. The gates to each tier of cells were separately geared and automatically controlled from the central control station.

These light, clean cells provided all the factors of punishment that segregation and imprisonment can supply. But there was none of the squalor and degradation of even a decade before, when a prison itself was as much of a breeding place of criminal character as anything beyond it in a free society.

For most of us the depraved status of penology in the United States in 1930 seems like the backwash of a shameful long-forgotten century.

In that decade, while the nation was reading Elinor Glyn, dancing the Charleston and drinking hootch, prisoners at Albany, New York, were spending forty-three of every forty-eight hours in vermin-infested cells four feet wide, totally without light, with a reeking bucket for a toilet.

In Maryland prisoners were not yet being segregated as to sex, age, or criminal charges. In Pennsylvania jailors were legally extracting fees or withholding food from prisoners and pocketing every cent of the fees they could avoid spending. In the Jackson, Michigan, state prison the doctor was of such a calibre that he stood holding the pulse of prisoners being flogged, in order to give the signal for the flogger to stop just short of death and to wait until the prisoner revived enough to proceed. A 21-year-old lad sent to the Jackson prison from an insane asylum was given a total of 181 lashes within nine days at five different times—with time off to revive spent in a dungeon on bread and water.

In the famous "model" prison of Colorado men were being shackled over a sawhorse and flogged for stealing a few onions from the prison kitchen. Floggings such as this lacerated the flesh of the victim's back so deeply as sometimes to expose the ribs and spine. In the same prison at least one insane prisoner was beaten to death, his ribs crushed by heavy boots.

In Missouri prisoners were being suspended by their wrists for failure to complete work quotas. In the Minnesota state prison the inmates were not allowed to talk to each other at any time; in Wisconsin they were not allowed ever to raise their eyes from the ground; in Illinois the inmates in solitary punishment cells were handcuffed to the wall in one position for twelve hours out of every twenty-four, and in Ohio the solitary cell was a form-fitting strait jacket that excluded all movement. At both Leavenworth Penitentiaries blow torch squads made daily rounds trying to keep ahead of the vermin.

In this decade of Prohibition, Lindbergh's flight to Paris and the Teapot Dome scandal, 22-year-old Martin Tabert, a farm boy who left his North Dakota home on a trip "to see the world," was yanked off a freight car in Florida, sentenced on a vagrancy charge to serve ninety days as a convict or pay a twenty-five dollar fine. His people wired him the money. The sheriff returned it marked "unclaimed" and "sold" the boy for twenty dollars to a lumber company, where he was flogged to death by the prison boss. The sheriff had a contract with the lumber company at twenty dollars a head.

This was the decade of the Capones and the Druggans and their ilk. It almost seemed that the courts and prisons who were responsible for these inhumanities and injustices were trying to make the general prison population, who were schoolboys compared to the gangsters on the loose, pay for the crimes of those gangsters, while the gangsters themselves, beyond the law, continued to defeat justice.

Finally, in response to the pressure of reports by The American Prison Association on one hundred prisons, Federal Investigator Fishman's report on 1,500 jails and 50,000 prisoners, Tannenbaum's, Mrs. O'Hare's, and other shocking exposés, the House of Representatives appointed a committee to investigate Federal penal institutions, and in this instance the wheels of democracy turned rapidly. The committee reported in 1929 and by 1930 the face and future of Federal penology in the United States was changed, the first significant reform in one hundred years.

Since before the Revolutionary War the Quakers had been tirelessly working toward prison reform. Finally, under the efforts and presidency of Herbert Hoover, sweeping legislation established a separate and powerful Bureau of Prisons, which terminated the spoils system of political appointments and established Civil Service requirements and a training school for prison personnel. The entire penal medical service was unified and turned over to the United States Public Health Service. Appropriations were made for a large hospital for the criminally insane at Springfield, Missouri. The Porter Narcotic Farms were established for the treatment of drug addiction. For the first time in American history the rehabilitation of convicts, rather than punishment and revenge, became the goal of Federal penology.

The Federal reforms had some salutary influence on state

37

and municipal institutions, but these are still perpetuating many of the evils and brutalities of the twenties in spite of reports such as the Wickersham and Seabury commissions and the Committee of Fifteen.

Pending the building of new Federal penitentiaries, Fort Leavenworth Penitentiary, referred to in Governmental and penal circles as the Annex, was used by the Bureau of Prisons to relieve the hopeless congestion in the existing Federal prisons and to begin the study of drug addiction and criminality under the USPHS.

To a research man an appointment to the USPHS is a highly prized plum. The USPHS is the unsung hero of medicine all over the world. It was founded in 1798 when John Adams was President. It has more than a century of service behind it and is respected by scientists everywhere for its monumental work in pellagra, malaria, venereal disease and Rocky Mountain fever. It administers the Leper Colony at Carville, Louisiana, the only organization in the country currently wrestling with this disease. Much of the progress in the treatment of tropical diseases has been made by the USPHS, which also figures prominently in research on cancer. It works closely with the Narcotics Commission, one of the few surviving agencies of the League of Nations. It is known to play no politics, to be generous with research facilities and moral support, and to keep its hand strictly off a research man's activities as long as he is working at his job.

The new research hospital at the Fort Leavenworth Annex was the first of its kind in the history of American penology, and in those years of reform and research I would have traveled considerably more than a thousand miles to work in it.

3

THE CAPTAIN was right. Connie reported to me during my first week, and he worked like a dog. I was glad to have a convict with Connie's prestige "front" for me with the general population while I pursued the more obsequious role of getting acquainted. He hung around the suite when I could not be there during the remodeling, and everything had to go strictly according to specifications or Connie started barking.

He had never worked in an office before, in or out of prison. He did the secretarial work on the requisitions I prepared for the CMO, and talked at the rate of three hundred words a minute at the sight of our joint initials at the bottom of the first letter: DPW/JC. He praised all the democratic processes of life that day.

At first he hacked away awkwardly at the typewriter with two long middle fingers, but I found him one evening on a special pass up in the schoolrooms, trying hard to master the ten-finger system, his bulging eyes glued on a keyboard chart before him. He was still typing with two fingers at the end of three years —though with marked improvement in speed and accuracy.

It was a great day for him when my phone was connected and he began to answer it for me. A penitentiary phone service is a closed circuit limited entirely to departments within the institution. Only the warden's private phone is connected to outside trunks. One day shortly after mine was installed I returned from an errand in the cell block just as Connie dropped the phone into its cradle. He sank into a chair and sat there staring happily into space. He jumped at the sound of my voice when I asked him who had called up.

"Oh—that? That there was the warden." That there was the exceedingly small and unbeautiful flea on my dog's hind leg was about his tone.

"Does he want me to call back?"

"Yeah," he said, after thought. "Yeah—as near as I could make out that's what he wants, all right."

After calling the warden, I turned to Connie.

"The warden says he had a very interesting talk with you just now." What the warden had said was that Connie had got far out of line on the phone, and that he, the warden, had led Connie on to see how far he would go. In the warden's mind there was no limit to how far Connie would go.

"Hell, it wasn't so much," said Connie. He'd had better in his time. "Warden kinda blowed his top toward the last. He calls up, see? Is the doctor in? Well, you know me, Doc—let 'em down easy. So I says, No, he ain't here at the moment, but this is his Executive Assistant in Charge o' Bugs speakin'. So when the warden sees how it is he says cagey-like, Well, where *is* the doctor? So I says, Well, I can't rightly say where he is right now, warden. I been havin' a little trouble with the good doctor, he's been gone a lot lately an' I been handlin' most of the stuff, is they anything I can do for you? Then he says, When do you expect him? I says, Well, sir, I ain't instructed to make no statements about that. An' that's when he gets snotty an' starts talkin' like a head waiter. Well, he says, *When* the doctor comes in, will you tell him to *call* me! Why, sure, I says right off, I sure as hell will if he ever gits back, he's been spendin' a unnatural amount of time in the psychopathic ward. At that the warden says maybe him and me better have a little talk soon, and—"

He shot me a quick glance.

"—and then he hangs up?" I asked.

"Yeah, he sure does. That's the best thing he does is hang up. Ka-*wop!*"

I looked thoughtfully at Connie. Such a nice double cross. He tells the warden I'm A.W.O.L. and then tells me he told the warden. Just so everybody will understand how things are. Just in case I'm ever tempted to underestimate the Vice President in Charge of Trouble.

A month before the first load of new men were tested in the office I was still without a staff except for Connie. Following the warden's and the CMO's suggestion, I planned to test the new men exclusively for a while until I was generally accepted by the oldsters. I was expecting to choose part of my staff from the new men whose I.Q.s would test out highest, with the idea that my staff would eventually assume what part of the testing and scoring they could. But I knew it might take me a long time to get a staff of five or six. The average I.Q. in a penitentiary is 80. The average in a college classroom is 125.

One morning I looked at Connie with my first serious thought of his possible role in the office. He still didn't look like research material to me. And I do not refer to his almost daily nicking his Adam's apple while shaving and stanching the flow with a tab of toilet paper. Connie was bright and industrious when he wanted to be. But no convict opens up like a rose before another man; there was a lot I didn't know about him. So I gave him the battery of tests I was going to use with the new convicts.

I say I gave Connie a battery of tests. It was not quite that simple. It was like coaxing a two-year-old into a barber's chair for his first haircut.

"You got the wrong man, Doc," he began stubbornly. "I ain't puttin' nothin' down on paper. No, sir. Why, most of the trouble in the world is because somebody says too much, 'specially in writin'. No, sir."

"Look, Connie," I said, "Did I squeal when you took my picture?"

"No, sir," he said respectfully, "but you knowed all the time what I was doin', see?"

"The hell I did, Connie! For all I knew you might have let go with a cannon ball from that camera when you pushed the button."

He admired the thought briefly. Then he looked aghast. "Now why would I do a thing like that?"

"Then what makes you think I'm trying to frame you with an intelligence test? Look. You asked to work in this office. Right?"

"Yes, sir."

"Was that because of your broad experience in psychology, Connie?"

He gulped.

"So you either thought you'd like me or that the job would be an easy go. I don't care which it was, Connie, but I can't use you if you won't learn. You've got to know damn near as much as I do about these tests or you won't be any help to me. How are you going to give tests to the new men and score and interpret them next month, if you won't take them yourself now?"

His eyes popped. "You mean *I'm* gonna be givin' tests to these cons?"

I reminded him of the stacks of tests he had helped me store in the cabinets. "I'd sure hate to give them by myself, Connie."

He stared at me in unbelief. I couldn't believe I hadn't made the point clear before. He took a short turn up and down before my desk. Then he stopped, his face wrinkled in profound concentration. "What kinda tests are they again, Doc?"

"I can't tell you before you take them, Connie, it would in-

fluence your score. But I'll tell you afterward. I'll tell you anything you want to know—in fact, I want you to know all about
them," I assured him. "Afterward."

His face closed up on me.

"I know, Connie, it sounds like a line," I admitted.
". . . . Okay. I want to know your intelligence quotient, the
ratio between your chronological age and your mental age, your
percentile rating. And what your personality indices are of
neurosis, extraversion-introversion, dominance, emotivity, complexes—"

I glanced at him and felt guilty before his look of pure de-
light at those high-sounding words. He sat down in a fog of
thought. Anyone with an I.Q. of 90 could have guessed the particular circuit on which the wheels of his mind were going round.

"You mean if I stick around here I'll be talkin' like *that?*"

"Connie, I'd say by November fifteenth you'll be throwing
those words away with your left hand, and that in six months
you'll have five hundred words just like them in your vocabulary! Wouldn't they come in kind of handy for a barker on a
midway? Like calling the fat lady a *viscerotonic endomorph*—"

Why go on? I had him. He rubbed his hands together. "Doc,
you don't know what you're sayin'. You just don't know! Well,
what in hell are we waitin' for? Gimme a pencil!"

His tests gave me an encouraging profile. He could have
passed college entrance examinations with his I.Q. He was high
in self-sufficiency and had but few neurotic tendencies. He was
gregarious and, of course, a healthy extravert.

Punch Pinero's tests showed a different picture.

Punch checked in one morning about a week after Connie
had completed his tests. I found him standing in the hall doorway
smiling ingratiatingly when I looked up from my desk in my
private office.

43

"Hiya, Doc." He lounged at the threshold, his body easy against the door jamb. "I see you're hard at it."

"Hello there, Punch." I hoped I sounded cordial.

He did not come into my office. He walked over to Connie's desk, the only one so far in the large room immediately off the hall where eventually all my staff would work. Connie had been at his desk the greater part of the time the last week, poring over textbooks which explained the administration, scoring and interpretation of our tests. Connie looked up at Punch, and deliberately closed his book.

Punch scowled at him and then at me. Then he settled for a smile.

"What goes on here? Secrets? Is them the stoolie records?" he asked facetiously.

"Glad you came, Punch," I said brightly in lieu of an answer. "The captain told me you might check in."

"How come you to wait a week after your transfer came through, Pinero?" asked Connie. "You chicken?"

I looked at Connie in surprise. On the other hand, why had I supposed he wouldn't know Punch had requested a transfer? Wasn't he practically Chairman of the Grapevine?

"You want to start work today?" I asked quickly.

"Work? I didn't aim to *work* in a place like this. I been workin' in the machine shop, threadin' pipe, gettin' m'pinkies all dirty."

He held up his hands and considered them thoughtfully. "Y'know, Doc, I used to have the prettiest hands? Like a pianna player." He dropped his hands. "No, I aimed to just sit around like Connie here, with m'butt on the feathers, readin' ten-buck books an' writin' notes to myself. Some go, eh, Connie?" He favored Connie with a flat, humorless show of teeth.

"Yeh—some go, Pinero," drawled Connie. "Now take this here little book. Probably nothin' you don't already know, though, you bein' such a *reader*."

I tried to catch Connie's eye to warn him to lay off. Failing, I stepped in. "Connie's just reading up on some tests—"

"Hold it, Doc." Punch was eyeing Connie who had gone back to his book. "Let this wise-ass ham hang hisself."

"Sure thing, Punch." Connie played it like a college professor. "Doc has some little tests here. Let's see, there's the Otis Classification Test, the Pressey X-O Test for Complexes, the Bernreuter Personality Scale—"

"Cut it!" Punch turned on me. "What's the matter with him?" he demanded. "What's that crap he's peddlin'? Somethin' you taught him?"

"Somethin' I read in one o' them ten-buck books," Connie said easily. "Now, here's a great little volume. Rorschach's Psychodiagnostic," he read languorously. "An' here's just the thing for your nightstand, Punch. Willoughby's Emo-tional Matur-ity Scale."

Punch made a move toward Connie.

"Don't you laugh at me, you cheap punk. You wouldn't be so goddam wise with a shiv in your neck!"

Connie looked lazily at Punch. "That there's big talk for a man's temporarily outta guns, Pinero."

Punch wavered. Then he tightened and growled, "Start talkin', ham."

"Well, y'see," said Connie, "Doc's gotta get himself a mob here in the office, Punch. You oughtta know how it is, when a guy moves in on a new racket. Doc ain't so dumb, see—he's gotta know what he's gettin', and quick. So he's got hisself a kind of a third degree, here. An' he finds out things in about five hours it'd take you twenty-five years to learn. Some o' this stuff you'd never find out. You oughtta understand that easy, Punch. You've softened up a lot of hoods in your day. Okay, you take Doc's gimmick, you're in. You don't take it, you're out."

After brief and furious thought Punch stomped over and stood in my doorway.

45

"That how it is, Doc? That your pitch? Last time I filled in some papers a smart-ass D.A. tries to have me shipped back to Italy." He laughed shortly. "Anything you want t'know about me, you ask me!"

"The thing is, Punch, everything I want to know is on those tests," I said. "Besides, you learn how to give a test to somebody else by taking it yourself."

"Not me!" he said flatly. But on a second take he asked. "Whatta you mean give it to somebody else?"

"That's what we've been trying to tell you, Punch," I said. "Next month every new man will come to this office after his physical examination. We'll give him the tests Connie's been talking about."

Finally he was listening.

"You mean *I'd* be givin' those tests?"

"That's right, Punch."

"Jeez. . . . What kinda tests you say they are, Doc?"

Connie answered for me. "Can't tell you before you take 'em, Pinero," he said to Punch's back, "it'd influence your score."

"Huh?" Punch strode back to Connie's desk.

"It'd affect your answers."

Punch exploded. "Look, Lowlife, it'd sure affect my answers *not* to know what I was takin'!"

Connie tipped back in his chair away from Punch's menacing face and spoke leisurely.

"Okay, you ast for it." And I listened with as much fascination as Punch. "Doc wants to know your intelligence quota, the ratio between your chron-o-logical age and your mental age, if ya got any. An' what th'hell the personality—indexes is of neurotics, extra- or intra-version, domination, emoti-vity and—uh—complexions."

"Can it!" Punch's complexion was black with fury.

"Sure, Puncho." Connie eased his chair back in place with a contented smile.

46

Punch rubbed the back of his neck while he stomped hotly up and down the room. He came to a halt in my doorway.

"I still think the punk's blowed his wig!"

And he sailed past Connie and out of the office.

Connie instantly raised a rasp that could have been heard in the solarium on the roof.

"Just like I said, Doc. Big fat-mouth Dago—no guts."

That brought Punch back, looking like a hungry shark.

Connie jumped up. "Right this way, sir! Please remove your coat and leave your shoes at the door!"

"Not you!" roared Punch. *"Him!"* He jerked his thumb at me. "Well—what'n hell are we waitin' for?" he growled. "Gimme a goddam pencil!"

I glanced at Connie, who gave me an okay with his thumb and forefinger. I got to my feet and came into the room.

"You can keep your shoes and coat on, Punch," I said, "let's use this first cubicle."

I glanced at Connie as I followed Punch into the cubicle. He was smiling into his ten-buck book.

Punch's I.Q. was higher than Connie's, but because he lacked Connie's emotional stability to see him through a crisis his brightness only led him into trouble. Punch operated almost exclusively on two emotional levels: at dizzy heights and in abysmal depths. Strange things could hurl him from one level to the other, strange things according to the popular picture of a gangster. A word, a criticism, a personal slight, a blow to his vanity, and Punch would fall to sulking at a six-year-old level. Connie was too busy dreaming up new exploits ever to sink into distemper.

Punch was abnormally high in dominance and aggression. He left Connie far behind in these qualities. In performance this meant that Punch got what he wanted by force, while Connie used his wits. The latter, of course, shows more resourcefulness

47

and flexibility. Connie could talk his way out of a tight spot. Punch let his guns talk for him. Connie had never taken a gun into either a bank or a second-story window. Punch had always carried two: one on his hip and one in a shoulder holster. Gangsters are frequently babies about pain and danger. What makes them brave is their gangs and their guns.

Connie rated higher in self-sufficiency and resourcefulness. Life was a sideshow to Connie. To Punch it was a pitched battle. Connie would have enjoyed being shipwrecked on a hostile South Sea island. In three hours, what with his pulling rabbits out of hats and one thing and another, he would have been offered the chieftain's favorite daughter. Punch, on the other hand, would have ambushed himself for a last stand or bullied his way into their midst, with the result that Connie would have met Punch in his soup that night.

The two men were equally respected in the penitentiary, but for different reasons. Punch's few followers were men of his own cloth, big shots. Though always not quite as big as he, of course. They weren't chummy with him. They were polite. They gave him room. Connie's influence was wider. His wits and diplomacy made him a good man to know. He could get a man out of trouble. He could also get a man into trouble, of course, as some of them learned to their edification. It didn't pay to dally with Connie. On the other hand, he was a happy-go-lucky good for a lot of laughs and a lot of connections which nobody quite understood.

I was amused at the feeling between Connie and Punch during their first few days alone together in the office. Each was successful on his own level on the outside, and on the inside too. They bore each other a grudging respect. Punch could have enjoyed Connie's clowning, but he could never quite let himself go. He could not forget that he was *the* Pinero. I think Connie could have liked Punch, too, despite his distaste for Punch's long-arm tactics. Punch had some qualities for which I always liked him,

48

even in the period of my last year when I had good reason to fear him. He was generous, immediate and direct in his dealings, boyish in his enthusiasms. He might have had a different history if he had not come to believe that the only people he could trust were babies—*bambinos*—and corpses. He could be reduced to Italian gibberish by a picture of somebody's baby. He had none of his own, his wife having been too busy running his blackmail racket to have babies. But some day, he swore softly, he would have them one way or another. What's the difference who a baby's ma is? he reasoned. It's his pa that counts.

I asked about his own youth. On this he was voluble. I learned that he was beaten all through his childhood, mercilessly, regularly and senselessly, and then forbidden recourse to tears. How did he feel about his parents now? He flashed his dazzling smile. Everything was fine now, he assured me. His mother ran his girl-racket and his father the gambling. His wife handled the extortions and Punch himself ran the smuggling and shakedown rackets. None of his businesses were seriously interrupted by his imprisonment. He took care of them through the grapevine. Yes, Punch was a great believer in nepotism. "Keep it in the family," was his motto. Sure, everything was fine now.

But when his smile passed and he changed the subject abruptly, I had a quick flash of two aging, tired people with all their beatings of little Punch far behind them, who hadn't meant to get mixed up in crime, who only wanted in their old age to sit in the sun and dream of Italy. Instead now they would have to work until they dropped of weariness and age, paying off to little Punch, wondering stupidly as they looked at their beautiful black sheep of a son if maybe they should have beaten him more. . . . .

When I learned about Punch's childhood, I was reminded of the theory held by many psychologists and supported by many case histories that most of the sadistic criminals of history have been beaten and mistreated as children. Beatings may subdue a willful child, but they do not always produce a gentle adult.

Word was getting around that I needed more men in the office. But the impression was shortlived that it was an easy go. The expansion of Punch's and Connie's vocabulary set most of the population to wagging its head over how buggy can a guy get. The institution was set on its ear by both Connie and Punch checking in so quickly with me. In some quarters this did me good, in others it did me harm. The men who thought Connie could do no wrong thought Punch could do no right and vice versa, and here they were working together. How was a man to know?

One day I went to the cell block for a haircut from the convict barbers. A frost fell when I entered the shop, and when I sat down in the chair among scissors, razors and silence, I experienced a brief relapse to my childhood prayers.

"Shave?" asked the barber, brandishing a long blue blade near my obviously clean-shaven face.

"No, cut, please."

"Cut *what?*" he asked.

"What did you have in mind?"

A wave of sniggering passed over the men. The barber gave me an appraising look and went to work. He gave me a good haircut and before I left I had a date with him for the following day. I could see that I would never have any standing in the barber shop until I had passed their little third degree—a shave. After that I was "in" with the barbers.

I frequently met and chatted with the captain in the shop. He was taking chances under the razor that few of the guards hazarded. With the latter a razor had been known to slip—just a little. Nothing like that ever happened to the captain. His Irish bluster and warmth paid off handsomely. These were first generation convicts under the 1930 reforms. A captain who trusted himself to a barber and swapped stories with them had not been long in their books. He was much too genuine to be taken for a ride.

When I left the cell block after my first shave I picked up a stocky middle-aged convict who had been standing at the barber shop door when I left. He followed me for a few discreet paces across the yard. Then he joined me.

"Mind if I walk with you, Doc?" He wore a clerical-looking pair of round eyeglasses, but his eyes were alert behind them. "I got a buddy in the hospital."

"That so?" I waited.

"He had a little accident yesterday." The tone in which he said accident took all the chance out of it.

"Too bad. What happened?" I asked politely.

I was wise by now to the roundabout way the convict's mind approaches an objective. This man didn't just want company crossing the yard. Whatever he had on his mind would come out in due time.

"It's a kick," he began, "the guys that get sent up. Now take Scott. That's his name. No alias either." He looked at me. "Mine's Gibbs."

I held out my hand. "Wilson."

We shook hands.

"Well," he went on, "Scott's been here about three months on a narcotics rap. He's a Square John (non-user). Innocent as a baby. He's takin' the rap for some dame. On his own, I mean. He wasn't framed. He got contempt o' court for that." Gibbs shook his head. "I ain't met no dame I'd take a rap for." He glanced at me to see if his cynicism was going to be rebuked.

I said, "She must have been quite a 'dame'!"

Prisons are full of "innocent" men, which frequently means only that they were not guilty of the charge on which they were convicted, but that they were guilty of some other offense that escaped detection. "Innocence" in the sense a prisoner uses it is a very relative concept. I didn't know about Scott's innocence, but I went along with Gibbs in order to get the story.

"How's he taking to prison life?" I asked.

51

"Doc, you won't believe it. I ain't heard him gripe onc't about bein' sent up or the jernt or anything. He seems t'think it's all a big joke. I don't get it. He never puts on no airs on account of bein' different. He never asks no favors, just acts like he's one o' the boys. Well, y'know, in this jernt actin' like you was one of us, if you *ain't,* can get you into a hell of a lot of trouble. The cons get suspicious—think you're phony. So I been kinda watchin' out for him, see?"

He glanced at me.

"Hell—" he said, "somebody's gotta wise up these new guys. Some of the things which happen to 'em ain't good, Doc. No use makin' a criminal outta a guy just because he gets sent up, is there?"

I looked at him. "There surely isn't, Gibbs," I said quietly. "What happened to Scott yesterday?"

"Well, it's like this. One day Scott takes me to one side in the laundry which is where we work.

" 'Gibbs,' he says, 'how long would it take me to learn to smuggle?'

"Before I can shut my face I'm askin' him, 'Whatta ya figger on smugglin'?

" 'I don't care what it is, Gibbs,' he says, laughin'. 'I just feel conspicuous not knowing how to steal or smuggle. Besides, I bet it's fun. Let's make it a sandwich out of chow hall'—all that trouble for a sandwich!"

"How did he make out?" I asked.

"It's a kick, Doc. The kid just ain't got the feel. Where d'ya think he hides it? In his hip pocket. This half a loaf of bread sittin' there like a goddam bustle." He chuckled. "The second time it's a apple. He's bright this time, he's learned about hip pockets. Nothin' dumb about Scott. So he puts this pippin in his shirt pocket. The guard thought he was seein' things."

While we waited for the guard to come and unlock the hos-

52

pital gate I asked, "What about yesterday? Was that a smuggling job too?"

Gibbs spat. "I don't know how he got mixed up in that deal. I musta been lookin' the other way for a minute. It was the first time he'd had anything really hot. He stuck it under his jacket. I was standin' right behind him when the guard yells, 'Hey—you. What you got under your jacket?' Scott didn't know hisself, it wasn't his job, the stuff was planted on him, see? I taps him on the shoulder quick, to pass it to me. But you know what he does? He just hands it over to the guard. You shouldda seen that guard." Gibbs smiled broadly. "He drops it. He won't open it. He backs away, thinkin' sure it's a bomb. No con ever give anything up before, without he was searched. The guard calls another screw an' they open it from eight feet away, with poles."

"What was it?" I asked.

"Electric pad made in the power house. Somebody wasn't sleepin' for cold feet in the second wing," said Gibbs with a straight face. "When they're openin' the package I ask Scott how come him to give it to the screw. He says, 'The man asked for it, didn't he? Besides, I was as curious as he, I wanted to know what I was carrying.' You see what I mean about Scott, Doc? Well, it was then this big bruiser decides to wise him up, so he eases up to Scott and kicks him—where it hurts most," he said delicately.

Inside the hospital gate, on the way to my office, Gibbs quickly made his point.

"You can see how these new guys get it in the neck," he said confidentially. "I even been worryin' about you in there, with that Pinero. How you gettin' along? You need any help, Doc?"

When I did not reply immediately, his voice dropped even lower. "You need a nice clean boy in your office, Doc? A college boy?"

"Scott's a college man?" I asked, interested now.

"Sure, he's quality, Doc. He shouldn't be mixed up with

53

them butchers in the shops, now, should he?" He turned to me again. "Jeez, Doc—I got a kid of my own about his age—"

So then I knew. It could have been a stock story, but I was sure it wasn't. Gibbs knew I could check on it in five minutes. How much he was agitated for Scott and how much for his own boy on the outside whom Scott represented, I didn't know. Whichever way it was, it was a valid incentive. Worry and guilt about families is a real emotional load with many convicts. I felt Gibbs was on the level.

I asked him if there wasn't a regular procedure for changing jobs. Sure, he knew. You go to the captain and ask for a work transfer.

"Fine. You tell Scott to go to the captain then. I'll have a talk with the captain too."

"Yes, *sir!* . . . . Jeez—thanks, Doc. Thanks a lot! I'll sure tell Scott." And he was off.

"Oh, Gibbs."

"Yeah?" He turned around.

"You and Scott a team?"

"Well—like I say, somebody's gotta look out for these kids."

"Then suppose you go with Scott to the captain," I said.

"*Me?* Jeez—ya mean that, Doc?"

"One more thing, Gibbs." I told him about taking the tests.

"Yeah, I heard. Anythin' a bonehead like me can do to study up on 'em, Doc?"

"Not a thing, Gibbs."

"Okay, Doc. . . . . An' Doc—ya won't be sorry, this ain't no bum steer."

In the few minutes between the time I went to bed and the instant of falling asleep that night, I suffered a twinge about having encouraged Gibbs to seek a work transfer. I already had two incipient scrappers in Connie and Punch. What kind of assimilation was I hoping for in adding to them a solicitous old maid? However, by that time I knew that of the two thousand in-

54

mates it was wishful thinking to ask that more than twenty be potential researchers. I could do worse, as the captain had said of Connie. Especially if that nice clean college boy of Gibbs' turned out to have even one of those three qualities.

With such a possibility in prospect I fell asleep.

Scott, a handsome Southerner with a profile like Scott Fitzgerald, came to see me a couple of days later, still walking gingerly. With some flinching and swearing at his predicament he made it into a chair opposite me at my desk.

"Ah. . . . Last time this happened to me I was playing Georgia Tech." He smiled. His whole smooth unlined face smiled, including his wide gray eyes. Smiling was quite an operation with Scott. His entire expression seemed to shift into a higher key, even his ears responding to the beam when it hit.

"You should see the other guy. He's still upstairs in ice packs." He shook his head. "That Gibbs doesn't know his own strength."

"Gibbs?"

"Didn't he tell you what he did? I saw it from a reclining position, naturally," he said. "From the laundry floor, to be exact. Gibbs walked up to the mug who had just kicked me and said, like some damn patriarch, 'You shouldn't have *did* that, McGowan, it ain't *nice!*'—and he brought his big knee up into McGowan's crotch—" Scott slammed his fist into his other hand and winced at the thought. "McGowan's still in hydrotherapy. I got off easy, don't you think?"

"Maybe you better give up smuggling," I suggested mildly.

"That's what Gibbs says. But I'm getting to be a hell of a pickpocket. And I'm going to take up lockpicking next. That'll come in handy, I'm always losing my car keys—that is, I was."

It was, as Gibbs had said, all a joke to Scott, even getting "kicked in the balls." The only time the amusement in his eyes clouded was when I made oblique inquiries into his background.

55

There was a clean break in his mind between his life before his sentence and his prison term, and he would not bridge the two spheres. I did not try again.

I expedited his and Gibbs' transfer because I wanted to get the four men ready quickly to proctor the first tests. I checked their records that day and cleared with the captain.

Scott was a college man, and of good family, from the Blue Grass country. His record indicated illegal possession of narcotics, but the real story was supplied by the grapevine. The girl for whom he was taking the rap was a member of fading Southern aristocracy. She had been misguidedly trying to recoup the family fortunes by a shady track deal: the drug had been intended for "the ponies." Although the girl was not Scott's sweetheart, the families of the two young people were old and loyal friends, and in the tradition of loyalty nurtured in the South, Scott stepped in between the law and the girl. He was serving a four year sentence, the stiffness of the sentence being largely due to his contempt of court in refusing to divulge what he knew about the case.

Gibbs was a carpenter, but he signed in at the penitentiary as a "sub-contractor." His "business" had been largely transporting stolen cars across state lines. He facetiously called this traffic "interstate commerce." There was smuggling of other stolen goods on his record too. He was a sub-contractor in the sense that he did what he was told by his bosses. He "disremembered" why he had left his legitimate carpentry business, which meant he remembered very well. He rationalized his life of crime by pointing out that the common sharp practices of business, including his own contracting and building, were every bit as shady as his "interstate commerce," but that they just happened not to be constituted as illegal on the statute books. For that matter, he pointed out, the Big Fellows he worked for in organized defiance of law had never yet seen the inside of a prison. "I'm just a little guy an' it's hard to keep out onc't you been in." He had a

56

powerful body; nobody fooled with Gibbs even when they called him Grandma. He was not a violent man and had never carried arms. He just had worked for the wrong people. Otherwise he would have made a fine Sunday School superintendent.

I gave Scott and Gibbs the battery of tests when they reported for work. Scott now led the four in I.Q. Gibbs was at the bottom of the list, but he was going to pay his way by other means. Scott's story of Gibbs' patriarchal rebuke to McGowan reinforced by muscle was a good indication that he would be the mentor of the group in matters of etiquette and sobriety. He was a doer, a fixer-upper.

But he also liked a good rousing game of playing the end against the middle, like Robin Hood's Friar. If a man were momentarily down on his luck, Friar Gibbs wouldn't be above accepting a bribe from the Sheriff of Nottingham for disclosing the whereabouts of Robin Hood, but not until Robin Hood had first been forewarned—and later reimbursed from the reward!

Gibbs' encyclopedic memory fascinated me. In the field of social injustices he devoured statistical abstracts, prison reports and national exposés, and retained most of what he read. He had staggering volumes of facts and figures at the tip of his tongue. It was his considered opinion that crime too often paid. "Which is why there's so much of it," and he backed up his opinion with facts. But he was not one to gloat over this incongruity. It offended his strong moral sense. . . .

4

IN THE days before Scott and Gibbs were added to the staff Connie and Punch were like school kids competing for my favor. Neither of them knew anything about psychology, but they tried to conceal their ignorance from each other. They had their pride. They read everything they could get their hands on. Connie went at the problem of self-education by means of indirection, trial and error, and by considerable eavesdropping, while I openly instructed the more direct-hitting Punch who had to have quick answers.

But when the opportunity came of initiating Gibbs and Scott, Punch and Connie forgot their mutual antagonism and had a field day displaying their knowledge before the two novices. They also displayed wide swathes of ignorance, but I would not have spoiled their fun or their first experience of legitimate superiority and functioning for anything. I just sat by watching Scott and Gibbs look from Connie to Punch like a row of spectators at a fast tennis match.

During the following days of instruction the men's interest in pencil-and-paper tests sometimes lagged. They couldn't visualize the research as a whole yet, or the fun they would later have with statistical curves and growing evidence.

But they never for an instant lost interest in the performance tests and form boards: fitting blocks, running mazes and completing pictures, by which the I.Q.s of the illiterates and feeble-minded would be measured. They played with them as though they were toys and looked upon them as a huge joke. They could not believe I was serious about using them. They expressed absolute incredulity that I thought any convict could be so "stupid" and "dumb" that he couldn't match blocks or complete a picture such as the famous Mare and Foal, the Ship, or the Manikin.

"Look, Doc," said Gibbs earnestly, "I don't know about them college people of yours. Maybe this stuff's okay for them. But a con—" he smiled condescendingly, "why, a con's gotta be smart. How d'ya figger he can beat the cops if he can't tell a circle from a square? You're just wastin' your time, Doc. This ain't no college."

I couldn't very well point out that a man in prison had obviously not beaten the cops.

"Maybe you're right, Gibbs," I said soberly. "But you men go ahead and practice on them anyhow. It's a good way to learn how to use your stop watches, isn't it?"

"Oh, sure," said Connie quickly, "only we thought you oughtta know."

One day Punch read some of the finer print on the instruction sheet of the Otis test and came storming into my office. This goddam thing, he said, was made for school kids.

"Ele-ment'ry, it says. Ain't you *psychos* got no tests for men?"

I explained that we had, but that we would use the elementary test until we had some idea of the average educational level of the men. There was no point in giving a high school level I.Q. test to a man who had a second grade educational level.

Second grade! "So they ain't been to school. They been livin', ain't they? Ya can't live for twenty-five years without you learn a little somethin'!"

To this I made no comment.

I reminded him that we could tell from a man's score if his

I.Q. was higher than the grade school level. If it was, we would call him in and give him a more difficult test.

Grade school level! "I suppose you think I got a gang of school kids workin' for me on the outside? You think I been runnin' a kindegarden?"

No, I said, probably not.

He swore. "How d'you like that—*probably not!* Why—" But he dissolved into a withering smile. "Of course we'll never know until we give 'em all a I.Q., will we, Doc?" And he walked away, his back bristling with anger. Somebody around here was sure gonna get hisself a surprise. Second grade!

The day before we met the first consignment of admissions we went carefully over the procedures for the last time. My four men were seated at the school desks in the large testing room, and I was perched on one of the desks in front of them.

I planned to administer the tests for the first few times. The men were to serve as proctors. Each of them would supervise one row of not more than five men. Their duty was to see that the testees understood the directions and progressed properly from one part of the test to another. I wanted them to observe that the test must always be given in the same way, under the same conditions, within the same time limit, with the same attitude on the part of the testor, and always with exactly the same directions. The results could be standardized only if the procedures were uniform.

I made a special point of the fact that they must not help the testees with the answers—not even with an expression of approval or disapproval. That was a lot to ask of four pantomimists. What I wanted from them, I said, as they walked up and down the aisle, was about the expression they gave me when they dummied up.

The four faces went into a gross deadpan.

"Wonderful!" I said.

We discussed the resistance we would run into at first, about which the men exchanged smug glances that made me a little uneasy. I told them I could see several violent objections. The new men would distrust me because I was not only a stranger, but also a psychologist. And whether the test proved hard or easy for them, having to take it would be an insult. Again, they would be suspicious of how the information they gave would be used, and they would fake answers. And they would resent being stuffed like children behind school desks in a schoolroom situation. Distrust, offense, suspicion, resentment. It would not be easy. And I couldn't take a week out to work on them either, I pointed out. That was why I wanted my assistants to give the tests as soon as possible. They would go a long way in breaking down resistance.

I was careful not to point out that they could also go a long way in creating resistance. They would have thought of that. . . .

"Okay, that's all. Take it easy the rest of the day. You're all as tight as fiddle strings."

The next morning a convoy of twenty men were seated before me in the testing room, to take the Otis Classification test. My proctors were standing at the back of the room. I made the introductory remarks the boys and I had worked out in explanation of the procedure. I said that the test was given in an attempt to assign them to work details in keeping with their abilities and aptitudes. Also, to those hoping for eventual parole I explained that the tests were requirements which would be repeated at intervals, and again at the time of their release. This, I added, was also true of those hoping to accumulate Good Time (time deducted from the original sentence through good behavior).

I then proceeded to the technical instructions regarding the test itself and explained the time limit. My proctors distributed the tests with the testees exuding powerful. disinterest. We labored through the sample questions on the first page. Five minutes after I had set my stop watch and given the signal to begin, only eight of the twenty men were working. Wasting five minutes of a total of thirty wouldn't help their scores.

I saw my proctors catch one another's eyes; then, with the dignity and precision of a Presbyterian deacon proceeding down the aisle for the Sunday morning tithes, Punch marched to the front of the room and turned. After a moment of electric silence he asked, "Is they anything you mugs don't understand about what Doc here said?" His smile could not have been more beguiling or his tone more menacing.

Nineteen faces looked at him with recognition and respect. The twentieth man, a thin, dark, intelligent-looking fellow, paid no attention to the interruption, but went on working.

"Therefore," Punch announced stentoriously, "I will kinely ask you to get the hell to work!"

"*Now!*" added Connie, from the back of the room.

The mutineers bowed morosely over their tests, and the proctors moved majestically up and down the aisles. Punch eyed his men as though they were prospective corpses. Connie's lips moved in a silent stream of sarcasm and raillery. Gibbs padded from desk to desk like a shaming mother hen, holding his tongue at great personal cost. Scott took turns aping his three coaches, never able quite to hide the amusement in his face. All of them were having a good time.

I guessed there would be four tests with valid scores and four or five near-illiterates and feebleminded who would require retesting with individual form boards. The other dozen subjects worked under the constant handicap of the proctors' incipient threat, and their scores would be useless.

The dark slender man in Punch's row finished first and began doodling in the margin of his test. Punch walked up behind him and looked archly at the drawing. His brows went up and his mouth puckered for a whistle while he unabashedly watched the moving pencil. When he straightened abruptly and walked away with a thunderous expression, I did not understand why until later when he showed me the test. Apparently our man, King by name, had expressed his opinion of Punch's kibitzing in a caricature of him drawn in four swift wicked lines.

When I called time the proctors swept up the tests and scored them eagerly. There were only four scores above 100, and four illiterates of indeterminate status. The I.Q.s of the twelve who had operated under coercion ranged from 45 to 72.

"Well, fry my ass!" cried Gibbs, begging my pardon. "From high-grade imbecil-ity to high-grade moron-ity! Where they pickin' up these type gonifs?"

Punch delivered another of his relentless threats: "Let's us don't do no playin' with this sorry mob. A couple fast smacks in the butt'd raise their I.Q.s fast!"

"Oh, that's not so bad for the first try," I said soothingly. "They wasted time, and they didn't really put their minds to it when they did settle down. These scores aren't valid. We won't enter them on our records."

"Maybe Doc won't," Connie ventured, "but these here scores is gonna be real interestin' to the boss of the road gang detail. Serve the bastards right. They had their chanc't."

"That's right, Doc," said Gibbs the mediator, "it'll learn 'em that we ain't kiddin'. They don't play with us, so we queer their easy go. When that gets around, their scores'll raise, you just watch!"

I shook my head. "Remember that impersonal scientific approach I've been telling you about? You can't bully a man into a high score. We'll call in those twelve defensive men for individual tests. Each of you can take on three of them and see what you can do in an hour with them at a form board."

They received the idea in horrified silence. Then Gibbs tried to reason with me.

"Aw, Doc—we're tellin' you this ain't no college. You're missin' a big chanc't. You can't handle them thugs like that. You gotta rough 'em up so's they'll know who's boss around here."

"I'll see my three after they leave the hospital followin' an 'accident'," said Connie.

"I'll take mine on after a little chat in the shower room—with a lead pipe," said Punch. "Y'know, Doc, there's nothin' like gettin' off on the right foot in a jernt like this. There's no cooperation like what you get by throwin' acid on a hundred dresses of a smart-ass dry cleaner who don't wanna join up, or by scarin' his daughter on her way home from school. You can take it from me—"

"It's no go, guys," I said. "You're still talking like third degree cops. You're scientists now, remember? So we leave the brass knuckles outside. They're probably expecting to get roughed up, so let's give them a surprise. There were four illiterates today. Tomorrow let's start with them, then tackle the other twelve. That's a hard day's work, so maybe you better set up the form boards and polish off your style."

None of them made a move to go. They stood very still, staring me down in a long, foreboding silence. Six against one—and suddenly a very lone one. What to do? I couldn't stand and stare back. I couldn't capitulate either, without serious loss of face. The silence became uneasy. They weren't going to help.

Then I noticed Scott. So did the others. With a great show of nonchalance he had begun to roll a cigarette. It was a thing Connie did blindfolded with one hand in five seconds. But Scott was as adept at it as he was at smuggling. It had been one of his projects ever since he arrived at the penitentiary.

He finally got it rolled and sealed with spit. We watched intently while he put it into his mouth and lighted a match with his thumbnail. It was the first time he had succeeded at the match chore. This gave him courage. He put the light to the cigarette, drew deep and exhaled without taking the cigarette out of his mouth. Ah. . . .

But his victory was brief. He was surveying us with a cool

64

eye when his cigarette got the bends and buckled in the middle. A little shower of tobacco sifted to the floor. Scott gazed forlornly at the limp fag in his lips.

The comedy relief cleared the atmosphere. Gibbs chuckled. Punch swore in florid Italian. Connie stamped over to Scott, grabbed the cigarette out of his mouth, and threw it into the wastebasket.

"Honest to God, kid," he said, playing it big, "I think you *better* spend some time at them form boards! Talk about illiteracy! It's like I been tellin' you, kid." He took his own tobacco sack and paper out of his pocket. "Not enough tobacca, not enough pack, not enough spit! Now you come along and let's us see how long it's gonna take you to pin the tail on that there donkey."

He shoved into Scott's lips the cigarette he had been rolling while he talked, and led him toward one of the cubicles.

Scott winked at me as he followed Connie. Gibbs noticed it and smiled to himself. I'm not sure that I did not wink back at Scott, I was so grateful for his having dispersed a gathering rebellion.

Punch's conversion to the change of pace was slower than the others. He sulked around and muttered about doing his talking with a length of pipe. Later in the day I asked him for the test of the young man who had finished first, the dark slim one. I was thinking he might be staff material, I would need someone to make diagrams and graphs eventually.

Punch gave me the test. "At least *I* got a bright boy anyways," he said loudly to catch the ear of the other three. They joined us. "Exceptin' for that drawin' of me, for which I will teach the jerk some manners. He's got a I.Q. of 127, and jeez— look at this dame he draws. Least I guess it's a dame, with plenty bumps an' stuff, even a extry one—looks kinda weird. Jeez, Doc —how horny can a guy git?"

The drawings were all of the same girl, phallic abstractions, but without pornographic content. I turned the test around so that the other three men could see the girl. They admired it in their individual ways.

Scott picked up the test first. Gibbs watched for his reaction to a "quality dame." Scott raised his eyebrows and said nothing. Gibbs took it from Scott and gave it a real try.

"I don't get it," he said at last. "When it comes to a picture of a dame I like somethin'—"

"Somethin' you could hang in a high-class cathouse parlor," said Connie, taking the test from Gibbs. "Gibbs, you got the soul of a pig." He held the picture at arm's length, covering first one eye, then the other. "Ah—me!" Then with a quick change of expression he brought it up close, turned it upside down and righted it again. "Which end is up anyways?"

He returned the test to Punch. "Now my taste runs more to *your* pitcher there, Pinero," he said jovially. "That I'll buy."

Punch flushed, and Connie had just time to jump clear of Punch's foot which was aimed unmistakably at Connie's groin. Connie grabbed Punch's foot in mid-air and up-ended him in a mean fall. Punch showed an instant of pure surprise, scrambled to his feet, and made a rush for Connie. This time he ran into Gibbs' powerful body planted indignantly in his path. Gibbs' hand closed hard on Punch's arm.

"You goddam fink! You got a high I.Q. You better start usin' it. You ain't got no two-bit torpedoes backin' you here, you wop bastard. In a beef with Connie you wouldn't go so good!"

Punch tried to wrench himself free of Gibbs, but Gibbs wound him up and sent him spinning across the room, where he crashed into the door of the vault closet. He landed in a backward sprawl on the floor. For a dazed moment he lay motionless. Then he began to laugh. Connie and Gibbs looked questioningly at each other. Gibbs walked over to Punch.

"Why, Grandma!" said Punch. "Who would of thought my

own sweet little Grandma would lift her hand against me!" He tried to laugh again.

It was a quick grab at face-saving, not too convincing.

"You shouldn't get so excited at your age, Grandma," he said, "you oughtta see your face. It's awful red. You should remember about your blood pressure!"

"Git up, Pinero," snapped Gibbs. "You ain't spendin' the afternoon on the floor. We got work to do. What the hell will Doc think of us?" he asked, glancing apologetically at me.

"I think—" I said, after I had swallowed my Adam's apple, "that King fellow would make a good subject for a Rorschach. How about it, Punch?"

So ended our first day of testing. Two mutinies. One fight. One tired psychologist.

The above conversations—in fact, all conversation in this volume—represent stringently expurgated copy, the original of which jangled harshly upon my academic ear at first. Every American male has been exposed to a vernacular of sorts in barber shops and shower rooms. But to find in a penitentiary such a wide knowledge of certain parts of the human anatomy and their proper functions was a surprise. This jargon went on, of course, twenty-four hours a day.

Those two little four-letter words, for instance, without which we could not conduct a war, have been deleted completely. So have most of the loving names the men called each other. As time went on and their professional vocabularies expanded, their vernacular took on a new face. The two little words began to appear in various forms of the highly respectable verbs, *defecate* and *cohabit*. The effect was startling.

Seriously, the renovation of their speech habits was, relatively speaking, spectacular. I suppose that, for one thing, they wanted to conform to a new environment. But it was more a simple matter of displacement. They suddenly had several hundred new words (not all of which would convert as easily as the two mentioned); and as any semanticist will tell you, the thalamic level of life on which a vernacular such as theirs develops is usually an inarticulate and non-functioning level. As my men became articulate and began to function, the gross obscenities were displaced to quite an extent. Except in a crisis of any kind, when they quickly reverted to local color. . . .

The next day the men met first with the four illiterates, and then with the twelve stubborn subjects. Some of the latter did much better on a retest, but not all of them.

By midday my staff was in mild shock. They had to admit that there were convicts in good standing who couldn't tell a circle from a square and couldn't fit a horse's head on a horse's shoulder. They looked at me with hollow-eyed respect.

They proctored the second convoy of new admissions like sleepwalkers, afraid to look into the men's faces for fear of finding another moron. The cooperation of the second group of testees also was poor, and so were the results. This led to more sessions the next day with the illiterates at the form boards—and a fresh blow to the staff's ego.

The trauma continued for three days. They did nothing but give and score the tests. I needed help in cross-indexing the vocational records of all the inmates which the warden had recently turned over to my office, but the men were useless. They could not shake off their stupor.

It was at this time that some of the implications of a "dumb con" hit Punch. He now reasoned that he was in stir because of the low I.Q. of one of his henchmen whose arrest Punch was avenging when he himself was picked up. When his stooge had been run in by Federal men for peddling dope, Punch was furious. Who did they think they were? His retaliation had been to defy the authorities in their own territory. But his enthusiasm overstepped the bounds of caution, and he was picked up personally peddling a single 15-grain shot of morphine in the Federal Building. This was the rap for which he was now doing time. Four years in stir, all because of a low type gonif with no I.Q!

The situation had always amused him before. Of all the crimes of which he was guilty, to be sent up on a peddling rap had all the incongruity and sting of being kicked by a pet rabbit. But it was no longer funny, now that his dumb stooge was responsible. And only two days ago he had been ribbing me about "maybe he oughtta give all his goons an I.Q." Now he was saying about the same men, "Them cretin sons o' bitches!"

I summoned the artist King for additional tests on both the first and second days of the men's trauma. I took care of him myself, giving him a more advanced battery of tests, among them the Rorschach, which is considered much more indicative than the standard personality tests. This was the "jerk" to whom Punch would teach some manners, but he passed almost unnoticed in and out of the office while Punch and the others sweated away at the form boards.

King was interested in the prospect of working out the tabulations and graphs of our data, although he had never done anything in the field before. The captain's records showed that King was a counterfeiter who had been transferred from another crowded Federal penitentiary to The Annex. He gave as his occupations artist and bellhop. In criminal terminology a bellhop is rarely just a bellhop. He is usually an accessory to crime dealing in girls, hiding loot, harboring criminals, or blackmailing. King's bellhopping turned out not to be a front for any of these activities. Nor was it a necessary means of livelihood. The grapevine said that King had more money than any of the tycoons whose bags he carried at the hotel. Why wouldn't he? He was a counterfeiter.

The explanation of his bellhopping lay in his pathology,

which came to light gradually as I knew him better. However, I sensed from the beginning a compulsive current in his nature which he was holding in check, and which moved beneath his highly integrated front of fastidiousness, precision and aloofness.

On the afternoon of the third day of the staff's shock Gordon dropped in and immediately commented on the gloom.

"Involutional melancholia so soon, boys? Maybe some of the things I hear about this office are true."

He met a barrage of eyes.

Maybe, he said, the new men were being told it didn't pay to act too bright on those tests. Maybe they had the fear of God thrown into them before they ever reached the office. Maybe somewhere along the line, he concluded mysteriously, we were being sabotaged.

Connie began to blink.

Shortly after this he disappeared. He returned a little later, looking very smug.

I learned in due time that he had paid a surprise visit on a forged pass to the delousing and clothing details that afternoon. It was about the only place where sabotage could occur before the new men came to our office. These two details employed several convicts, and it would have been fine sport for them to haze the incoming convicts about being "bugged" and ending up in a strait jacket.

Following Connie's visit, the testees evinced a marked change in attitude and some improvement in I.Q. I learned that Connie had given the two details the alternative of becoming active propagandists for our office, or being abducted one by one and subjected to the tests themselves and having their scores widely publicized throughout the penitentiary. Their capitulation was instantaneous and unanimous. Even the continued hazing of the guards could not successfully counteract the propaganda of the newly converted convict assistants on those details.

This incident broke up my staff's three-day trauma. With

70

the return of perspective they suddenly realized they had been overlooking their own intellecutal superiority as compared to the I.Q.s of their fellow-inmates. Whereupon a new danger threatened the integrity of the daily intelligence quotients. The lower my men could make the scores read, the more superior they themselves felt. They tried to outdo each other in reporting the outlandish answers of the feebleminded. It was no longer a mark of pride for them to turn up with a high I.Q. among their tests. The distinction now was the lowest score. I had to supervise their work closely to prevent them from "forgetting" to record an answer, or to shade the stop-watch timing. When I was suspicious of a score, I called in the inmate and retested him myself.

Finally Scott found our lowest man, "I.Q. 33", a low-grade imbecile, a sweet, happy vegetable. Connie, Punch and Gibbs each insisted in checking the score by giving the candidate three different form board tests. The score remained substantially unchanged.

We placed the man in the psychopathic ward for his own protection. The more agile inmates helped him dress each morning after approaching convulsive seizures a few times, watching him spend two hours at the job. I don't know that his vocabulary of forty-nine words was much changed in that ward, but after months of coaching he learned to play a passable game of checkers, although he took as much as two days to conclude a game.

My men made surmises about the ingenuity necessary to get him into a Federal penitentiary. They thought it probable that the combined resources of the FBI and the city police prosecuted a charge of "stealing a manhole." Actually "I.Q. 33" was guilty of possession of postage stamps and blank money orders with which he had papered the walls of his packing-box hovel at the edge of the city dump. Among his forty-nine words were none with which to explain where he had found the stamps or the blanks. Tough luck.

71

Weary Willie was another case whose I.Q. was stimulating. Willie, a low-grade moron, was the subject of excitement, conjecture, study, examination and exasperation.

He could not stay awake.

This happy state of affairs afforded him periodic psychiatric examinations. He was observed for encephalitis, but the staff concluded that it was a personality set rather than a disease. He was just born sleepy. The hospital repeatedly discharged him as being entirely harmless. He certainly was no criminal. He was in for possession of stolen goods, a fact which Willie couldn't illuminate. His confederates probably left him holding the bag while he was asleep.

He so frequently was missing at cell count that whenever escape alarms were sounded everyone first thought of Weary Willie. He never tried to escape. He would just fall asleep, in the cornfield, the hay mow, the grainery—wherever he happened to be when he found something to lean against. Eventually, therefore, when Willie was missing, no alarm was turned in. Instead the guards would check the last place Willie was seen, and they were sure to find him not far away fast asleep.

Although he never initiated any mischief he was always in trouble through the good-natured baiting of the men. When this baiting campaign became apparent to the captain all marks against Willie were erased and his Good Time re-established.

He proved such a bothersome charge on the farm that they sent him back inside the wall. This decision was reached by the medical staff after treating him for exposure. He had gone to sleep without reference to weather.

His mental candle power equipped him for only two vocations, toting or sweeping. However, he was taken off street detail after several incidents of guards rushing up to his reclining form, thinking someone had been stabbed or clubbed. He was then attached to the loading gang at the railroad gate. This proved a very nostalgic pastime for Weary Willie, who had spent most of his life on the rods. Inevitably, Willie was found missing one night. This time he was nowhere near the railroad gate, where he was last seen loading a freight car.

Later in the night, remembering Willie's somnolent propensities, the captain traced the car number through the dispatcher's office and telegraphed an alert to the freight's next stop. When the yard detectives and brakemen spotted the car, they found Willie asleep on the rods.

The captain was inclined to believe that Willie had been innocent of intent to escape; nevertheless, the act constituted a technical break. He sent Willie to my office, and I found a completely innocent record on the lie detector. Willie explained to me unofficially that the appeal of an old car had been too much for him.

"You see, Doc, all the modern freight cars don't have no rods below. They're just steel girders—no place to ride. But here was this old, old baby and—well, I just wanted to see how it would feel again, so I climbed under. I guess the homesickness was too much, and I just naturally went to sleep. The next thing I knew I was six hours and a hundred miles away and the brakeman was pulling me off.

"Gosh, Doc, I don't want to escape! I want to spend the rest of my life here. It's the easiest go I know. No begging for food, free clothes. And it's a funny thing, I'm even getting used to the showers. I don't mind them so much any more. The hot water is kinda soothing."

The following week Willie was missing again. This time they found him sleeping in the corner of the shower, a tiny stream of warm water spattering down from his bald forehead over his round pug nose.

Weary Willie wasn't entirely alone in not wanting to escape from prison. These *O. Henryesque* stories of men who didn't want to leave the penitentiary, and who wanted to come back when they did leave, were not uncommon. They pleaded not to be discharged, and would try to "escape" to get a longer sentence. Failing in this they would request their foreman to hold their jobs and the captain to hold their cells until they returned. Some of them, before they were released, had already picked the crime they planned to commit in order to be returned to prison, and some of them had chosen the judge under whom they hoped to be tried. In states where there was a recidivist's law they quickly accumulated their three sentences in order to get life for their fourth offense. In aiming for a Federal penitentiary they would commit a postal "crime" in an area that would put them in line for the penitentiary of their choice. Federal penitentiaries were favorite berths for these unresourceful, inadequate Weary Willies following the 1930 reforms.

Perhaps eventually society will commit them to a hospital, for they surely do not belong in prison. Their irresponsibility results from their low I.Q., not from their moral culpability. This makes them naturals to take the rap for somebody else. It is ironical that the law which appears so flexible in the prosecution of big-time crime is so inexorable in dealing with Weary Willies.

The desire to keep their same cells in consecutive sentences was accompanied by all the emotionality that surrounds an ancestral mansion. The cell seemed to mean home to them. It was in many instances the only place in the world that was theirs. They were disturbed and angered when a work detail shifted them to another wing or tier. When a new and modern cell block is erected in a penitentiary, it is usually filled with incoming men because so many of the old prisoners don't want to give up their original cells. It is good warden policy not to move them.

The ordinary prisoner tries to delay his trial and to stay out of prison. But these star boarders were impatient of delays and studied which crime could be most quickly apprehended and punished. They tried to ascertain which judge's docket was the least crowded, so that they could request trial before him. I

74

sometimes received letters and telegrams like the following: "Hope to be back by March 15. Tell my foreman to save my job and tell the captain to have my cell swept out!" There was great warmth of greetings among pals when they finally returned.

My men expressed their feelings about penitentiary life in that decade of depression and unemployment in a joke about a Chamber of Commerce who tried to sell some city fathers the idea of building a wall around the cemetery. The Chamber representative depicted with color and enthusiasm the beauty and function of such a wall. When the Chamber had no more inducements to offer the unresponsive city fathers, one of them spoke up.

"What's the use of a wall around a cemetery?" he asked. "Anybody inside gonna get out? Anybody outside wanna get in?"

One afternoon about closing time a high-grade imbecile named Brody came into my office where I was talking with a staff doctor. In the bantering conversation we held with this feeble-minded chap it developed that he had been caught four times by the same deputy sheriff in the same mountain community for the same attempted job, and was sentenced each time by the same home-town judge. He had attempted to rob the country store and post office, above which the deputy lived. But he had gone about it so thick-headedly and made so much noise breaking in that he was invariably caught. After the first two lugubrious attempts the deputy had stopped laughing at him and preferred charges. Brody was now being released and meant to try the job again. "That little store has the best cheese in the country, Doc, and do I like cheese!"

The staff doctor tried to argue him out of the idea, but Brody's resistance was definite and well-organized. He was going to prove that the job could be done, and done his way. It was such an obviously stupid plan that finally the doctor took paper and pencil and jokingly drew up a much better strategy. Brody listened respectfully and said he would think it over.

Two days later he came back and said, "Doctor, I know you fellows are smarter than me because you're out and I'm in. An' I know you've got a lot of learnin' an' things, but you don't know nothin' about criminals. I'm goin' to go and do this job just the same way I done it before, just to prove it can be did."

A few weeks later I received a letter written for Brody by a friend. Brody couldn't write. "Dear Doc: Please get me my same job, I'm coming back."

He had tried to pull the job, all right, and got life this time for his trouble. He was very happy.

King had been with us in the office about a week when I added another man to the staff. Gordon sent Davis down to me saying that he was a trouble maker, did I want to take a hand with him, maybe I could do him some good. Two factors recommended Davis as a staff member. He was alert and well set up in looks and bearing, and he was a laboratory technician. He had been working in the laboratory just around the hall from my suite.

I asked Davis why he had requested a work transfer. He replied that he was sick of the smell of urine and stools. He superciliously pointed out that I should be glad to get someone with a medical vocabulary and his knowledge of psychological procedures. I took him for those qualifications and his I.Q. of 130, and not for his personality profile.

He was King's age, about thirty. This was not his first stretch, but it was his last. He was in for life. He had been in before for assault and robbery. This time it was for murder.

The fact is well established that the one-time killer, who is frequently a lifer, who didn't kill sadistically or with premeditation, but who struck in a moment of provocation, rage or drunkenness, presents the fewest disciplinary problems of any inmate. His is the most nearly normal personality in prison. But Davis was not one of these. Hate was too basic in his nature. He could kill again. He hated people, and that makes a convict dangerous.

When he first looked at me his eyes were cold, suspicious and contemptuous, and the look in his eyes never changed as long as I knew him.

None of my men liked Davis. He added nothing to the affability of the staff. He rarely joined in conversation, even when he was spoken to. When he did, it was to quarrel, ridicule, or provoke.

King and he would have nothing whatever to do with each other. Their eyes locked once in hostility, and after that they never looked at each other again, to my knowledge. During the short time he was with us the two did not exchange a word. I began to wonder if the reason for their instantaneous dislike of each other was that, whatever the current of pathology in King, it might also be present in Davis and, as is frequently true of psychopathic individuals, they both were sharply aware of this fact. Whatever the force in them was, it was malignant and unpredictable, something they both feared.

The other four men had accepted King at once. An artist-counterfeiter lent a lot of "class" to the office. But the tension between King and Davis made them edgy. Much of the rapport and spontaneity that had begun to develop before Davis came gave way to restlessness and irritability. Davis had a way of setting the men at each other's throats by nothing more than his contempt for them. They left him alone, but the unrest which he provoked in them was turned upon each other, since they were not prepared to handle it in any better way.

After several unsuccessful attempts at getting next to Davis, I concluded that the men would never accept him and that I should take the first opportunity to have him transferred.

In spite of Davis, however, Connie the safeblower, Gibbs the smuggler, Punch the gangster, Scott the innocent, and King the counterfeiter were turning in amazing performances in response to their first chance in a penitentiary to work under a legitimate challenge. They had been exposed to an entirely new and complicated field of learning far beyond their formal education, except in the case of Scott. The fact that they found psychology within their grasp gave them a great sense of superiority. They knew they were valuable to me and would be hard to replace. They knew they could go ahead in their work as fast as they wished, that every inch they gained was theirs as long as they could hold it.

This was different from a few years ago when some of these same men were sitting in idleness and filth, hatching up mischief and breeding resentment. Gibbs still bore the scars of having been beaten until the bones in his back were laid bare because he couldn't fulfill a work quota on a rock pile.

All this sudden positivity threw them back upon their old defenses once in a while. They were self-conscious about their enthusiasm, and suspicious of having been taken in by me. They had had little to be grateful about in previous sentences. This was too good to last, and if things went too smoothly they had to break it up with a petty scrap or some fisticuffs in order to assure themselves and me that they weren't going soft.

One source that was always good for an argument was their expanding vocabularies. They showed astounding resourcefulness in philology and semantics. Their arguments frequently pyramided to such a pitch that I had to come out of my office to mediate the crisis. When several cases of my books and journals arrived, among them some dictionaries, I gave the dictionaries a big build-up, hoping this would terminate the fisticuffs. There had been a couple of bad fights over the meanings of words that had sent the losers to the hospital.

However, the introduction of the dictionaries could not have been more uneventful. To look up the meaning of a word would have settled the argument, and nothing was further from their minds. Occasionally one of the men would surreptitiously consult the dictionary, but only for his own satisfaction, never to settle an argument. If the dictionary proved him wrong he would be that much more on his mettle to defend his retreating position.

The dictionaries did serve one purpose, however. It was through them that the crudities and vulgarities of their jargon were translated into correct medical terminology. They practiced hours on these newly-framed insults. Punch gleefully reported a run-in with a rival gangster. "I called him a *coiting cunnilinctor* an' he never tumbled!"

I was at my desk in my office one day when I heard Connie's voice from the other room starting an argument that developed somewhat as follows:

"I don't know nothin' about *here-di-taments,* but any dope oughtta know what *in-cor-por-eal* means."

"Such as?" Punch challenged.

"What the hell! You a moron? *In-cor-por-eal* means *in the body. In* meaning in, an' *corporeal* meaning body."

"Corporeal don't sound like no *b'ody* to me," said Gibbs. "It sound like the army."

Scott laughed. "He thinks corporal punishment means when a corporal gets it in the end!"

This kind of argument was Davis' meat. "*Incorporeal* means *not pertaining to the body,*" he said patronizingly. "The *in* means *out of.*"

"Since when does *in* mean *out of?*" demanded Connie. "What the hell are you doin *in* stir? Maybe you're supposed to be *out of!*"

"Yeah, it's a hell of a operation when a word don't mean what it means!" said Gibbs.

"Then there's the word *inanimate,*" said Davis.

Nobody had ever heard of it, except Scott who was pretending he hadn't, and King who wasn't participating.

"What about it?" asked Connie.

"Nothing. Except *in* doesn't mean *in,* in this case either. It means *not!*"

"Who're you kiddin', Goggles!" Connie bristled. *"What's* not?"

"Animate's not," replied Davis. *"Inanimate* means you're not alive, sweetheart. It means you're dead."

"Who's dead?" threatened Connie. "Say that again, an' I'll show you who's dead, you phallicphile schizoid!"

"Aw—go cohabit yourself, you low-mouthed dirty fellator—"

There was some fast footwork, during which Connie apparently lifted the surprised Davis out of his chair, followed by a short scuffle and a blow, then silence.

When I walked into the room, the men were philosophically surveying Davis stretched out cold on the floor.

"Connie was reading one of your journals," explained Scott. "He came across *incorporeal hereditaments.*"

"Well, all I can say is, your man on the floor ought to study up on his," I said.

"His what?" asked Punch.

"His incorporeal hereditaments. It means a man's inalienable, immaterial rights."

"Yeah?" Punch scratched the back of his neck thoughtfully. "You mean like standing on the Constitution?"

"Something like that," I replied. "It means that your rights end where his nose begins. Why don't you look it up in the dictionary?"

"I'll take your word for it," said Punch, who at that time wouldn't have been found dead with a dictionary.

I'm afraid the Constitution lost considerable caste that day. During the next three years one or the other of them was found standing on his incorporeal hereditaments instead of on the Constitution.

Davis came to later upstairs in the hospital. He was sent back to the laboratory at my request. Everybody in my office was glad he did not return, including Davis, I'm sure.

I soon replaced him with another man, Ross, and the ranks of my staff closed. These six men were with me all through my three years, and the rest of this book is the story of these six, their world inside as I saw it, and my world outside as they saw it.

Ross, the last man, was in his late forties. He was a magnificent engineer—civil, electrical and mechanical—of considerable reputation and experience. He was a graduate of one of the finest universities in the western hemisphere. His specialty was electricity, but he had the frame and muscle to attest the fact that he had dredged swamps, bridged mountain passes and spanned rivers. But he was not just a mass of muscles, not with an I.Q. of 140.

There was a quality of tragedy in his face, the mark of his own hopelessness about himself. His record showed repeated sentences for illegal possession of drugs, and forgery. He had been in for almost a year on this stretch when I met him, and had a little more than three years to go. It was a long time before he would talk about himself.

Ross requested transfer to our office shortly after I had set up my polygraph in one of the cubicles. I tried repeatedly to assure my men that the lie detector would never be used to establish anyone's guilt, but only to record the responses of addicts during denarcotization when their blood pressure and galvanic reflexes became erratic, and to determine areas of emotionality in men with complexes resulting in psychosomatic symptoms: heart attacks, ulcers, functional blindness, etc. Occasionally a man, like Weary Willie, would request a test to establish his innocence. But no amount of assurance won my men over to that mechanical conscience. They gave it a wide berth. They

81

wouldn't even use the cubicle in which it stood. If it was a lie detector it detected lies, and being expert liars they wanted none of it.

I told them not to worry, that it was still in an experimental stage, still full of mechanical bugs. It was Scott who contacted Ross about working on the machine, and Ross put in hundreds of hours on it, on calibrations, circuits, leverages.

The staff had real regard for Ross. A criminal has a fanatical respect for quality and integrity. They never referred to Ross as a forger or an addict. He was an engineer.

Their arguments did not stop with the transfer of Davis and the addition of Ross. Their disputations over words and their search for an I.Q. below 33 gained such momentum that I began to think of counter-measures. I concluded that they were not playing games strictly for laughs, but as a test to see how far they could go before I would crack down, and how I would crack down when the time came.

I could not backtrack or appease them, of course, but the pattern of standing my ground while they stood theirs could get tiresome. Soon the ground being held would get tougher and tougher, and the problem would resolve into who could get tougher, they or I. That was no resolution at all. That was the old philosophy of penology, the story of punishment. So I cast around for something better.

I felt they liked me as much as their brief acquaintance and native suspicion would permit. Perhaps they might respond more to leadership within their own caste, self-government. To appoint one convict to a position of authority over another was still considered a fine way to insure miscarriage of justice and insubordination, in spite of Warden Osborne's spectacularly successful introduction of it at Auburn and Sing Sing in 1915. But I decided to try it.

So I said one day, "Look, fellows, I'm new at this business

and I don't want to learn everything the hard way. How about wising me up and learning me the ropes?"

Sure, sure.

"In the meantime, we've got some work to do," I continued. "Now, Connie, you've been around. You've been in more penitentiaries than anybody here." Connie always swelled visibly at this distinction. "From now on you're Number One Boy around here. It's your job to keep this place straight, and no more rough stuff."

As the days passed I began to wonder whether my experiment was not going to work, or whether there was deliberate insubordination, because most of the orders I routed through Connie were not being carried out. I called him into my office.

I shut the door behind him and we sat down. But Connie promptly excused himself and returned to the other room "for a pencil." When he came back to my office he left the door open. I asked him to close it. He did, but immediately remembered that he had forgotten to give one of the boys some instructions and excused himself again. When he returned he again left the door generously ajar.

We sat for a moment watching each other speculatively. He was dummying up, his face was a mask of no-aid. I was beginning to realize that I had put Connie on a spot with the other men by closing the door and singling him out for secrets. Also, my appointing him Number One Boy had been a radical departure from custom, and he was probably hesitating to assume responsibility over his fellows without further public confirmation from me.

I picked up some irrelevant papers from my desk and walked out of my office into theirs, with Connie at my heels.

"Connie," I said into the listening silence, thumbing industriously through my papers, "I appointed you Number One Boy around here the other day, but nothing's getting done. I've given you several jobs, but your men haven't carried them out.

What's up? After all, they're being paid four cents an hour," I added whimsically, "and you're supposed to see that they earn it."

"You heard the man!" boomed Connie at my shoulder to anybody who *happened* to be listening.

I was on the right tack, then.

"Another thing, Connie. About your dialectics."

"My *what?*"

"Dialectics. Arguing about words. Your men are still at it. I don't care how much they argue, but they don't know when to stop. We can't always be mopping blood off the floor. Tell them when they get in that mood, they've got to use the dictionary!"

"Listen to the man!" boomed Connie.

In the months that followed, Connie's "You heard what the man said!" became tantamount to a performance to the letter of the word. If a staff member demurred or did a poor job, the other boys dealt with him in varying degrees of severity. They would see that for a week he didn't get his meat, his movie, his shower, or his ball game.

This deviousness and indirection, which is a component in criminal personality, extended even to written notations. At first I left memos for Connie on his desk at night until I realized that many of them were never put into operation. After two or three such infractions I recalled the closed door, and knew I would have to follow the same procedure of public informing. Connie could never allow the possible accusation to grow that he was in league with me, that he was lording it over his men, or that there was any special privilege or dispensation in his case. I therefore evolved the plan of writing the memos to Punch or Gibbs and telling them to give it to Connie. Or I told one of the boys to tell Connie what I wanted done.

This became my *modus operandi*.

Viewed positively, indirection proved a way around red

tape. As in the army, all Government institutions are buried under myriads of quadruplet and quintuplet forms, budgets and requisitions. This was especially true in a penitentiary where the "leakage and shrinkage" of stock was very high. All departments had to make their estimates for a year in advance on some items, semi-annually on others, and quarterly on others. If one miscalculated on estimates, one couldn't get the supplies in advance, regardless of how critical the need. The hospital was sometimes in the preposterous position of lacking an anesthetic or a specific medication, which resulted in postponing a crucial surgery or delaying treatment until the next quarterly requisition.

My staff found ways around this annoyance.

In our research we needed colored inks, colored paper and cards for convenience in tabulating and filing. I could not expect to get them for three months. I must have mentioned this fact in the office, as well as the alternative of delaying the project until the next quarter, unless I dug down into my own pocket for the materials.

I thought no more of the matter until a few mornings later when I unlocked the cabinet. There on the shelves were reams of colored paper, stacks of different sized cards and pints of colored inks.

"Where did *this* come from?" I asked my Number One Boy.

"Well—whatta ya know!" exclaimed Connie innocently. "Punch, where did this stuff come from?"

"Haven't the slightest idea, Honey Chile," drawled Punch. "You know anythin' about this, Grandma?"

"Never saw it before," said Gibbs. He turned to Scott.

A week later the incident was still good for a laugh.

"Beats the devil where that stuff came from," Gibbs began one day, his nose in his work.

A minute or two later Scott picked it up. "I'm not used to this mystery stuff. How do you suppose 'they' opened that lock?"

Silence for a couple of minutes. Then: "I'm a second story

man myself," said Connie, "I don't know nothin' about locks. I got my start openin' pullman windows an' if it ain't somethin' that can be jimmied it's outta my class."

"Hell—I'd of shot it off," said Punch. "That's the quickest way to open a lock. Nothin' like a .44 to pick a lock."

"Bein' a contractor," said Gibbs, "the only thing I could do would be to get a crowbar and pry it off. Or else get a saw an' saw around it."

"It couldn't have been Ross," decided King, the artist. "You know how he would have gone about opening a lock? First he would have to get a blueprint, then he would get out a table of logarithms and figure out the leverages and the fulcrums—he would still be at it. Couldn't have been Ross."

"Couldn't have been Scott," said Ross, the engineer. "When he sees a lock he thinks it means you should knock on the door. No answer. So what would he do? He'd go up to the warden's office. 'I say, warden, I need a master key to open a cabinet—' Couldn't have been Scott!"

It was months before I fully appreciated the ingenuity and effort represented by my bulging cabinets. The old army game behind bars is a different colored horse.

If somebody needs anything unusual, he makes his need known through the grapevine. The convict clerks first check to see if it is in stock. They may have to go through literally dozens of boxes and shelves. If it is in stock, the guards must be diverted while the boxes are opened, rifled, and faultlessly re-sealed. The "hot stuff" may be relayed to another point, or it may be re-packed with cornflakes or shoe leather or light bulbs.

If the article is not in stock, a confederate on the outside "lifts" the material and sends it in through a dozen channels. The unloading crews must separate the marked boxes and stack them until they can be distributed. Getting it to its destination may mean passing it through five gates and risking five possible searches, but it is all done in the name of the brotherhood.

Some of my colored paper came from outside, I was told, through the machine shop to the shoe factory in a shipment of leather, then to the laundry in with dirty aprons, then to the hospital kitchen in dishcloths, then to the basement in empty cartons, and finally to the office. My ink hit the power house along with cans of oil and the paint shop with cartons of turpentine.

Indirection also accounted for the episode of the Ediphone which occurred a few weeks later.

The ennui of prison life made the smallest event a foil for the boys' inventiveness. They laid feverish plans upon the promise of an Ediphone from the head office.

While waiting for its arrival they settled among themselves the matter of each man's responsibilities to it according to office seniority and personal qualifications. Unless seniority and rank were observed, infantilism would creep out and somebody would have his feelings hurt and sulk, long and hard.

The momentous question posed by the promised Ediphone was, who would shave the cylinders? Now, *there* was a problem cut to just their size, one that demanded long deliberation and clear thinking. . . . The job offered great distinction to the man who would take the used cylinders upstairs to the administrative office and shave them. They must therefore choose their delegate with caution and sobriety. It was positively exhilarating to watch full-grown men turn this triviality into a full-sized production.

But after several days of deliberation they still could not agree upon any one man's being permanently assigned to this important job. They finally compromised: they would take turns daily. This was one of the rare occasions when seniority did not operate. Instead they flipped coins to establish serial order.

Immediately a cylinder shaving schedule was made and a chart posted on the wall above Gibbs' desk.

This innovation promptly produced an epidemic of charts and calendars. Each man had to have his own calendar on which his Good Time was accumulated and his parole anticipated. "Only 720 Days Till Parole." Mail days, shower days, shave days were charted—no event was too large or too small.

One morning I found my men standing around the maze of calendars. One of the latter was giving them trouble.

"Goddam!" murmured Connie, "Now, what the hell d'you suppose it was?"

All their names were there, with series of checks after each name, but they couldn't remember the purpose of the chart. After all, there were so many of them. . . .

A week later they were still asking, What the hell d'you suppose it was? Finally they quietly removed the chart and said no more about it.

Eventually the wall became so cluttered with calendars as to be impractical. Ross and King were commissioned to draw up a master chart with dozens of columns to absorb all the calendars. It was most complicated and impressive. Men came down from other departments to gather ideas for their own charts. It was shown great respect for a while. But a master chart somehow destroyed the sense of individuality, so that gradually the calendars reappeared and everyone was happy.

Having settled the schedule of cylinder shaving for months in advance, they were considerably unhorsed by a memo from the head office: there was no Ediphone in the storeroom or on order, and it would be over six months before we could expect one through regular channels.

This was bad, I could see. They had been boasting to the men in the cell block about the competence of their office. It was not just an ordinary office with clerks and typewriters, but one with an Ediphone. And now no Ediphone. A sorry deal indeed!

There were a couple of days of brooding, and then things became bright again. I put it down in my mind as just another evidence of the emotional immaturity of the prisoner. But one morning when I walked into the office I found Gibbs powerfully preoccupied with adjusting a pair of head phones, taking off a record from a transcriber sitting beside his desk. In my office was a new dictator.

Punch came stomping in. "Jeez, ain't it wonderful, Doc? I guess the C.O. or somebody got this on a fluke."

But the mystery cleared when he added in dummy-up style, "The orderly said to say nothin' about it, Doc. They can't put it on the budget until next year."

I talked to Gordon about it later in the day.

"Well," he said, "I guess you're in with the boys. Either they like you enough to take a chance, or else their pride was so hurt that they just had to deliver."

Probably, he said, something like the following had taken place. In some distant city a distributor or a warehouse was now short one Ediphone transcriber, one dictator and forty-eight records. The men wouldn't have got it in our vicinity; it would be too easy to trace. It undoubtedly came in on a bogus inventory and the slips would never reach the front office. Or it might have come in labeled catsup and have been carried down from the hospital kitchen. The theft would not be reported by the company because it wouldn't be discovered till the year-end inventory; in any event there was probably a confederate in the warehouse who would raise the count by one to cover the loss.

"Anyway," he concluded, "the numbers on your machine are probably phony."

I had not thought of that, but the boys had. There were no number plates on either instrument.

Months later, when I felt I knew my men, I asked them for their rationalization regarding the Ediphone. Gibbs undertook to explain.

"What a guy don't know don't hurt him, Doc. As long as you have a lot of stuff, you don't miss a little. The railroad has thousands of shovels which they keep in warehouses. As long as they don't need 'em an' think they're there, it's all right. Now, if I took your shovel from your garage, that would be stealin', since you only got one. But what the hell is the difference, one girl more or less in a harem?

"It's like they teach you in economics. Credit is built on faith, or some damn thing. Lots of banks stay open when they're really busted.

"For instance. A express shipment of a couple canvas bags of dollars is sent to a bank. So they dump 'em in the vault and nobody thinks no more about it. A few months later the teller goes down to get some dollars, an' whatta you know, nothin' in the bags but iron washers. So they check back with th'express company and find the shipment got mixed up with a order for a bolt-and-nut company. The bolt-and-nut company went out into their yard, an' sure enough, there was the two sacks of dollars leanin' up against the fence. You see, as long as the bolt-and-nut company thought they had washers, they was happy. An' as long as the bankers thought they had dollars they was happy. Now, that's the faith of credit.

"*You* don't know whether the Gov'ment's really got any silver to back up your dollar bill, Doc. You just think they have," he concluded brilliantly. "As long as they say they have, nobody is the wiser. Maybe even your dollar bill is made by King here, but if nobody knows it's counterfeit, what the hell?

"So here's a warehouse, an' they keep a backlog of two hundred Ediphones. So they get fifty in and they send fifty out, and they still keep their two hundred. Now, what's the odds whether they are short one or not?"

King, the counterfeiter, concluded the argument. "The moral of this story is: don't keep your money in a bank."

Although operating the Ediphone became commonplace in time, shaving the cylinders never lost its appeal. Since caste was established by the number of cylinders a man shaved on his day, the count was religiously kept. Zeal was at such a pitch that half-filled records were spirited from my dictator to be transcribed and shaved. They were impressed with my perspicacity when all by myself I uncovered their tracks.

Soon it became obvious to everybody that the count was being falsified. They constituted themselves a Board of Censorship and Control and established an auditing and checking committee. This guaranteed the count, but overlooked a new racket. New and unused records began to find their way into the shaving basket. Several had been shaved down to the burlap before I discovered the practice. Since my supply of cylinders was fast dwindling, I wistfully called their hand.

In their words, the air was electrocuted. Their immediate reaction was one of stunned silence and consternation. It was plain to see that they were all equally guilty, except Ross and King who had no time for such games. Then they found their tongues.

"Thieves! Sneak thieves! What a low goddam operation!" sputtered Gibbs.

"Chicken stinkin' heisters!" yelled Connie. "Pinch their old lady's last cow!"

"Some smart bastard's beggin' for a fat lip!" muttered Punch.

The gall and ignominy of it was that they themselves had flubbed the deal. None of the experts had detected the other's deception. All were guilty, and each had failed to check on the other from sheer overconfidence in his own cleverness. Their admiration of anyone who could put it over on someone else was mixed with chagrin this time at having been taken for a ride by one another.

"You stupes belong in stir," said King, from the sidelines. "If *Doc* can catch onto a deal like this, you wouldn't be safe on the outside."

91

Later they came around to his point of view.

"I'm scared to git out," moaned Connie. "Why, a flatfoot could be sittin' on my shoulder an' I'd never know it!"

"We're outta practice, no kiddin'," said Gibbs, "when Doc here puts on them specs of his an' picks it outta the air both times."

"Yeah—Doc's not so dumb. He knows more than he lets on. Fact is, you never know what the hell he knows!" said Punch reproachfully.

Thereafter all four men descended upon each cylinder and personally thumbed it before it went to the shaver.

As in the paper and ink episode, my men were "entirely innocent" and "in no way responsible for" the appearance of the Ediphone. This was true in the sense that no department does its own raiding. Some other department steps in, and later, when the other department lacks something, reciprocity is in order.

I was not aware of this reciprocity until one day I heard a convict orderly from the surgery ward remark in the presence of my men about the shortage of ether. He guessed they would have to "dig into that new gas the docs are hoarding" (cyclopropane) for some jobs coming up the next week. This led to a long beef on red tape and requisitions. I got the point two days later when the same convict came back with a grin on his face and an invitation for me to watch some brain surgery. They had ether now and could save the precious cyclopropane. I knew then that the surgery ward had pilfered our ink and paper for us and that my men had reciprocated in anesthetics.

5

ONE MORNING in December of my first year I arrived very late, fully expecting to find the quota of new admissions restlessly stacked up in the hall awaiting processing. Instead I found everything assigned, the group of admissions being tested, and Connie and Punch strutting around like martinets. I was pleased that they felt their initiative would be approved. But the fact that gave me pause was the realization that the vault was open, the cabinets unlocked, and the records from my desk were out.

This second demonstration of the futility of locks—even of the vault combination—brought into question the disposition of my extremely confidential records.

Building rapport with the general prison population and establishing a consultation program had progressed slowly. For the first several weeks I was left strictly alone. I was still the Squirrel Guy waiting to "bug 'em." Then I had a run of unsavory squealers who wanted me to get even for them. Listening to them would have put me in an enviable position to wake up dead some morning. The next to beard the lion were the sob sisters who wanted a shoulder on which to cry. I had the impression that these were sent in by the men at large as test cases to see what my line was. I sent them to the social workers.

Some of the cases were hard to classify.

"Doc, I didn't sleep much last night," began one patient. "I got a problem. I get out next Saturday an' I came to ast you whether I should kill him or her or both of 'em."

I asked clarification on the pronouns.

"Oh, this guy, he's my pal. An' the skirt, she's my gal. He's been takin' care of her since I got sent up."

"What do you mean taking care of her?" I baited him. "Is she ill?"

"Oh no, Doc. You see, she's too good for the streets, so I always got men for her. None o' this taggin' around cheap speakeasies or workin' for a house where she has to pay cop protection. I picked 'em out and brought 'em to her. So my pal says he'll pimp for her while I'm sent up. An' now he's layin' her."

"Well, if she's a prostitute, what's the difference?"

"Hell—she ain't no prostitute!" he protested, "I got her outta that class!"

"Oh?"

"Y'see, I got her two bedrooms and a sittin' room, so's if two guys gets there at the same time, they don't have to meet. She can go from one room to the other."

"Oh. . . ."

"Now m'pal has moved in with her an' it cuts down on income. It's a double cross! An' that's not all. I think she's beginnin' t'like him better'n me. She says he's gettin' her more money. Maybe so, on tricks. But she forgits the guys we used to jackroll. They paid off big. Them dirty double-crossin' rats—I oughtta bump 'em both off!"

I finally realized with shock that he really meant to kill. In three days he would be released with murder in his blood. I quit bandying.

Later, after some spontaneous therapy on my part, he asked philosophically, "Well, if I ain't supposed to kill 'em, shall I try to get her back, maybe? Or punch this mug's face in? Or should

I look me up another floosy? They're hard to git as good as her, y'know."

One of the early cases involved Doctor Fellows, our surgeon.

As Gordon had said, the men loved Fellows for his character and religion. But they would have ignored his beautiful character, probably, if he had not also been a fine surgeon. Fellows was kept as busy sewing up one kind of lesion as I was another. They *would* come apart at the seams.

They had a housewife's pride in their operations. "See this?" displaying a scar, "Fellows." "Sure, Fellows sewed me up, I wouldn't let no other croaker touch me." Many of them, unable to get into the surgery ward by faking appendicitis, would check in for circumcision. This scar was as proudly exhibited as a skull suture.

One morning the door of my consultation room flew open. I had just time to notice that the outer office was deserted before a burly convict walked in and began talking.

"We're wised up that you're a square guy, see? An' we got trouble, see? The captain's a square guy too, but we can't tell him, see? Maybe you can tell him indirect-like an' get his screws to lay off, see? It's like this, see?

"I'm the cook, nobody monkeys with me. I got the knives, see? Things are missin', maybe some cans. I don't get the rap, I can't let my men get the rap, so who gets it? The screw on the job, see? He checks stuff in an' it don't check out. Monkey business, see? So the captain yanks him off an' puts another screw on, see? That's all right, I don't care for no screw. But now they're doublin' 'em an' things is gettin' too tight, see? You can't move easy, see?

"Now, Doc Fellows ain't got much money, see? An' he's got a big family, see? An' Christmas's comin' up an' it don't cost the Gov'ment nothin', see? What's a turkey or a ham to them with all them bums on relief?

95

"Know what Doc did last summer? Spent seven hours on a guy I carved up. It was a bum steer, I got the wrong guy. Doc could've just throwed up his hands, see? But no. After he saves this punk's life he works and he works, slow and patient, on the guy's hand. He goes half way to the elbow after muscles and nerves an' slits every finger almost to the tip, see? an' ties every goddam muscle back so the guy's not only got a hand, but he uses his fingers, see? They don't even hurt. He don't have to do that kinda thing, see? It's all right, a croaker can just let 'em go, see? But not Doc Fellows.

"Now you go tell the captain everythin's all right, see? Nothin' much is goin' to get out of that refrigerator, see? Nothin' is goin' anywhere except just a little once in a while, an' it's goin' to the right place, see? An' the records will be patched up an' he can take off all his extry screws.

"An' the captain don't need to know nothin' about this, see? An' I don't know nothin' about it either. I just dummy up. But it's okay an' the captain don't need to worry about nothin'. In fact, I dare him to take all his screws off if he wants to see somethin' work real smooth-like. It'll check out even. When I take a seven-pound hen out of the stew the flunkie'll put in seven pounds a water, see? An' that checks, see?"

And the cook was gone.

I couldn't have reproduced my conversation with the captain ten minutes after I left him that afternoon. I tried to make it a model of double-talk. It had neither unity, coherence nor emphasis. I hoped he had a vague idea of what I was talking about. He couldn't have had more.

Apparently he understood me. At an after-lunch bull session the next day Connie remarked to Gibbs over the top of a newspaper, "This goddam Gover'ment don't know what the hell they're doin' half the time. Why can't they make up their stupid minds? Last week the captain triples the watch in the kitchen, an' today he takes 'em all off an' sends 'em down to the paint shop. What the hell—if you want some sense you gotta go to the funny papers!"

Another case that came to me was an addict who turned up periodically in the narcotics ward after getting his hands on the small caches of dope that were smuggled in once in a while. His resistance to cure was strong, and I soon learned why.

After the passage of the Harrison Narcotic Law in 1914, he had gone voluntarily to a "sanitarium" where cures were guaranteed. Instead of being cured he became the victim of a racket which still exists in some of these charlatan sanitaria, and which for fiendishness can hardly be equaled.

He became fond of one of the nurses. She was excessively friendly with him, and after her rounds at night would return in great secrecy to spend a hectic fifteen minutes with him. He had great mental conflict over these interludes, however.

"Every time I mounted her," he said to me, "I just couldn't go through with it. She was such a nice kid—she was a virgin."

But one night temptation was too great, and he spent the next few days in remorse over having molested a virgin. His remorse was dissipated quickly, however, when he discovered that he had contracted both gonorrhea and syphilis. His disillusionment in a "representative sanitarium and doctor" threw the balance against society in his mind, and the man became a more or less constant small-time criminal.

The prostitutes, dressed as nurses, would infect all the men in the sanitarium. They would then require treatment for venereal disease, which in turn required money. My man said he began stealing to pay for the shots.

In this way many sanitaria kept a constant flow of money coming in, and when a patient became suspicious of protracted treatment or refused to pay, or wanted to change doctors, he would be threatened with being turned over to the narcotics authorities.

When my case load of voluntary consultations increased I wondered what would happen when I finally began to get the real thing, the serious personality pathologies involving life and death and implicating other people. Any leakage from these records could precipitate catastrophe. Distrust or suspicion of me would awaken a persecution complex in the men that would build to a mass psychosis and paranoia. It was absolutely imperative that the men in the general population feel their confidences were inviolate. I hadn't forgotten the warden's warning about exercising my immunity.

Inevitably, questions of trust were in the minds of my staff concerning me. They had quaint methods of coercion.

Opening my desk one January morning, I found a gun lying in plain view in the center drawer. It was new and neatly polished, and I'm sure without a fingerprint; although I can think of nothing more foolhardy than to have carried it to the captain's office for a fingerprint test. The cylinder of the revolver didn't seem to be loaded. Using my handkerchief to avoid prints, I opened the gun. Whimsically there was one bullet in the chamber. At least it didn't look much like preparation for a jailbreak.

As I mused Dick Tracy-like over the open drawer, I wondered if they were testing me to see if I would report the gun as contraband. Or perhaps the gun was "hot" and my desk was considered safe from search. But even Dick Tracy would reason that, if this were the case, the gun would have been placed at the back of the bottom drawer and well concealed from sight. No, it was clearly a warning to me. They knew the kind of story I was getting in my consultation room, but they didn't know what use I might make of the things I was hearing. The gun was by way of saying I had better be a bright guy and keep my mouth shut or

I might be a dead one. It was by way of reminding me that I had said I would guard the confidences of the prisoners with my life. I had no inclination to underestimate the cold gleam of that gun. My life was only as good as my discretion.

None of my men were in the office when I made the discovery. This delicate phenomenon, I learned, always announced an event of any proportion. They reported one hour late, saying they had missed the early work convoy and, of course, had to wait until the next detail of men checked through. They were so sorry. There was nothing unusual about their manner when they did arrive, or about the rest of the day, except that they displayed unprecedented concentration in their work.

The next morning the gun was gone. The incident was never mentioned.

Did I say they knew the kind of story I was getting?

A few weeks later I tried to move my desk out of the progressive path of the winter sunlight and discovered that it was bolted to the concrete floor. I distinctly remembered moving it freely when I had arranged my office that fall. Upon examination I found a microphone beneath the desk, the wires of which led into the desk leg and probably through a hollow bolt to the tunnels beneath the half-basement. Where it terminated I could only surmise. I took a quick memory inventory of what might have been overheard during the past weeks. That was no good, everything that happened in my office was volatile.

Going into the outer office I told Ross, the engineer, that I had kicked some wires loose in my office and asked him if he would take care of them.

He looked at me and flushed. "I'm sorry, Doctor," he said quietly, as he rose. "But I want you to know the mike has already been dismantled."

Gibbs rose too and said quickly, "I'll take over, Doc. Ross wouldn't know where to look for the stuff." He wanted to clear Ross with me.

But Ross wanted no special privileges. "I think I can find them, Gibbs," he said.

The following day Gordon came down to the office.

"I was O.D. last night. What the hell's wrong with this wing? I couldn't sleep for the pounding. That's twice in a month they've torn up the laboratory plumbing. That's bad enough, but why the drilling through concrete?"

"What's the lab got to do with us?" I asked.

"Well, they're next door, and I've been here long enough to know that where they're working isn't where the mischief is, and there's no one else but you in this wing. What goes on?"

Yeah—what the hell goes on? echoed my men innocently.

The plumbing stoppage was, of course, deliberate, I learned later. Somebody had "accidentally" spilled a chemical in the sink which ate through the pipe and into the concrete. Then, while the repair crew chiseled out the concrete in the tunnel under the laboratory, four holes were surreptitiously drilled in my concrete floor and the desk bolted. The microphone wire was run through the conduit to the outer office wall plug, where it was connected to the Ediphone headpiece by a concealed secondary circuit. Dismantling was done in the same way. While the crew repaired the laboratory the four holes in my floor were cemented and the wire removed from the conduit. Nothing remained but four skillful patches in the battleship linoleum.

Questions of my integrity also existed in the minds of part of the general prison population. The possibility of my keeping incriminating notes and carrying them home arose. Davis, embittered by his experience in my office, was creating considerable speculation about me among the prisoners. I knew nothing of this until later, but my boys told me they had been gravely concerned for me. I learned that my person had been frisked by pickpockets a half dozen times, but that nothing incriminating had been found.

One night when I returned home from a staff party I found

that my new residence in town had been thoroughly ransacked. Everything had been systematically moved, looked into and under, even to the point of loosening carpets and going through books. Order had been restored for the most part, however. And suspended from the mouthpiece of the phone was a card which read: PASSED INSPECTION.

The search included my garage and basement, which were less painstakingly restored to order. Even my car had been searched while I was still at the party.

Two days later I learned that Davis had cracked under the hazing of the other prisoners after my integrity had been established by the house search. When this did not silence him he turned up at the hospital with a fractured skull.

My men allowed me the dignity of opening the vault and cabinets in the morning and locking them at night, even after the episode of my late arrival, until this became a rather hollow ritual. At any rate, early in the game I was still doing this janitorial work.

One February evening at closing time I discovered my key ring was missing. Connie was voluble and coldly furious. Some insufferable meddler was disturbing his smooth-running administration.

"It ain't the goddam keys, Doc. It's fer Christ sake the discipline in the joint! We gotta hang this thing right now. Some jerk gets the idea he can pull a little deal like this an' the joint pops its lid. This guy's gotta be oriented quick!"

He procured the roster of the new men who had been processed in the office at the three o'clock period that afternoon, the last time I could remember using my keys. One glance at the roster and he said, "Ah-ha! Gimme a pass, will ya, Doc? An' you chase on, I'll lock up."

Reaching for my fountain pen I found that was gone too. Connie swore loudly and procured another. I gave him a pass. I was putting on my coat to leave when he said he was sorry, some ink had spilled on the pass where he was going to write in *third wing,* would I write him another?

But he didn't return the blotched pass and I didn't ask for it.

There are two attitudes open to a staff member in a penitentiary. Like the guards, he can trust absolutely no one. That's playing it safe. Or with his eyes wide open he can take a chance on someone against very long odds, hoping it will pay off.

I was beginning to believe that one can trust a criminal implicitly in certain areas. And if I was going to gamble in something in my men, I didn't dare show distrust, just as I didn't dare show fear.

Sometimes, in a crisis, Connie would give me a cue in a look or a word. At other times he would dummy up and throw the ball in my lap. I learned that the less proportion he gave an incident, the more important it was. I left the second pass on the desk and started home.

When I reached the exit, the gate guard was solicitous. Connie had reported the loss of my keys, he said. Somehow I hadn't thought of my car keys. "We've sent for Simms, he'll take care of you."

Simms was a lock-picker on the outside. On the inside he was a lockmaker, and a very busy man. He was never seen without a large noisy ring of a hundred keys which he carried only for effect. He closed his eyes, chose a key at random and opened my car door. He repeated the ritual for the ignition.

"Shame on you, Simms!" I said. "*Two* keys?"

He grinned.

"One key, two keys, no keys, same difference. You want I should use a bobby pin, maybe?"

I had dinner at the club and bowled a couple of games with Gordon before starting home, expecting to crawl in a window. Such skepticism! My house was blazing with light, the door was unlocked, and inside on the telephone table were my keys. For a moment I looked back wistfully on my quiet professorial life.

The next morning my fountain pen was on my desk and the boys were singularly quiet. I went out into their office and stood in front of Gibbs' desk. "Gibbs," I said poignantly, "what was my address before I moved here and how much money do I have in the bank?"

"How should I know, Doc?"

"You heard the man!" boomed Connie.

"Aw—1244 Center Street," grumbled Gibbs.

"And my bank account?"

He glanced at Connie and squirmed. "Which you want, Doc? Savings, or commercial?"

I began to understand the mystery of my keys when later in the morning Gordon asked me to see a new convict suffering from retrograde amnesia and a hell of a bump on his head.

I asked the convict ward attendant who the patient was. He said he was Dewey the Dip, a new convict who had come in yesterday and had fallen down the steel stairs in the third wing this morning.

"Third wing, did you say?"

"Yeah. I guess he's not used to the catwalk yet. You know, Doc, most of these new men get a bump before they get wise to the joint." He gave me a broad look.

"That's quite a bump," I said. "Must be quite a joint."

After lunch my men engaged in a bull session in which the incident of Dewey the Dip was illuminated.

"It's a kick," explained Gibbs. "You'd honest to Christ think that a guy in that quicky-foot profession could creep down a stair one at a time without woppin' off into the air. More like dove off, the way I heerd it. Hit about the middle of the stair an' bounces right down to the landing, screechin' like an unpaid whore all the way."

"Is this his first stretch?" asked Scott.

"Naw," growled Connie. "He's a three-time loser. He oughtta know better."

"Like I say," said Punch, "some guys just don't have no sense of proportion, no finesse."

Then the cigarettes were put out and they went to work.

I was usually apprised of strategic events by some such unorthodox business as this. As I have said, when I found the outer office deserted, I knew it meant that my men were busy somewhere distracting a hospital guard or raiding the kitchen, or creating a disturbance at the other end of the hall, so that someone with something on his mind could enter my office unknown or unwatched, and leave the same way, without record or witnesses of the visit. I would then be brought up to date on the denouement of the visit during what I came to call their *post-mortem* sessions held almost daily after lunch. The more important the information they had to convey, the more innocuous would be their double talk, and from it I was expected to make my own deductions and find my own clues, as in the case of Dewey. If the boys came to feel they had talked too much or too revealingly, they would dummy up for a while.

Poor Dewey. There is a pattern in the criminal code that requires a completed circuit. It is not so much that they demand a personal retribution for a personal injury, as it is their belief that Fate is not rightly served until retribution has been done. It is their religion. The pattern is so compulsive that they lose sleep and sometimes become ill until the circuit is completed and the episode is somehow appropriately closed. The issue is not merely the settling of a personal score; it is not as fatuous as Tarzan's Law of the Jungle or Tracy's Crime Doesn't Pay. It is a cause-and-effect concept, a stimulus-and-response bond completely apart from ethics. They believe that implicit in whatever a man does is a resulting fate. Frequently these retributions and disciplines couldn't possibly be effected by the avenging party himself. The deed will be done by a confederate, and only when the real avenger is safe behind an air-tight alibi.

My men were angry at this pickpocket episode, but not because someone had muscled into their territory. They expected this, for they did it themselves all the time. But they couldn't have advantage taken of me, or have me placed in a ludicrous light. To them the sting was that a low caste sneak thief had penetrated their wall of protection around me and done this ignominy under six pairs of skilled and watchful eyes.

But apart from their skill and in a more personal sense, any mischief done to me was mischief done to them. I was fast becoming their alter ego. Of course, they would never have admitted such identification with me; to allow such an insidious influence was called going soft in the head. It was not hard for them to conceal the truth from themselves; that was their special skill.

The caste system among criminals is just as fantastic and irrational as a caste system anywhere in society. Dewey would have said regarding his pickpocketing: "No rough stuff for me, I'm an honest guy. I don't carry any guns or knives. I'm on an equal basis with the guy I frisk. If he finds my hand in his pocket he can stop me, can't he? No rough stuff for me. I'm honest."

Says the bank robber: "I'm an honest man. I go out in broad daylight with a gun, where anybody can see me and shoot me. I take my chance and fight it out. I'm no sneak thief."

Says the stick-up man: "I'm an honest guy. I don't go robbing banks, shooting people. I just stick a guy up, and if he comes across I don't shoot. Banking is a legitimate business. If this guy did his business in banks and wrote checks, he wouldn't have any money for me. It's his fault. But I'm not going around in broad daylight interfering with legitimate work."

Says the forger and check artist: "I'm an honest man. I live by my wits. They can check the endorser, can't they? They can find out about the bond issue if they want to buy that stuff. They do it of their own free will, don't they? I'm not sneaking up when they're not looking."

Says the shoplifter: "I'm an honest guy. I don't take things from poor people. I lift a shirt from a store where they've got lots more. And anyway, I only take what I need. A guy's got a right to live, hasn't he?"

Says the kidnapper: "I'm an honest guy. It's a deal. I got something to sell, they want to buy it. They don't need that money, so I take ten grand and release the man. If they don't keep their part of the deal, if they tell the cops, I can't help it if the guy gets hurt."

I've had "honest" bankers tell me in reference to their embezzlements: "My bank was covered by insurance. Nobody lost anything. Insurance companies make a 200% profit in a theft. They benefit by a robbery or a fire because everybody who didn't have insurance goes and buys it, and that increases the insurance company's business. I didn't hurt anybody."

There is an inflexible adherence to these rules, codes and guilds, and a total inability to see any incongruity in them.

The pathology in their lack of perspective is seen in its full flower in their attitude toward pederosis. When I was at the Annex the guards once had to rescue a sex offender (who had molested a seven-year-old girl) from a beating which the guards were amazed to learn was being administered by other sex offenders. The explanation of the avengers was that *their* activities had been restricted to little ladies no younger than *nine!*

Although the boys were undertaking my education on the convict level there were times when I needed enlightenment from a staff member. I couldn't go to the warden or the chief medical officer with some of my questions without putting them on the spot. And it seemed grossly inefficient to sweat them out alone when men were available with experience in these matters.

My confederate was Gordon. I told about the search of my house and the recovery of my keys. He grinned as he listened.

"Those jobs are done by confederates on the outside," he explained. "Go down to Jake's Pool Room and look at the hangers-on. Drop into Mac's speakeasy, and when you're in Kansas City go by the union hiring halls. You'll find discharged convicts everywhere."

But more important than these are their pals who have never yet been sent up. These people are valuable because they do not have a police record. They are chosen because they are not suspect with the police, and either don't know or have had no previous association with the convict in the penitentiary who wants a job done. The grapevine operates through them on the outside, and a trusty, a truck driver, a chauffeur, or one of the boys on the farm, acts as liaison man. Someone will make a telephone call in cryptic language, and these people on the outside start moving. *Ergo*, my house was searched.

Most new staff members are subjected to negligible investigation by the convicts, who only want to know into which staff man's trouser cuff they can safely drop an encapsuled message which can later be picked up by a confederate on a bus or in a bowling alley.

The ordinary doctor presents no problem; he sews them up or gives them a pill and never reports them. He has immunity. The ordinary guard always reports them. A priest reports nothing; he too has immunity and can always be trusted. A social worker reports everything and is rarely trusted. Because of my peculiar status, I was in a position to know more incriminating facts than any other person in the penitentiary. They had to be sure of me.

"If somebody came to you and you squealed—" Gordon drew his finger across his throat. "So when they checked up on you they really gave you the Blue Plate."

"But how could they get my keys out of the penitentiary and back to my house in such a short time?"

"Let's reconstruct it." He reasoned that Connie went on my pass to the cell block and found Dewey. He "scared the hell out of him" and got the keys. He couldn't take care of Dewey then or he would have got himself in trouble. But Dewey knew he would get it from someone else. Then Connie undoubtedly used the pass he claimed he had blotched to contact someone going outside: the bus driver, the last mail run, the milk truck. Through this envoy the keys reached a saloon or a bus station where they were given to another confederate. My keys probably passed through a half dozen pairs of hands, the last of which laid them on my telephone table.

The simple way to have taken care of the keys would have been for Connie to give them to a guard or the captain, saying that I had forgotten them, or that he found them under some papers after I had gone. An official runner immediately would have delivered them to me at the club.

"But that's no fun," said Gordon. "Here it's always the hard way, the devious way. It would be a shock to them if you suggested such a course. Their exclamation, 'God—I never would have thought of that!' would be absolutely honest."

That night as I went about my routine of locking up to close shop, I thought of the paper and ink in my cabinet, the incident of the open vault, the search of my house and car, the Ediphone, the microphone and gun, and now the key episode. Suddenly I asked myself: why am I making these silly motions?

"Aw, the hell with it!" I said aloud, "lock up the stuff yourselves!"

"You heard what the man said!" boomed Connie.

After that everything was wide open and work was in progress by the time I arrived each morning.

This pattern had not been in operation long when one

108

morning the captain stopped at the office on an inspection tour before I arrived. "Sure and I know the doctor is here early this morning," he said, "otherwise you scalawags would be in trouble, instead of at work."

He was a wonderful captain!

However, this development posed some problems. I knew the men realized it when during the noon *post-mortem* that day I overheard their discussion about coming over on the early work detail and staying on late assignment. Otherwise, they reasoned, someone would end up on the carpet because of their unofficial opening of cabinets.

Presently Connie brought Gibbs and Scott into my office with the suggestion that I sign a work request putting the whole staff on early-and-late duty to take care of any eventuality. I signed the request and thereafter the keys were left at the hospital guard station in the evening and picked up in the morning, a gesture which amused my men. In the words of Simms the lockmaker, "One key, two keys, no keys—same difference." The men piously appointed Scott of the pure conscience to bear the keys to and from the guard station, which rite he performed with a puckish smile. The keys were rarely used.

Although I said nothing about it, I was perfectly aware that the official opening of the vault was not the only end to be served in their request for early-and-late duty. It would also mean two additional hours out of their cells each day, supper in the hospital where the food was better, and it would add prestige to their already imposing stature in the eyes of the general prison population.

However, there was a deeper reason than this for their request. The volume of work was becoming such that I planned to increase the staff. But by this time there was growing up between these disparate and pathological personalities a tremendous feeling of belonging and functioning as a unit. Keeping the original staff intact was a matter of great importance to them, so that what they were really saying in requesting twelve additional man hours per day was, "To hell with a new guy—we'll do his work."

And they worked well, without supervision. King couldn't resist an occasional remark when I would arrive in the morning. "We didn't see your coat anywhere, Doc, but we knew you must be around because the files were open and everyone was at work. . . ."

After the episodes of the gun, the house search and the microphone, a man would begin to suspect that his life, liberty and pursuits were hardly his own. Or was that what they meant to say by all their slue-footed tactics?

One day I said, "Correct me if I'm wrong, boys, but I think I've passed my examinations so far. How about working out a place where I can keep my love letters, bank statements and confidential records?" I also suggested that when I had some confidential records to dictate, perhaps one man could handle the Ediphone and be responsible for it; and that if I didn't have one private drawer or file somewhere I would begin to feel like a naked goldfish in a public bowl.

"Listen to the man!" boomed Connie at once.

Perhaps there was the answer. They liked to be put to a test too.

"Scott," he went on, "you're the confidential secretary in this here office an' you don't have to tell nobody what goes on, see? An' the rest of you guys, lay off him, see? because he'll dummy up."

To me he explained, "Scott's the only guy in this office with no chip on his shoulder and nothin' on his conscience, see? He thinks like you do, Doc." Then he added gruffly, "Come on, guys—you heard what the man said!" So Punch, Gibbs and Scott followed Connie out of the office in a sober and orderly file.

There were unused steel cabinets in the office, but I wanted the boys to be responsible for the choice. When the four men left the office I supposed that they had some special file in mind, perhaps one with an unusual lock (sic) or a specially designed wooden cabinet which was being made at that time in our furniture factory. But they soon returned carrying two pasteboard cartons from the kitchen, one bearing the legend, *Solid Pack Tomatoes,* and the other, *Regular Grind Coffee.*

The choice of labels was no accident, Connie was exuberant.

"You can tell 'em apart, Doc, see? You can put your office stuff in the *Regular Grind* box, an' your personal gimmicks in the *Solid Pack!*"

They all grinned proudly at the play on words.

Turning to the men Connie told them flatly, "Hands off. Nobody gets in these here boxes but Doc, see?"

I was momentarily taken back. Where were my fancy wooden files? Then I realized that what the men were telling me was that no file or lock in the world was safe from them if they wanted to rifle it, but that no file in the world was as safe as those pasteboard boxes, because they didn't want to get into them. It was a great moment for the men and for me. I don't know which meant the most to them, trusting someone, or being trusted.

It was hard to thank them. I did not even look at them. That would have made them self-conscious. A lot of inane things came to mind, one of which found its way into speech.

"Let's fix those boxes so we won't need a bobby pin to get into them," I said. They could rig up the damnedest Rube Goldberg contraptions.

"Now how the hell d'you suppose we'd get bobby pins into this man's penitentiary?" scoffed Punch.

I had now been at the penitentiary for six months. I always felt that the period of my testing ended with this episode. There was no further question of rapport or trust or any incident of question between the boys and me—until the middle of my last year, when Punch gave me a scare.

Certainly there was never any leakage of confidences from either the *Regular Grind* or the *Solid Pack* boxes. If the men knew the contents they said nothing outside the office. If they had talked there would inevitably have been reverberations and consequences. It is my conviction that the privacy of those boxes was never invaded.

The next day I found that shelves in the vault had been cleared for my two boxes, the flaps cleverly arranged as doors. Ross and King, kibitzed by the other men, had designed a fastener from a notebook clip and a hairpin.

Each man also had his own private space on the shelf, the confines delimited by chalk. His name, printed flourishingly by King, was pasted on the front of the shelf. Day by day the intimate treasures of each man accumulated on the shelf. A comb, a hairpin, a picture or clipping from a newspaper, a dime store trinket, a cigar, free garden seeds sent out by congressmen.

Under pressure of increasing work, and when my men began to teach in the prison school, I added two relief men to the staff. It was then that I first became aware of the discriminatory size of the space allotted to each of us. I measured the spaces and found that I was given an exact three feet, Connie twenty inches, Punch nineteen, Gibbs eighteen, Scott seventeen, King sixteen, Ross fifteen, and the relief men twelve inches each. Presidential succession was definitely established.

Later, after an episode that tested and demonstrated our cohesion and unity, there was a change in the shelf alignment. I now had an entire shelf to myself, as a token of respect or admission of differentness. My original six men occupied the next two shelves; and although there was unused space at the end of the shelf, the relief men were relegated to the bottom shelf and still kept their allotted twelve inches. The original six had gained three inches each. . . .

One day Ross and I were working in the vault. "Mister Engineer," I said, "you're a mathematician, explain this shelf business to me. Why are there several unused inches at the end of these shelves when some of the spaces are crowded? Why isn't the space divided and utilized?"

Some days later Ross came to me. "You know, Doctor, I've been thinking about that shelf line-up. Not only that, but about a lot of things—how our minds work. That shelf allotment doesn't mean a thing to me, but I can understand that it does to men like Connie and Gibbs. That's the way they develop a feeling of importance. That's something a penitentiary doesn't foster. You begin to think like kids. Since nothing at all is important you make something important out of nothing at all. Our minds jump around on the same crazy little circuit all the time —maybe these inflexibilities of ours explain why we're in and you're out, sir." It was a valid insight, and one that saddened Ross in relation to himself. "Even with these reforms, it's going to take a long time to forget the past," he added, "when the only way we could keep from losing our minds completely was to sit and count the buttons on our clothes."

My men played their infantile little games with a charm and perspective that was not typical of the general prison population. Admittedly my six represented the upper one percent of the general population. The run-of-the-mill prisoner falls under the army and navy classification of *psychopathic personality,* a concept which holds that in an individual of constitutional psychopathic inferiority there is something structurally or functionally inadequate, so that the individual cannot make proper adjustments to his environment. In World War II the army alone had a neuropsychiatric load of over three million cases for rejection, hospitalization and discharge.

The psychopathic personalities that fill our prisons have

been described by criminologist Barnes as the least intelligent, the least fortunate, the least resourceful, and the least influential members of criminal society. It is an easily demonstrable fact that few of the "smart operators" are in prison; they are still operating on the outside. It is the "dumb operator" who gets caught. The smart operator may also be neurotic in that he is antisocial, but he is not inadequate.

Shortly after I left Fort Leavenworth Penitentiary I was asked to address a lay group on the character of the criminal. The implications of criminal character reach so deep into social phenomena other than lawlessness and crime itself that very little generalization on the subject can be conscientiously indulged. There is no criminal type *per se*. I was doing the best I could, restricting my observations to the convicts I had studied in my own research experience. I enumerated certain personality factors which I found present in those convicts, factors which it will be seen are not criminal in content, but neurotic.

Criminals are emotionally immature and unstable. They are self-reflexive egoists. I have seen big tough criminals sitting in their cells in a puddle of tears because another criminal's capture was given bigger headlines or more inches of text in the papers than theirs. (This kind of thing, I am told, happens among movie stars also.)

Their sense of proportion and sense of values are either totally absent or badly distorted. They will gladly exchange a million dollars in bonds next Tuesday for ten bucks in cash today. Or like Punch they will sentimentalize about a baby and kill a man in cold blood.

They are mentally and emotionally inflexible and impoverished. Only an upheaval can precipitate a change in them, and they do not learn from experience. Dewey would always remain a pickpocket, Connie would never frisk a man. Brody would have gone on robbing the country store year after year because he liked the cheese.

Lacking other drives and ambitions, they are preoccupied, as Ross said, with the importance of nothing-at-all: shaving Ediphone cylinders and measuring shelves.

They make generous use of Freud's seventeen defense mechanisms, notably rationalization, projection and compartmentalization, in an attempt to relieve themselves of personal responsibility for their conduct. The jackroller who rolls a drunk reasons that it's the victim's fault—he shouldn't have been drunk.

They are bristling with antisocial aggressions, for which mill anyone can always find grist. Many of their gripes are legitimate and a great shame on society. The convict thinks very little better of our conscience on the outside than we do of his.

These aggressions produce their bumptious philosophy of Me Against the World, and their suspicion and paranoia, the most devastating of human emotions.

In the absense of real self-respect, they cultivate a ludicrous sense of superiority through lying and deceit and deviousness. More than one prisoner has said, "Honest, Doc, I've lied so much I don't know what's the truth any more."

Finally, despite their protestations and boasts, they are sexually inadequate individuals, and compensating for this inadequacy in an unconventional life explains much of their behavior.

I remember the startled exclamation of one mother of a six-year-old as she surveyed the above neurotic catalogue. "My God—my child's a criminal!"

These factors in a child—try them for size on your own—are normal because he is not yet maturated.

But in an adult these factors of inadequacy and immaturity mean trouble. It may lead one man into alcoholism or drug addiction, another into insanity, another to suicide. Another becomes a hypochondriac, a prostitute, or a chronic invalid. Another, with sufficient emotional and economic irritation and opportunity in his environment, becomes a criminal.

Sanitaria, hospitals, doctors' and psychologists' offices, pastors' studies and institutions for the insane are full of these maladjusted individuals, but *their* outward manifestations of neurosis have social approval. We have no legislation outlawing them, desirable as this possibility sometimes appears in view of the nasty tyrannies fostered by some neuroses. The manifestations of neuroses in the man who tangles with the law instead of with religion does not have social approval, although the criminal may not wreak any greater misery on any more people through his crimes than does the tyranny of the chronic invalid in your home —who would find her legs soon enough if a pot of gold lay at the end of a brisk walk.

One is said to be neurotic, the other is said to be criminal.

Sometimes a neurotic is salvageable, sometimes he is not. This is true of the hypochondriac and the drunkard; it is also true of the criminal. He is not always salvageable, in which case segregation is most certainly indicated. But it is doubtful that a drunkard would ever recover without help if every time he "went on the wagon" his friends threw a bottle of Scotch at him. Yet the criminal in discharging his debt to society is often given no aid. He is thrown in prison upon his own pathological resources for recovery, and is expected to emerge from isolation, filth, brutality, hunger, idleness, loneliness and monotony, a changed man.

He may be changed. He will not be cured.

The prison school is probably the most effective rehabilitating agency within a penitentiary. If the staff is competent, the school may enroll as many as 80% of the inmates. The principal at Fort Leavenworth Penitentiary was outstanding in every sense and conducted an excellent school.

The Government assumed no obligation for classes beyond the fifth grade. Day attendance was compulsory for those who tested out below the fifth grade level, but was voluntary thereafter. In those days in order to staff high school and college courses, any inmate who could present anything constructive was given an opportunity. By spring my men had considerable prestige in the penitentiary, and when the principal asked them to teach for him they accepted at once. Their preparation for their teaching assignments was prodigious, and the two relief men were shamelessly overworked.

Attendance in the evening courses was desultory, indulged in by the majority only to escape long evenings in their cells. My boys would have none of this. They required term papers and examinations, collateral reading in the library, and quickly dropped loafers from the roll.

As I remember, Ross the engineer taught mathematics, Friar Gibbs criminology—a little warped toward social injustice. Connie the barker taught the psychology of sales and advertising; and Scott the innocent, history. The first year Punch refused to become a schoolmarm, but by the second year he had developed a course in business psychology. King, the counterfeiter, taught art, and was not discouraged by his small enrollment.

"I got quality, Doc. Bankers, importers, counterfeiters. No army of the great unwashed hanging from my doors and windows. No yokels that fall for a hula and a barker!"

Connie would flare out at this. "What the hell're you doin' in stir if you're so almighty good?"

The men even petitioned inter-library loans from the university. They devoured the sixteen professional journals that came to my office each month, and delved into back issues I had brought in for them. I was proud of my satellites and the way they used this chance to function constructively.

It was about this time that I noticed the pride of my men in the expertness with which they dispatched the scientific procedures of a research office. This was beginning to have wide reverberations in their personalities. Habits were being renovated.

The office, for instance, became a spit and polish affair. Being orderly myself about such things, I would simply have beheld this phenomenon with gratitude. But that was not all. Most of the prisoners went around looking like the African bush and belched loudly at social finesse. There was little incentive to keep up one's personal appearance. My men therefore really caught me off guard when they began reporting for work with their hair combed and parted, looking pink under daily shaves, and with a crease and a break in their denim pants which suggested they were deep in the debt of the laundry detail. All this was no particular innovation for Ross, Scott and King. King had a compulsion for cleanliness. He missed meals more than once to slip up to the physiotherapy ward for a shower, a massage, and a few minutes under the sun lamp.

But only a profound social upheaval could have impelled Connie to begin examining his teeth critically in the office mirror and squander part of his commissary credit on his first toothbrush. About that time there was an unexplained run on toothbrushes at the prison commissary. I'm sure they were all purchased under duress—that would be Connie's way of silencing a scorner.

The day came when the boys' critical eye fell on me. For the next gradient in their social evolution was to study the clothes habits of other civilian staff members who were in mufti and compare them with mine. They were bothered by the fact that I was the only man on the hospital staff not in uniform. A small Congressional crisis had been brewing in Washington for two years over the choice of an insignia for this interloping hybrid, *genus psychologist,* in the sacrosanct commissioned ranks. My men used an oblique approach to the problem, something like this:

"Wonder how many more years it'll take the Navy Brass to decide whether Doc should wear a star or an acorn on his sleeve?" asked King.

"It ain't the Navy, stupid, it's the Surgeon General," said Punch.

"Well, somebody in this goddam Gover'ment better get the hell off the dime. Doc's suit ain't gonna hold out much longer," said Connie.

After quite a pause Gibbs picked up the ball. "Now whatta you s'ppose made Erickson [a shop superintendent] get a brown suit?"

"Yeah, you'd think a albino like him would know enough to stick to blue or gray, now wouldn't you?" asked Little Italy. "It takes a good clear brown eye to wear a brown suit. Someone like Doc, here," he added charitably.

"Yes-*sir!*" boomed Connie. "One o' these mornings Doc's gonna come bumpin' down the hall in a nice brown suit with white stripes, with them new shoulders—"

"White stripes!" scoffed King. "Can't you get your mind off stripes, you stupid con! What Doc wants is a soft brown, hand-stitched, double-breasted flannel, with a long lapel. And none of those vulgar shoulders!"

"That what you want, Doc?" Connie asked. "Okay, make it one hand-breasted, double-stitched, hollow-chested brown flannel!"

"Oh, I don't know," said Ross, generously, "Doc always looks pretty nice on Tuesdays and Saturdays when he's issued a clean white coat."

"Thanks, Ross!" I said.

"Well now—it ain't that ya ain't neat and clean, Doc," said Connie quickly, "it's just that ya ain't *sharp!*"

I fearfully opened the wardrobe in the office every morning for a couple of weeks, fully expecting to find a hollow-chested brown flannel waiting for me. Then the agitation was dropped, and I relaxed. To keep up with the crease in their blue denims I would not have to give up my old Hart, Schaffner and Marx after all.

But their calm was more devastating to my peace of mind than the storm had been, and, before anything could happen, I rushed out one day and bought a suit.

There was more than normal pride in their sartorial ambitions for me, however. There was pathology as well.

A criminal's life is a game of wits. His superiority over the sucker—the honest man—is measured in the relative gains of the two, since it cannot be measured by respectability. A criminal's obsession not only to keep up with but to excel the Joneses is a deep psychological necessity. Actually criminals are jealous of the honest man's respectability. They feel inferior to him. Since they can not have respectability, they seek superiority on some other level. They will take ridiculous chances to get their girl a fur coat the same week that some debutante appears in one at a night spot. But their girl's must be better than the deb's. It's all mixed up with self-respect in their eyes—very mixed up.

I got mixed up with their self-respect too, representing about all they had in that commodity. Well, I got a new suit out of it, and I needed it.

6

"WHO'S YOUR best safecracker, Doctor?"

The warden's voice came over the phone at eight-thirty one morning.

I automatically turned to my vocational index. Then I turned back to the phone.

"Best *what,* sir?"

"Safecracker."

I passed the question on to Connie. He beamed modestly at me.

"I have one right here, sir—"

"Be*sides* Connie!" said the warden before I could say more.

I looked at Connie. "Connie doesn't know anybody else," I said.

Connie smiled. The warden groaned.

"Ask him if he wants to go out and do a job."

Connie did. But where?

The warden reported that the vault was jammed at one of the banks in a nearby city, their Diebold expert was in Chicago, and they couldn't get another man until the following day. It was pay day for the local factories, and they had to have the vault open before banking hours that morning.

Connie's Adam's apple tobogganed wildly. Did I mean he'd get to open a safe with the lights on, that he could make noise? And didn't have to listen for the lookout? Jeez—he'd never had no experience that way. He thought fast. Then he said loftily: "Okay, Doc. You tell the warden I'll do it, just for him."

"Thanks," said the warden drily.

"Wait a minute!" cried Connie. "Tell him I'll make a deal with him. I'll go if I can have tomorrow in Kansas City. Go on—you tell him, Doc."

The receiver vibrated with the warden's reply. "He's crazy! He's not a trusty—how could I let him go to Kansas City?"

Connie waited until the phone was quiet, then he outlined his deal to me and I interpreted it to the warden. A day in Kansas City, under guard, ten dollars cash folding money (usually given to a convict when he is released), and a suit of clothes. Where, he demanded, could the warden get a man with his experience for the job?

"One more thing, Doc!" said Connie. "Tell the warden I get to sit in the front seat of his car today and operate the siren!"

"I think you better say yes, Warden, before he gets any more ideas," I suggested.

"Send him to the front office," growled the warden.

Connie's report of the affair, as I remember it, was delivered before a captivated if sometimes skeptical audience in the office when he returned a few hours later. I wandered in and out of these recitations, but the whole thing seemed coherent and verifiable. For once Connie did not have to use his imagination in telling a story. His flare for hamming had never had a better vehicle.

"Talk about big shots!" Connie crowed. "Here I was, in the front seat of the warden's own car, see? Workin' the siren for all it was worth. It's a kick! Always before, either I was runnin' from the siren, or else I was in the paddy wagon with the siren going out front. The guards in the back seat was yellin' for me to lay off, but I told 'em this was the warden's deal—I made that clear before we left. I hadda get somethin' out of this job!"

They arrived in town in a cloud of dust and drove up in front of the bank in grand style. Inside, the cashier, the tellers and the president of the bank were standing around helplessly, waiting for Connie.

"The joint's crammed with legit characters, all these guys standin' around with vests on. So I go over to the safe an' I kinda line up and tinkle around for a while. Then I turn around and I say to the most important lookin' o' these guys, 'Okay, Jocko, hand me the tools.'

"That takes the air out o' this substantial-lookin' citizen. He puffs a while, an' then he says, whiney-like, 'W-well, what do you mean, tools?' 'Banker's tools, fer Christ sake,' I say. Imagine! Here's a bunch of punks runnin' a bank, and they don't have no banker's tools!

"The guy's gettin' a little hot, so I kinda lay it on. 'I figgered you wouldn't have none,' I say, 'so I had some ordered. They'll be here any minute. There'll be a little fee—taxi fare, rent, fixes, stuff like that.' "

Connie had them right where he wanted them. They could not quite understand what was happening. The guards were getting uneasy, too; it looked as if Connie was taking them for a ride. But in a few minutes a Kansas City taxi drove up and out stepped Big Ben—all of sixty inches high—in a Western Union uniform, carrying a nice new canvas bag.

He took out a receipt book. "Dat'll be twenty-five bucks," he said like an uptown banker, "an' I'm to wait an' bring 'em back."

This was quite a hurdle for the cashier, but what was there to do? The bank was about to open and the tellers had no money. He agreed to the fee.

"So I go to work. An' boy, you shouldda seen them tools. New an' shiny, like Benny'd been honin' and sharp'nin' 'em— man! was he proud of 'em! I could see his hands twitchin' in his pants, an' his bad eye waterin'. He came over to give me a lift onc't, but I jumped him. 'You wanna give yourself away, you goon? Go on back an' sit down!'

"Things didn't go so good for a while. Then I realized what it was. 'Look, screw,' I says to one of the guards, 'You make me nervous lookin' over my shoulder. You should go out an' make a fortune on my ability! Go 'way!'"

The guard sat down with a look of bewilderment on his face. Then things fell into place. Connie even had time to notice a comely secretary with nice blonde hair.

"Mm. . . . Was she stacked! An' y'know, I got to thinkin' about the first time I was sent up. Did I ever tell you guys how that was?"

The men obligingly shook their heads.

"There was a gal that time too, and this one reminded me of her. I watched her standin' there, her little tiddies stickin' through her dress, her little face all pink an' her eyes bugged out like doorknobs. She was seein' a real honest to God criminal, a crook, a bank robber, right in front of her eyes. It was a big day for her. An' I thought to myself, why disappoint the gal? Why not give her a real thrill, somethin' she could tell her grandchildren, y'know? Also, I didn't like the way the cashier was givin' her the eye. So I worked hard with my ears, an' I sanded my fingertips a little bit more. An' I couldn't get nothin', see? So I said I needed some help. I went around an' looked at their fingernails. I needed some long ones, see?"

The men exchanged glances. Sure. Naturally. The longer the better.

"Well, all the men's nails is cut. But to my surprise this girl's nails is nice an' long an' pointed."

The men looked at each other again. Imagine! What a surprise!

"So I asks her, demonstratin' I wasn't able to hear nothin' or feel nothin', I asks her, would she come up? She was scared, an' tickled pink. The cashier looked real unfriendly. But I take her hands and say, 'Now, you listen careful when I turn the dial against your nails, an' when you feel a jolt or a click, like this . . . . lemme know.' So I place my ear against the safe, an' fix her hands on the dial. Then I turn it. She feels a click an' makes a little squeal.

"The bankers didn't like that. An' I looked at Big Ben, an' his face was purple for wantin' to laugh. He was just about to bust out, so I made the cashier read off the combination slow-like. It's a kick, him readin' that combination to *me!* I kept the girl there while I twirled the dial. She heard the tumblers fall into place. I hollered, 'I think I got it!' An' I told the cashier to stand ready to twist the bolt an' jerk an' pull hard on the door when I say 'Ready,' so it wouldn't slam and lock again. 'Hard, mind you, an' quick,' I told him, keepin' the girl there, with her ear against the safe. Then I stopped."

Connie looked over the men.

"I ain't so dumb. You gotta make your deals with suckers before, not afterwards. So I said to the cashier, 'Look, cousin, I get out in three years. How about me comin' down an' collectin' a hundred bucks for this job?'

"Well, he hummed and hawed and said, No, he couldn't, that the warden told him it was illegal to give any—what the hell did he say? *honorarium,* or some damn thing. Anyway, he made it clear there wasn't no mazoola. So I said, 'Okay, cousin, have it your way.' Then I yelled, 'Pull away!' So he pulled like hell, an' the door opens an' spins the girl around, an' the cute little keester lands right in my lap!"

The men grinned. Whatta y'know!

"I don't get no dough," said Connie, "but I get, like the book says, maybe a little *flotage.* . . ."

The cashier thought it was all over and was looking relieved when Connie yelled, "Wait—stand back a minute!" And with the help of Big Ben he took the glass plate off the inside of the vault door. When the bankers protested Connie said indignantly, "You don't want it so you can't lock it tonight, do you? Your expert can't get here till tomorrow. I gotta fix it so it'll shut, don't I?"

With the glass door off, Connie told the cashier to let the tellers get their money. Quickly the tellers filed in and each came out with his money tray.

"An' y'know," said Connie, "it's funny, but I got a feelin' those fellas is gonna be just an even, exact, precise hundred bucks short tonight. That's one o' the penalties of bein' legit. It's a absolute requirement, you got to be stupid in the head!"

The truth is, Connie would never have gone back for his hundred dollars. If he had gone back at all when his time was up, it would have been in the grand manner, waving the money aside, just to swagger a little. "Remember me? I'm the big, bad con. How's every little thing? How's the little old vault?" Or perhaps he would have asked, "How's my gal?"

"Well—" he went on, "some guys are sure stupid. They never get wised up. They never know when they're well off. Now, these goddam bankers. You ask 'em for a loan. Will they give you one? No, they want collateral. Or you get a loan an' you can't pay. Will they give you time? No, they foreclose. Now, here's a legitimate deal: a hundred bucks for openin' a safe. They'd have to pay their own expert more. They're just a bunch of goddam *anal erotics,* like the book says. Ain't that right, Doc?"

"That's what you said, Connie," I answered.

"I sure as hell did! Well, we fixed it an' put the glass door back on. An' I really mean 'fix.' That expert'll never untangle it in the mornin'. But of course he'll never know what happened, either. They're either gonna have to pour soup on it, or else they're gonna have to take their torch an' cut her off the hinges, an' it'll take a derrick to lift her outta place. Jeez—ain't it a shame how a delicate mechanism can get all loused up?"

"How come you didn't use a torch or soup?" asked Gibbs. "You ain't pullin' our leg, are you? How could you hear them tumblers if it was jammed? Why didn't you keep on usin' your tools after you started?"

Connie's face spread with a beatific smile and his narrow chest barreled like a bullfrog's.

"It's a kick," he said, "you know what was wrong with that baby all the time? The set screw was a little loose on the time lock. It just slipped a little when they banged the door shut. It was just delayed a coupla hours. While I was workin' on it, just before I called for the gal, I heard it go off an' snap to. A baby could've pulled the bolt from then on."

After the hubbub that created had subsided Gibbs said, "Connie, you're a card. You kill me. You shouldda been on the stage! How come you was never a actor?"

"Actor, hell!" said Punch. "He's an actor, ain't you just seen? A ham. What's a sideshow barker but a ham?"

"Connie," said Scott, "maybe if you'd been an actor you wouldn't have been such a phony."

King, the counterfeiter, looked up from his work.

"Phony, hell! What's an actor but a phony? You do make-believe on the stage and you get your name in lights. You do it on a dollar bill and you get your name in numbers! The whole damn world's phony."

That was my first clue to King and the currents of his mind. A man with an obsession for perfection—everything King did was flawless—had realized at some point in his life what we all know, that there is phoniness in the world. Some of us are embittered by this fact. King was one of those. Instead of avoiding the thing he decried in the world and in people, he expressed his bitterness in a game of spite, by counterfeiting. By making phony money. Beating the world at its own game.

Suddenly there was a howl from Gibbs. He was ogling something in Connie's hand. The men gathered around Connie who was underplaying the whole thing.

127

"Spoils of war," he murmured, "keepsakes. . . . mementos of the Ball an' the Opera." It was a girl's yellow comb. "You don't suppose she'll miss it, do you? Hell—I don't think she'd mind if she did," he added cockily.

He took the rest of the day off, sitting with his feet up on his desk, fondling the comb and patting a cigar given him by one of the bankers.

After the men had gone that afternoon I was sitting at my desk thinking about Connie's story when the captain came in. His face was moving in quiet excitement.

"I see Connie is gone." He sat down. "You know, son, here's something strange. This bank business of his. Did he tell you? Well, sir, that same bank was Connie's first job twenty years ago. He got sent up from that bank! . . . . I wonder how he felt to-day. It sure is a strange world."

The warden made good his promise to allow Connie the next day in Kansas City. I guess he felt Connie would play it straight. He knew Connie wasn't anxious to escape—he was having too good a time running the show in the penitentiary. More probably, since Federal experiments of putting 9,000 trusties on road gangs and farms had paid such unexpected dividends in prison morale, the warden was trying out Thomas Mott Osborne's precedent of allowing an occasional prisoner to be away for a day.

Connie did not talk much about this trip. Some of the events meant too much to him. From the guard who went with him and from remarks dropped by Connie himself during the next week, I pieced together the following story.

On the morning of the trip he dressed in his choice from the clothes stock room, a loud checked suit three inches too short, with a size 18 shirt for his size 14 neck to accommodate his long arms. He wore the same brown derby hat in which he had arrived three years previously. He looked fine except for the tag of toilet paper bobbing on his Adam's apple.

A guard, Higgins, whom everybody liked was assigned to him. Higgins was dubious about the whole thing. He told me in Connie's hearing that he didn't like the assignment. But Connie swore submission to Higgins. A minute later he flashed his ten dollars and warned everybody that Higgins would be worn down to a nub when they returned that night.

Connie did not want to blow any sirens this time. He was James Connie, private citizen. He and Higgins took the train. The trip was somewhat of a nightmare to the conductor and Higgins, the latter said, Connie being simultaneously in the baggage room, engine, and all points south.

In Kansas City Connie treated Higgins to endless streetcar rides with endless transfers to nowhere. They went on endless elevators in tall buildings and wandered in and out of chain drug stores and dime stores.

On two occasions Higgins discovered Connie lifting merchandise, and much to Connie's sorrow forced him to return it.

"Look, you have ten dollars," Higgins pointed out, "why don't you buy that stuff?"

"What? When I can get them for free?" Connie was scandalized. "Jeez—money is to use only when you *have* to!"

They were in the lingerie section of a department store when Connie turned to the guard. "Okay, Higgins, you want I should do a job legit? On the counter? Come on!" Connie assembled some expensive lingerie and started to pay for it with two twenty dollar bills. Higgins remonstrated. Where had Connie got that kind of money?

That? Oh, that was an *honorarium* he got for a little favor he did the warden yesterday.

"I'll just bet it is!" said Higgins. Or could it be that some poor devil on the train was now traveling considerably lighter?

129

Connie took the guard off to a corner. "Look, *Mister* Higgins, you got only one job an' one order from the warden today. All you got to do is to watch me so I don't escape an' bring me back tonight, right? If you turn me back by nine o'clock watch you're clear, right? Fine. So—money's contraband in the pen, but I'm not in the pen now. You can frisk me in there, but you can't frisk me here. You've got a right there to know who I write to, but out here it's none o' your damn business who I send this to!"

But Higgins was not easily intimidated. Connie became exasperated. "There's nothing worse in this world than an honest Irishman. In the first place, how can an Irishman be honest? An' when they are honest they can be the damnedest people! A honest Irishman an' a dumb Irishman are the same thing, an'—" He looked significantly at Higgins. At this Higgins became understandably belligerent. "Okay," sighed Connie, "you win. Pick up your marbles an' let's go."

They walked out of the lingerie section into the men's department, where they wandered around for some minutes. Then Connie announced that he wanted to see the floorwalker.

To the floorwalker, in a corner, Connie said: "I feel it my duty, sir, to tell you that this man with me has several pieces of merchandise in his pocket."

"I have *not!*" yelled the horrified Higgins.

"Some cuff links, a stick pin, a pair of sox, two ties—Go ahead—look an' see!"

Higgins himself reached into his pockets and dazedly pulled out the loot, piece by piece.

"*Well!*" breathed Connie. "Now, what do you do with a man like that?"

The floorwalker was afraid he would have to call the store detective. Higgins tried to explain, and flashed his badge.

"It's a phony," said Connie.

As the floorwalker raised his hand to summon the store detective, Connie addressed Higgins in an undertone.

"Hey, won't the warden think it's funny, you liftin' stuff? Won't the cons think it's funny? Come on now—how about that linger-ee?"

Higgins threw in the towel.

"Just a moment, sir!" Connie said to the floorwalker. "After due reflection we have reached a private agreement. Everything's all right." Whereupon Connie divested himself of several items concealed in his own clothes and piled them on the counter. Higgins told me that he couldn't understand how pockets could hold so much and not bulge.

Connie talked easily to the mystified floorwalker. "It's no misdemeanor, y'know, to collect merchandise in a store. You can't arrest nobody till they get out on the street with it. After all, they might be intendin' to pay for it. Thank you, my good man, for your trouble, and for your assistance in our little joke. Good-day, sir!"

And taking Higgins' arm Connie walked him sedately out of the front door, doffing his hat at the portals.

Connie did not think it would be healthy to go back for the lingerie; they would find a smaller shop somewhere. "An' listen, Mister," he said to Higgins, "on my word, I ain't gonna put you on the spot about this. I just wanna buy somethin' for a girl friend an' get nobody in no trouble, see? an it's strictly on the up an' up."

"I'll just bet it is!" croaked Higgins.

Then they had lunch. Connie told us that he ate just one thing: oysters. One dozen oysters raw on the half-shell; one dozen in stew and one dozen fried. Higgins told me this was true.

Then they boarded a bus, and after several transfers found themselves alighting in an exclusive residential section.

"Where the hell are we?" asked Connie happily.

"I haven't the *slightest* idea," sighed the guard.

They paused in front of a magnificent residence on a hill. "What a joint for a second-story man!" cried Connie. "I must remember this."

Higgins had the feeling that Connie had been there before. . . .

Looking down over the city from the hill, Connie suddenly grabbed Higgins convulsively. "Look, a ferris wheel! A carnival!"

At last, by this devious route, Higgins understood the reason why Connie wanted to come to Kansas City.

By way of a taxi they ended up at the carnival, where Connie greeted an appalling array of old cronies. He acted as barker for the freaks and the burlesque girls until he was hoarse, using a vocabulary that had never before been sounded on a midway. He rode every concession free, reeling from the ferris wheel and the merry-go-round to play every dart game in the roulette concession, loading the guard with hams, kewpie dolls, hula skirts and china bulls. Connie was delirious and hysterical. He consumed pink lemonade, hot dogs, popcorn and taffy.

His unconfined joy ended suddenly when reaching into his pocket for money to give in response to a hardluck story of one of his pals, he discovered his pockets had been picked. He was thunderstruck.

"Me! James Connie! For the first time in my life a dip got me! Fifty dollars—all that legit bank money too, not even counterfeit!"

He replenished his coffers by "borrowing" from his carnival friends and started back downtown. It was near closing time when he and Higgins left the toy department of a store and went to the best hotel in the city for dinner, still loaded down with carnival trophies.

Connie stood looking around before he chose not his table, but his waitress. She was young, pretty, and wary of men. Then he called for the manager.

"I don't care what it costs," he told the manager, "just gimme the bill. I want a slice of rare prime rib of beef a inch thick, an' with it on a sizzling platter a planked porterhouse two inches thick, some French fries an' some black coffee. An' on four plates, four different kinds of cake. An' bring it all up together."

He leaned back in his chair with a happy smile. Then he noticed the manager's face.

"Oh, I ain't gonna eat the stuff," he said sweetly, "I just wanna look at it."

As it turned out, he ate the stuff.

When he finished he called the waitress, and from an inner pocket extracted another twenty dollar bill over which Higgins shook his head sadly.

"This is for you, baby," said Connie to the girl. "An' give these two silver dollars to the hat check girl, an' will you please get me my hat?"

But he rose suddenly and followed her, with Higgins trailing. Standing by the hat check stand, Connie again addressed the waitress.

Connie was never shy, but at this moment Higgins said Connie did not appear over-bold. "Would you please do one more thing for me?" he asked.

"Well?" She was not one to look at life in a rapture.

"Well—right here, baby, in the middle of my forehead, I would like a kiss."

"You crazy?" she snapped.

"I was afraid of that. Look, it's this way." He pulled open Higgins' coat and pointed to the badge. "I'm a con, see? I been in for three years an' I won't get out for three years more. It's gonna go awful hard with me with the boys if I can't prove I been near a girl. I don't care about the kiss, baby, all I want's the lipstick. Whatta you say?"

The girl looked at Higgins. "Is he kidding me?"

"No, he's a con all right, lady. It's like he says, all right."

"Well, if that's the way it is—" She sized Connie up briefly. "Sit down, Mister, I can't reach your forehead."

Connie sat and pointed. "Right exactly in the middle, please. An' make it good—you know?"

"Yeah, I know. Close your eyes," said the girl.

She kissed him full on the mouth and was gone.

After a while Connie reached out his hand. "Lead me out, Higgins, I don't wanna open my eyes."

Outside he stopped and thoughtfully wiped off the imprint of the kiss with the back of his hand. . . .

The guard said Connie was quiet all the way home, pausing just before the gate to brush his mouth gently once more, this time on the sleeve of his checked coat. None of his accounts of His Day included any mention of The Girl. To one of his odd sensitivities it meant too much.

About two o'clock that morning Connie was carried to the hospital violently ill from acute indigestion, in an almost comatose state, mumbling, "Right here on my forehead—gotta show the boys. . . . Right here on my forehead—gotta show the boys. . . ."

"Holy Mother of God!" marvelled the interne. "All that in one stomach!"

It wasn't the taffy and popcorn and pink lemonade and peanuts and crackerjack, Connie explained the next day; he was used to those things. It was the steak and oysters and cake.

Two days later Higgins came in much perturbed. Large packages had been delivered to his children. They contained a large erector set and a bicycle for his boy, and a life-size doll with buggy, clothes and all the trappings for his girl. The gift card read, "From Daddy." Higgins insisted Connie had never been out of his sight in the store.

Higgins wanted to be rid of them because they represented

a possible bribe for which he would be liable to discharge by the warden. But how could he take them back now? The children had engulfed him with love and kisses when he returned home.

I told Higgins I would take it up with the warden. But he said, "He can't give his okay, it's against the rules."

"Who's going to ask for his okay?" I said. "I've learned a thing or two in this place—I'm just going to remark incidental to nothing that you're worried about keeping the toys. That way he'll know you have them, but it will be no secret, and therefore it can't be used as a bribe."

"Y'think it'll work?" he asked eagerly. "I'm sure on a hell of a spot with my kids, Doc!"

The same day the captain came in with two pinochle decks, a box of cigars and a long face.

"Connie knows I can't accept them, Doctor. And the cigars —my favorite brand too!"

Why not keep them? I asked. What were the odds? The men didn't have much opportunity of expressing their gratitude for his decency and fairness. What was the harm?

"You know perfectly well what the harm is! You accept something from them and you're bribed. Pretty soon they put on the screws and you're hooked."

I said again that I thought the trouble would come from secret bribes or gifts. Why not let this business be known?

He shook his head. "I can't set such an example for my men."

"Well, then why not give them to your lieutenant or your sergeant, just for the force?"

He brightened a little. "Maybe you've got something there, Doctor. I'll see the Father about it." Then he shook his head dolorously. "When that Connie's time is up I'll be a happy man! But you know something, Doctor? For the first time Connie says he's going straight when he gets out. And he just might. He refused to be a trusty, you recall. That's decent. That's honest. And now he says he's done with safecracking and is going straight. Maybe the Father will let me keep these things on that."

Connie kept Higgins' toy deal a secret, but his maneuver of the cigars and cards was definitely the event of the season. Here were incorruptible men playing with stolen cards and smoking stolen cigars. But the prisoners warmed toward the captain for his display of human frailty and feeling in a world of concrete and steel. My men told me afterward that it was this incident and the captain's behavior in it that saved his life in a prison break some months later. The breakers had expected to use the captain as a shield because they were sure no one would shoot near him. Instead they used the deputy warden, and it didn't go well with the deputy in that break.

Why did Connie show his gratitude to Higgins and the captain in such a way as to put them on the spot, the guard with his children and the captain with the prisoners? Why didn't he express his gratitude verbally, in view of the rules prohibiting the interchange of gifts between staff and prisoners? Such an expression would not only have moved his two friends, it would have astounded them. But as Gordon and the captain had both said, the men would never dream of doing things the simple, direct way. Although Connie liked both Higgins and the captain, his former boss, they were members of society, for which Connie as a criminal had contempt. Society to him was the greatest show on earth—a show in the sense of hypocritical sham, glaring inconsistencies and awful injustices. In the maneuver of the cards and the toys Connie accomplished two things at once. He penalized the men for being members of society by the same act in which he rewarded them for being his friends.

That was finesse in his eyes.

7

THAT SPRING the prisoners acquired an unusual interest in aesthetics. Flower gardening suddenly became a hobby of the entire outside work detail. Petition was made to beautify the paved courtyard with a large circle of flowers around the center flagpole. From this hub ran bordered walks, spoke-like, to every gate and building.

This meant that large areas of cobblestone and brick pavement were broken up, and in place of a colorless expanse of gray courtyard there were circles, triangles, squares, ellipses and octagons of color. Flower beds had never been so beautiful or so well watered.

Spring had never been so phony. . . .

My men were rapturous about this opulent landscaping.

"Imagine!" chuckled Scott. "All this in a penal institution, a house of correction!"

"It couldn't happen in Italy," said Punch with a straight face.

"It's a wonderful country, democracy is safe," sighed Gibbs.

"Jeez—ain't it *amazin'* what goes on under that flag?" said Connie piously.

I remembered this doubletalk vividly when during the summer, concurrent with all this flowering beauty, a visiting narcotics agent with one of our bachelor buttons in his lapel made his tour of the cell block—and smelled marijuana. Opening one particular cell he found a groggy novice trying to light uncured marijuana leaves.

The agent stalked out into the courtyard and discovered that growing between the hollyhocks and sunflowers were marijuana plants.

The captain's face was rosy with something besides Irish humor when he ordered demolition squads to tear up the beds. It was just as well, he rationalized, it was getting so there was no place to walk.

Following this vigorous housecleaning job the men's interest in aesthetics sunk to such an abysmal pitch that most of the legitimate blooms pined for water, and in a matter of days the place reverted to the original beds which were tended by the few real gardeners among the prisoners.

The men were not growing marijuana for the benefit of the addicts in the penitentiary. Like all their projects, the back-breaking job of tearing up pavement and tediously planting flowers was cheerfully done with tongue in cheek. They would do anything to "put it over" on the authorities and expose the Dick Tracy mentality of the guards.

Not long after the marijuana episode a window box appeared in our office. At one end of the box was one radish, at the other one onion, and in the center one marijuana plant. King prepared placards which read:

RAPHANUS SATIVUS   CANNABIS SATIVA   LILIACEOUS ALLIUM CEPA
    (radish)   *(marijuana)*   *(onion)*

Small delegations of prisoners visited us on occasion to keep abreast of progress. Punch issued bulletins on the marijuana's state of health. At the maturity of the plant a state funeral was held with rosaries and masses chanted by Connie, Punch and Gibbs. The plant was embalmed in alcohol and interred in the window box beneath a marble marker chipped out of the baseboard of a toilet wall.

Another seed was planted and the same burlesque started all over again.

The incident of the marijuana beds was too good to keep. The joke leaked outside as a minor scandal, with the result that a series of self-appointed reformers visited the penitentiary that summer.

Any interruption that would break the monotony of the cell block was welcome, but sometimes the prisoners would tire of visitors tramping up and down the galleries and peering in the cells. They could spot reformers a mile off and worked out some interesting routines.

"You seen the hippopotamus yet?" they would ask a startled visitor. "The giraffe is two cages down, nothin' but monkeys and buzzards up here, ma'am. The freaks is in the basement" (psychopathic ward).

Or, waiting until the visitors would approach the cell, a couple of prisoners would break into obscenities and cursings, and laugh hysterically at the visitors' quick retreat.

Or one of the men would quickly undress and come stark naked to the front of the cell asking sweetly, "Did you call me, guard?" And while the ladies gasped and ran he would complain loudly after them, "Goddam biddy comes along peepin' in an' here I am without no clothes on! No privacy in this place—damn biddies walkin' through yer bedroom without no warnin'!"

The reformers who visited the penitentiary following the marijuana farce registered a loud protest at the art on the walls of the cells. It was admittedly more realistic than not, and very plentiful. When the warden appeared disinclined to listen to them, they brought such pressure to bear that finally he had to issue an edict removing all girl pictures from the cells.

The pictures came down from the walls of the cells only to be put up in places of work. Leg art suddenly appeared in the machine shop, the paint shop, the shoe factory. Calendar art had long since been standard equipment in the garage, of course.

Punch brought his exhibit over to the psychology office. King took one look at it and called him an alley cat. Although King drew scores of provocative sketches of the same beautiful girl every day, he displayed no pictures in his cell.

A second order had to be issued banning girl pictures completely.

My men were philosophic about the action, but the rest of the population didn't receive the news with such equanimity. They championed their rights vehemently. They protested that the reformers were not living sexually impoverished lives, at least not of necessity, and that, as long as the pictures were not hung on the reformers' walls, what the prisoners wanted to look at was their own business. The warden inclined to agree with the men, but he had to bow to pressure.

At first there was sulking in the cells and slow-down strikes at work. Then one day three foremen reported that emery dust and monkey wrenches were being dropped into the machinery, the damage and destruction amounting to thousands of dollars.

The protest spread. Stitches were left untied in the brush and shoe factories. Trucks were breaking down on the road, tires were picking up nails. On the farm the cows were not being milked and were developing udder trouble. Hogs were losing weight because they were not being fed.

Then the men in the dry cleaning plant became suddenly "sick" and didn't report to work at all. The furniture factory struck next. In a matter of days the penitentiary was at a standstill.

The kitchen, power house and hospital details did not strike, the men feeling that these details were essential to the immediate welfare of the prisoners. But all other shops and factories were closed.

Idle, angry prisoners are capable of serious mischief. The warden locked them up. No prisoner left his cell at any time except for one meal a day, when they were escorted in small groups under heavy guard. The warden hoped the men would prefer working to remaining on strike in their cells. But they did not budge. In desperation the warden cut off the *Amos 'n Andy* radio program.

It was then the riot began in earnest.

Because of the monotony of their life they were fanatical radio fans, especially of a few programs, which they received through headphones from a master set controlled by the officials. *Amos 'n Andy* was their undisputed favorite.

The prisoners were not protesting the warden's action in the pin-up matter. They were protesting the meddling of the reformers, hoping by their strike to coerce the warden into coming out openly against interference from the outside. But when he took action on the radio show, their pent-up anger turned on him. Until that moment the reformers were the target, but now the warden himself was equally guilty in their minds. They struck out at him.

They instigated an eating strike and a noise riot.

There are two sounds in a penitentiary that strike cold terror to the most initiated. One of these is the mass silence of the men when trouble is brewing. The spectacle of a thousand men at the table making no sound in the hall except the unavoidable clatter of dishes creates a suspense that is paralyzing. The other is a noise riot, when the men are locked in their cells, but stand shaking their cell doors, smashing the plumbing, and shouting all through the night. It is a sound that makes a brave man quake. A prison break with sirens and shooting and pounding feet doesn't affect the adrenal glands like the noise of two thousand hands shaking the bars and a thousand throats shouting in a unified cacophony.

In the regime of oldtime penology there would have been shooting, beating, starving and solitary confinement until the riot was broken. In winter the heat would have been turned off and every man and bed drenched with a fire hose, until men contracted pneumonia by the score and the rest whipped into line rather than freeze to death.

The warden cursed the reformers for not minding their own business and called an advisory conference attended by his assistants, the captain, the school principal, the social case workers, shop supervisors and foremen, chaplains, and me.

As we talked at this round table it was agreed that everything had been going smoothly until the pin-up edict. We admitted that there was always some logical rationale, some injustice or abuse in question in a riot. The prisoners knew better than to riot for fun. There was always some stake for which they were fighting. The convicts had accepted unquestioningly the destruction of the marijuana beds. They knew the warden couldn't have condoned such a thing. They also realized that the pin-up crisis was not the warden's own idea, but that it came from outside pressure. And though they had regard for real religion and honest worshipers, they had a violent contempt for the religious fourflusher, the meddler and the hypocrite. They viewed the pin-up incident as an unnecessary and undemocratic infringement of personal freedom.

Talk at the conference thus pivoted around the ideology of riots in general and this one in particular.

One of the foremen ventured to say that I had some hoodlums down in my office who all of a sudden seemed to be full of brotherly love—what went on down there? I quickly protested that managing a handful of men in an office was very different from subduing two thousand men in a riot. But upon being pressed further I said that my principle with the men was largely one of self-determination, with opportunity for initiative and full responsibility for its use. I admitted I had taken some gambles, especially in the matter of putting Connie, whom they all knew, in charge of the office.

"Well, we've tried everything else," said the warden. "You're a psychologist. What do you suggest, Doctor?"

I said this was my first riot, I didn't know about these things, but had they ever tried a convict committee?

My words were lost in loud protests of *"Committee!"* "You gotta treat 'em rough in this game—you want 'em running the joint?" To this someone responded tartly, "Who the hell do you think is running it now?"

"Quiet!" shouted the warden in a voice that should have quelled the riot unaided. It did stop the table talk. After a moment he began more quietly.

"Maybe I better clear up something right now." His cold blue eye swept every face around the table. "I didn't call this meeting to pass out vomit gas and lead pipes. There's been a reform in this country and every damn one of us knows it! Maybe we won't appoint a convict committee tonight, but there isn't going to be any rough stuff. Of course we don't like riots and breaks! All right—let's admit it—we're scared. That's always been the time to start the rough stuff—when you're scared. Well, if we can't handle this riot without violence, I'm through!"

They were listening, even if not convinced. I noticed the expression of the school principal. He looked happy.

"This isn't news to you men," the warden resumed. "You know how I feel. And if any of you feel differently, maybe you better say so now." He waited briefly, but no one spoke. "Now, Doctor," he turned to me, "What kind of a committee did you have in mind?"

I suggested that it was usually true that when men like these had a chance to sit in judgment on each other, they were more merciless than an outsider. So how about a convict committee to decide what was decorous and proper in girl art for the cells?

The men sat in critical silence. So the warden reminded them that this was not the first time in penal history a convict committee had been used. Action much more revolutionary than this was used successfully in Auburn Prison as early as 1913 by Warden Tom Osborne, who established self-government among his prisoners and who later ran the 2,500-man navy prison at Portsmouth without a single guard. We weren't displaying that kind of courage today, our warden said. Some prisons have as many guards as they do inmates, and those are the prisons which have the most trouble. "There must be something in the idea that if you expect decency from a man you get it, and if you don't expect it you don't get it," he said. "Osborne let those so-called 'hardened criminals' run themselves as long as there was no trouble, and, by God, they did a better job of it than the officials!"

The faces around the table held equal parts of thought, rebellion, fear and indecision. Some had been with him from the first. He spoke quietly now.

"A lot of us around this table were brought up in the old school. We were told that the way to handle a criminal was to break his spirit. It was a battle cry. *Break his spirit!*

"I don't know what the hell's the matter with us that we don't learn. You break a man's spirit and he isn't a man any more. He's a wild animal. The spirit in a man is the only thing we've got to work with. We damn well better use our heads around here tonight, or we may lose them, by God!"

The final decision was that each wing of the cell block was to elect three of its own men to constitute a committee on art. As chairman we suggested my own counterfeiter and artist, King, and as secretary a man who was sent up on a pornography count.

Instead of an ultimatum, the following announcement was made to the men. The men were to have supper as usual that night, without restriction. They were requested, not ordered, to return to work the following day. The election of committeemen was announced and scheduled for the following night after supper, the new committee to meet immediately in the library for discussion and action.

The tension broke in the cells in a matter of minutes. In the days that followed, the men repaired the damaged machinery and general havoc throughout the place, doing extra duty to make amends. During the next few months production reached an all-time high in every department of the penitentiary.

The outgrowth of the committee was the establishment of an art salon in the library. The rigor with which the committee censored the art submitted, and the unreasonably high standards they demanded before pictures could be exhibited in the salon, put to shame the civic reformers who had started it all.

The counterfeiter would have no counterfeit.

The pornographer would have no pornography.

The captain was delighted with the administration's innovations in terminating the riot. He walked on air for days. It confirmed his belief that the men would act "like sons of men instead of sons of bitches if they were treated like sons of God, which they were." I gathered he was going to make an attempt to put his theory into practice.

He launched his experiment on the convicts in his office, much to the annoyance of his sergeant, who held no such gentle view about "them mugs," and apparently without sufficient explanation to his men of his intent. A girl's gold watch had been found one day on a new convict in the third wing. The captain purposely had not secured the contraband too well upon leaving that night, and the next morning the watch was gone.

The captain was heartbroken. He was also mad. It was nip-and-tuck for a while as to which would take over, his tears or his temper. He finally resolved into bristling indignation and summoned his men into the staff room. There were some trouble-makers among them, attached to his office as Connie had been, so that he could keep his eye on them.

They sat down and turned their wide gaze upon him while he paced up and down the room. Suddenly he stopped, lifted an accusing finger and bellowed, "Men—there's a thief among you!"

By the time the incongruity of his words struck him, the men had broken their stunned silence with howls of laughter. The wrath went out of the captain. When the men saw this they gathered around him in a circle, still laughing, and all but carried him back to his office on their shoulders like a hero. They wanted him to know that though he seemed to have lost he had really won.

His words, "There's a thief among you," became instantly immortal, as they should.

His men returned the loot the same day, in their own way. They planted it on the skeptical sergeant.

There was never a dull moment for the earnest captain. There was, for instance, the World Series.

A shouting baseball fan himself, with special loyalty to the Yankees, he anticipated the series in a glow of pleasure mixed with dread. The series closed our own baseball season during which anything could happen and often did.

The series had nothing on our ball teams for *esprit de corps,* provided the captain's office had first microscopically checked the grudge records of the players. If not, there was plenty of excitement in the way of unexpected plays. Too frequently to be explained by the law of chance, a teammate would accidentally fall afoul of a stray bat—just in the spirit of good clean fun. Three extra guards were always detailed around home plate.

I was once among the spectators at what appeared to be an unusually sedate game. There were no casualties aside from some raw shins, missing teeth, and a couple of black eyes, all entirely incident to sliding into second base, or a close squeeze play on third, of course. At cell check, however, one man was missing, and since he was one of the players the search for him began on the ball field. He was found doubled up in shock. He died later from a brain hemorrhage caused by a blow from a bat.

Following another game the guards called for a stretcher late at night for a convict found groaning in his cell. He had been suffering for hours, but had not reported to the hospital, fearing his fate if he squealed. He also had hemorrhaged internally and that night an operation was performed.

Some of the best hangovers in the world are acquired in a penitentiary. This was another of the captain's headaches.

I was periodically called to the emergency ward to study the delirium and mania incident to a convict's drinking shellac in the paint shop. Although this pastime generates terrific euphoria, everyone in the penitentiary knows that it also means death. Nevertheless every few months the craving for a jag would be so great that another victim would go on a binge.

More frequently someone would break into a warehouse and have a fling at wood alcohol, with resulting blindness or paralysis. This result was also well-known throughout the prison, but the knowledge acted as no deterrent.

Prison dipsomania did, however, have its lighter variations. Under pressure of time and secrecy, the kitchen crew could brew some of the world's most potent alcohol in one short day. Hairless Joe's Kickapoo Joy Juice is a related phenomenon, no doubt. All we could ever learn was that this alcohol was made of raisins, potato skins, yeast, and some undivulged chemical.

A bacchanalia was most likely to occur on a holiday when the privations of prison life were most keenly felt. New Year's Day was a natural for one of these festivals. It climaxed the Christmas holidays, which were really painful to the men, marked by nostalgia, homesickness, worry over families, remorse for their sins, and tearful resolutions. Two weeks of this undiluted emotionality was about all they could endure. By New Year's Day they were ready for a quick change.

On one New Year's the kitchen crew with this powerful bootleg on their palates turned into whirling dervishes and cavorted through the storeroom and the empty mess hall in a mad revel. The dancers hallucinated themselves to be flower girls, tossing cornflake petals into the air until they were dancing ankle-deep in them. When the supply of cornflakes diminished the ballet became more realistic: the dancers began tossing cans of condensed milk and soup instead of cornflakes, with an incidental decrease in the number of nymphs participating. Their marksmanship was deadly.

Solo dancers performed on barrels and tables, wearing prodigious numbers of towels and dishcloths as costumes. Those crippled with *arthritis deformans* or those with displastic potbellies disported themselves as nude nymphs.

Providing a static backdrop for all this choreographic movement, small clusters of men sat around weeping copiously into their beers, singing old hymns and ballads in lush uncertain harmonies, reaching back in their memory to days of indolence and peace, far past their tangles with John Law to the eternal innocence of childhood.

The captain was always surprised that incidents of assault and battery were rare during these bacchanals. This was hardly what one would expect from a bunch of pickled prisoners. It seemed a conspicuous occasion for them to vent their spleen on their fellows. Here they were, acting like children instead of criminals. There were many conjectures at the penitentiary about this docility, among them one that the undivulged chemical was some kind of love potion that neutralized the adrenalin in the blood. Those who held the popular concept that one's real self is released by alcohol had no explanation to offer.

One's "real self" is not released by alcohol. When one's critical faculties of judgment, evaluation, proportion and perception are deadened by alcohol, one conducts oneself in an uncritical uninhibited manner. In such conduct there are indices of personality conflicts. However, one's conduct under the influence of alcohol is not only uninhibited, but distorted and exaggerated as well. If there is sharp contrast between a man's behavior when his critical centers are temporarily deadened by alcohol and when they are not, he is described as having a high degree of personality dissociation. If the contrast is slight or absent, he is said to be a highly integrated personality. One's integration, however, is not always positive. It may be wholly negative, as in a violent personality. If a man is docile when sober and docile when drunk, there is reason to believe he is a docile man. If he is docile when drunk and violent when sober, we have one index of his conflicting personality drives. If he is docile when sober and violent when drunk, we have another index.

In the case of the prisoners' behavior when under the influence of alcohol, it may have been that they had expended so many of their antisocial aggressions through their criminal careers that when all their inhibitors were temporarily deadened by alcohol they had no aggressions left to release.

Originally, when these bacchanals first occurred, the guards were summoned to quell the festivities. Although the debauchees were harmless, they were also indefatigable. If ossification and catatonia did not overtake the performers, the guards did. In either eventuality the troupe ended up in the hospital. As the administration became seasoned to these holiday events, the guards compromised by herding the men into an open room and locking them in. This done, the guards formed a tight ring of faces at the gate bars to watch the revelry. It was better than a prizefight at Madison Square Garden.

The potent stuff would eventually embalm the performers,

whereupon they could be tossed like cordwood into a truck and backed up to the ambulance entrance of the hospital.

It took them several days to recover from the frightful stuff, at which point the warden gave them restricted quarters, and God gave them a five-day headache. At least, in trying to describe the headaches to the doctors, the convicts swore that only God could give a man such a head.

But the headache which bore down upon the captain's vagus nerve was the occasional case of homosexuality which he had to review for discipline. The captain, like most of the American public, was queasy about the whole subject, and he made no attempt to hide his lights when a rouged and predatory "wolf," having insinuated himself here and there on the primrose path, ultimately stood before him for judgment. He made short shrift of such. That boys would be boys he understood. That they would also be girls was something else.

But when an otherwise normal, wholesome man broke under prison frustration and loneliness, and came up on a homosexual charge looking as though he would gladly flee not only the captain but himself as well, the captain was dismayed. One such case, which broke him up for days, involved a former policeman, now a prisoner, whom the captain had known on the outside. (Whatever the frailty that sent up the erstwhile cop, it was not homosexuality.) The captain was badly shaken when his old friend was reported for having been caught in "an unnatural act." A prison psychologist never looked so good in the captain's charitable thoughts as when such a case was on his hands.

Homosexuality in prison is largely an American phenomenon, and only a little more than fifty years old. A little known and less assimilated fact among laymen is that segregation of sexes and individual cells did not exist in the early American

150

jails. To add piquancy to this tradition was the fact that jailers in those days did a thriving business in prostitution among prisoners. With heterosexual opportunities, prisoners took a dim view of homosexuality.

The penitentiary system, which appeared in the 1820s simultaneously in Europe and America, provided segregation by giving each man (or woman) a solitary cell, some being incredibly primitive for the decade of the Monroe Doctrine. Small individual stalls were conceived even for attendance at Divine services and for what passed as setting-up exercises. The prisoners were required to wear shrouds on their heads at these two rituals to forestall a chance glimpse of another human being.

Maine at that time by-passed solitary cells, instead digging pits ten feet deep into which a prisoner was lowered by means of a ladder, or in the absence of local ceremony he was pushed in, whereupon the pit was sealed with a two-foot square grating, and that was that. Connecticut used abandoned mines and kept the men chained underground, out of range of each other. Thus our forbears were not troubled with homosexuality, especially in winter, when the "institutions" were not heated and many convicts froze to death or died from exhaustion accompanying frantic efforts to keep warm by exercising.

Instead of homosexuality there was death and insanity.

The incidence of insanity from the solitary system was so high that most states began modifying or abandoning it by the middle of the nineteenth century. Charles Dickens aided these reforms by his now famous tirades in his *American Notes*. By 1855 universal solitary confinement was restricted to nine months in most states, and some states had abandoned it as a system, although Pennsylvania stubbornly maintained it until 1913.

By the time of the Civil War there were institutions where men worked without chains, and on July 4, 1864 the first assembly of unchained men gathered in the yard of a Massachusetts prison. This was also the date of the first relinquishment of the rule of silence. Prisoners were thereafter able to talk once a month!

By the end of the century congregate penology had demonstrated such superiority over solitary confinement that men were housed together, two or more, in a single cell (although to tell the truth the shift came more because of overcrowding than because of a change in penal philosophy).

With congregate penology came homosexuality. This abnormality is not specifically associated with what we commonly think of as criminal character. As found in prisons, it is the result, not of criminal character, but of our prison system, particularly such factors as restriction of physical exercise, the monotony of incarceration, and the deprivation of legitimate sexual expression.

It is a well-demonstrated fact that wherever men and women are segregated homosexuality appears: in a college dormitory, in the armed services, and especially when maladjusted men are locked together in cells with the abnormalities of prison life already creating an incipient prison psychosis. Add the punitive factor to the psychic pressures of depression, frustration, aggression, failure, privation and loneliness, and a natural energy is directed into abortive channels.

A very young child has an amorphous, non-specific or latent sexuality. In a boy from nine to fifteen years the normal homosexual period flourishes in the socially approved gang age: the period of idolizing ideals and deprecating girls. In the transition during the later teens come the heterosexual interests of sweethearts and marriage.

But many individuals never mature to the heterosexual point. Somewhere along the line they have been traumatized in some relationship and their psychosexual growth is stunted. They may be uncomfortable about the woman question and remain bachelors for life, or they may enter overt homosexuality.

Psychotherapeutically, the psychologist treats homosexuality not as a perversion, but as a problem of arrested sexual development and emotional immaturity, and treats the case by attempting to stimulate growth toward psychic maturity.

Occasionally the pressures of life become too great, as in war or in prison, and a once matured person regresses toward childhood, engaging in homosexual episodes on the way. Often this is a temporary, situational interlude which is terminated by environmental change, as in the case of the sailor who is homosexual on board ship, but heterosexual the moment he hits the water front. In fact, he frequently will have no shipboard episodes for several days in anticipation of docking. Many prison liaisons are terminated well in advance of release in sheer anticipation of heterosexuality.

Kinsey in *Sexual Behavior in the Human Male* reports that 37% of normal men have experienced overt orgasmic homosexual relationships, and many more have had abortive experiences. He states that over 50% of men who reach the age of thirty-five without marriage have had full homosexual relationships. He has excluded from these figures incompleted attempts and latent and sublimated affairs. However, this incidence does not represent a constant or continued activity.

The female is regarded as more natively bisexual than the male, both socially and scientifically, which may be one of the reasons for the greater prevalence of lesbianism over male homosexuality. There are no Federal or state laws against lesbianism, while all states as well as many Federal divisions have stringent laws against male homosexuality.

These same *mores* cause much less concern over women's more extensive homosexuality in prison than men's. While it is possible that Havelock Ellis' pioneer estimate of an 80% incidence of overt indulgence is still prevalent in reformatories and some women's prisons, it is far too high for a well-run men's institution. It is possible, in a restrictive state institution where brutality is still assaulting the personality organization of the prisoner, that one-half the population has engaged in homosexuality, but in a more ideal institution, such as the Federal penitentiaries, the figure is probably nearer 10%. Statistics on this front are hard to assemble. The problem was well under control at the Leavenworth Annex as I knew it.

The fewer the restrictions and the more areas of functioning offered the men, the less the problems of all kinds, especially discipline, insanity and homosexuality. A prison with a program of constructive labor, vocational training, school courses, athletics, a good library with something in it other than Louisa May Alcott and the Purity series, movies, radio, hobbies, superior medical services, a functioning practical religion, some female influence in the form of nurses, social and religious workers, theater troupes, and intelligent visiting rooms for relatives and friends, is making strides toward preparing the convict for a normal entrance into society upon release. As the hours in which he is engaged in constructive activities increase, homosexuality decreases. Again it is society's choice between revenge and recidivism, or reconstruction and citizenship.

Apart from Alcatraz, *none of the twenty-nine Federal penal institutions has had a break or a riot since 1932*. Overt homosexuality has declined to a minimum. More significant still is the steady decline in recidivistic crime of the parolee from good institutions: a drop from the old expectancy of more than 50% violators to less than 3%. Bates reports that *less than 1% of all fingerprint arrests are of men on parole!* These are among the unanswerable arguments for modern penology.

As has been said, homosexuality is an American prison phenomenon. Salvador, Mexico and Russia have solved the problem by bold moves. Russia has prison communities where entire families live and function within the compound area. (She is not so humane, unfortunately, to war prisoners.) It is reported that Australia is considering family communities for salvageable prisoners. Salvador and Mexico provide conjugal visits for husbands and wives, and, in keeping with their cultures, for unmarried prisoners as well.

As the United States becomes increasingly interested in creating citizenship rather than indulging revenge, a convict-operated town-and-country, home-and-family community to prepare selected pre-parole prisoners for re-entry into society is perhaps not too far distant.

8

BY THE time of the *Amos 'n Andy* riot that first spring my status with the men in the penitentiary began to look secure. I was disturbed to find that my staff was building me into a fantastic legend among the population, with only the purest motives, of course. The fact that their own status was greatly enhanced in the eyes of the population by such proximity to me—a very uncomfortable hero—was not purely coincidental. It was a maneuver that I should have liked to curtail, but I had to admit it was breaking down resistance among the prisoners at large. It seemed best to let well enough alone.

I appreciated the fact that Doctor Stevens, an old and wise institution man, had encouraged me to take the first few months to find my feet. It would have been foolhardy to have become too aggressive before the prisoners' feeling about me clarified somewhat.

My staff was won over to the testing technique by this time, and, having seen the results of the warden's action in the riot, they now relinquished all their skepticism regarding psychology and entered the second sophomoric phase of their education, an uncritical acceptance of the whole field and of me. Students pass through the same cycle, and it is a conscientious teacher's aim to develop critical and evaluatory processes that will give them some perspective on the field under study.

The critical and evaluatory processes were not highly developed in my staff: they are not highly developed in any neurotic or "criminal" personality. From my unofficial comments and lectures in our own semiweekly staff meetings, in which their antisocial aggressions were frequently ventilated, the men began to understand that many of the factors in "criminal personality" which had tripped them up could be explained in psychological phenomena. But I was careful to remind them that an understanding of these phenomena was only the first step toward cure, and that understanding alone would not necessarily produce the will to be cured, a factor which the individual himself must supply. Like many neurotic personalities, they were counting hard on psychology to produce some mumbo jumbo which would cure them without effort on their part, some kind of psychic colonic. This was a *laissez-faire* attitude from which they had to be disabused in time.

They were anxious to begin techniques in the drug research more dynamic than pencil-and-paper tests. They were hoping the staff would find a physiological basis for addiction that would absolve the addict from personal responsibility for the habit. For that matter, so was the USPHS; so was I. I think their real maturation started when as time went on, the evidence began to grow that there was little to support this thesis, but that the cause and cure of addiction were probably more psychological than medical.

In time the men even began to re-evaluate the efficiency of some of the paper-and-pencil tests, another step in their maturation.

In spite of the claims of publishers and the sanguine reports of uncritical users of standard pencil-and-paper personality tests, they are disappointing. It would be wonderful to have a test which could reliably differentiate, by their relative neurotic indices, sexual deviates from "normals" or sadistic killers from sneak thieves. Pencil-and-paper tests in personality do not differentiate the criminal from the non-criminal, the insane from the sane, the homosexual from the heterosexual. My men's enthusiasm regarding these tests diminished sharply when we found that our statistical curves on personality at the penitentiary could not be distinguished from those run on Stanford University sophomores. There was something wrong, either with the tests, or with Stanford sophomores.

Even today standard vocational and personality tests are not satisfactory. They throw little light on the vast problem of personality. They are frequently armchair tests, standardized on subjects not representative of a cross-section population, and on far too few subjects. A couple of hundred college sophomores are not representative of the general population of a nation, to say nothing of institutional deviates. And yet naive psychometricians blindly try to fit the patients to these tests, while their patients try to fit square blocks in round holes.

The projective techniques, such as the Rorschach, the Thematic Apperception Test, and the Association tests, pay higher dividends. Perhaps soon the enigma of personality structure will clarify.

Early in the drug research Gordon and I again talked about hypnosis. It seemed to us that it would be a good and valid entering wedge to help the men through the hardest part of their denarcotization with hypnosis.

Wherever men are restrained, institutionalized or incarcerated, there are predispositions to certain types of behavior: the scuttlebutt of the navy, the endless variations of the old army game, and the propensities for mischief on the part of prisoners. While the grapevine in a penitentiary is a startlingly efficient institution, it also predisposes to contagious behavior that mounts easily to mass hysteria. Because of the ignorance and credulity of much of the penitentiary population, superstition quickly takes root in weird tales and irrational attitudes. When one considers the lore of the Johnny Appleseed and Paul Bunyan stories, which grew in an unrestrained population, one is better able to appreciate the exaggerated beliefs and attitudes of the prisoner concerning the occult. Anything not understood is material for either fear or uncritical belief. It would be quite a step for the men to chance our extracting confessions from them under hypnosis, and then "turning stool" on them.

My hunch that Gordon would make a good hypnotist proved to be right. His good-natured domination of the subjects when he "put them to sleep" produced good results in the depth of trance he was able to produce. He therefore induced sleep, and I did the therapeutic work while the patient was in trance, and re-oriented the subject when he awakened from trance.

Gordon's training as a hypnotist was not restricted to me. He went east to train with two of the best men in the field. But I did have several preliminary sessions with him. For these we used members of our own families as subjects.

I recall one session in Gordon's home one evening. He had induced a trance in his wife. Before waking her, I made the post-hypnotic suggestion (a course of conduct suggested to the patient in trance, to be followed after the patient wakes) that fifteen minutes after waking she would believe herself to be in a movie watching a hilarious comedy. I have frequently used this suggestion in the college classroom in demonstrating post-hypnotic suggestion, because it breaks into the intensity and morbidity a student sometimes feels about hypnosis.

Upon a cue from me she woke up with no memory of the trance or of a post-hypnotic suggestion having been given. We were all pursuing normal conversation when, right on the dot of fifteen minutes, we "lost" Mrs. Gordon to the movie. Her eyes were on the wall, which she hallucinated to be the screen, and for several minutes she completely ignored us, alternating between provocative chuckles and loud gusts of laughter, while the private showing unfolded to her.

In the middle of the "movie" the door chime sounded. Gordon and I looked apprehensively at each other. It would have been a jolly scene for the warden or the chief medical officer to walk in on. It would have been difficult to persuade anyone, who had not heard the post-hypnotic suggestion, that Mrs. Gordon hadn't had too many after-dinner brandies.

Fortunately the caller was of no consequence and was promptly dispatched from the front hall.

The denarcotization period, which covers approximately 72 hours from beginning to end, was an exacting medium for hypnosis.

There are no major symptoms in the patient for eight hours following abrupt withdrawal of the drug, except a growing restlessness, but in the following twenty-four hours the restlessness increases. The patients are sleepless and thirsty. They all report muscle pain. They begin to lose their nerve because they know what is coming. The most rugged period is following the thirty-sixth hour after withdrawal until the end of the third day. During this time the patients cannot eat; their restlessness and muscle pain mount; they perspire through weakness, in spite of being dehydrated. Drinking water frequently precipitates vomiting which sometimes doesn't stop for hours. They lose several pounds of weight during this period. Their weakness is acute, but they cannot remain quiet. They have to keep on the move. They sit for a few seconds, stand up, walk, lie down, rub their limbs. Headaches are common, sleep is fitful. After about seventy-two hours the agonies subside, and the men quiet down.

It was in the second and third days that Gordon used baths, currents, and massage, and it was with these patients that we first tried hypnosis.

During the first few weeks of our work in the narcotic ward we limited our program to nothing but inducing sleep. At first only a third of the men obtained good results. Their restlessness made it difficult for them to concentrate. When we held a training period in hypnosis for the patients before their denarcotization began, the results were better.

As aids to relaxation we used the auto-condensation table in the electrotherapy ward. This current was used primarily to reduce high blood pressure. It created relaxation and drowsiness. To this we added ocular and retinal fatigue by having the recumbent patient concentrate on a tiny moving light above and behind his head. While he thus concentrated we talked to him about "the sleep machine," using this term instead of hypnosis because of the latter's negative connotations. We asked him to think of relaxation, drowsiness, heaviness of limbs and sleep, while we repeated such a phrase as "You are going deep asleep . . . . deep asleep . . ." many times, until the patient would sink into a hypnotic trance. While he was thus sleeping we gave the suggestion that he would remain asleep or stuporous until the denarcotization period was over, but that in the interim he would be able to rouse sufficiently to drink water (without nausea) and toilet himself.

The first few patients were wheeled back into the narcotic ward sound asleep, and they remained asleep for a period of hours, in spite of their beds' being surrounded by a ring of gawking inmates in gaping hospital gowns who poked and pinched them, shook them and talked to them in astonishment and unbelief.

"Hey, Joey—I rap this guy where it really hurts an' he don't even twitch!" one of them would exclaim. "If ya can't be coked up I guess ya just as well be rigid an' peaceful."

These first cases created no end of stir, and before long we had a line of new admissions wanting to be treated on the sleep machine.

Few subjects go into deep trance at the first attempt. It is necessary to train a subject in repeated sessions, each time trying for a deeper level of sleep.

161

We used some of our better hypnotic subjects in experiments with biochemical changes induced by hypnosis. We had covered the European literature describing the change of chemical contents of the urine in Bright's disease and the creation of lipase and pancreatic secretions by hypnosis. The biochemical research had heroic and dramatic proportions in the eyes of the prisoners, so that volunteers were easily obtained. However, the number of those susceptible to deep trance were fewer than for denarcotizing sleep.

There is much exaggeration concerning the ease and effectiveness of hypnosis. Many careless articles appear in professional and popular literature, claiming that almost anyone is susceptible to hypnosis and that extensive results can be obtained in the majority of cases. This is not true. Deep hypnosis is possible in less than twenty percent of subjects. Superficial hypnosis, such as is demonstrated in college classes and on the vaudeville stage, is quite another matter. But in such processes as changing body chemistry and solving emotional complexes by regression in time-space technique, the available subjects and ideal patients dwindle rapidly.

The time-space technique mentioned is the hypnotic process by which a subject is put into a deep trance and then given the suggestion that he is going to relive an episode, a crisis, a day, a conversation, an act—any strategic event that the therapist is led to believe is a possible clue to the subject's problem, any experience which out of fear or guilt or shock the patient has blocked off from his conscious memory so that he cannot or will not recall it voluntarily.

In time-space regression the patient actually does again relive the experience in time, place and content, with conversation and action, though never leaving the therapist's room. He does not simply retell an event—he re-enacts it. He has both positive and negative hallucinations, which means that he does not see objects or people in his surroundings which were not in the event

162

he is re-enacting (such as the room, the therapist, furniture, etc.), and he does "see" things which are not in his present surroundings but which were at the scene of the incident. He will hallucinate a chair, for instance, and will remain in the crouched position of sitting for a long period of time without fatigue or cramping. The time employed for re-enactment will be of the same duration as in the original incident, minute for minute, movement for movement. When there is conversation the therapist hears only the subject's comments and replies, and must supply from them the other side of the conversation. This technique of regression is possible only under deep trance.

Of the three hundred cases we hypnotized, the majority were not effective subjects for biochemical study. Of the twenty percent who were, only a few were ideal for controlled time-space regression—perhaps five percent of the total prison population. The percentages run higher in a normal private practice.

After a few months patients began coming to us requesting hypnosis for the removal of all kinds of complexes. Acrophobia and claustrophobia were torturous to men housed in the top tier of a cell wing. They were also suffering from fear of death, fear of being alone, fear of being with people, and from various hysterical effects: physical manifestations of emotional disturbances, such as functional ulcers, functional paralysis, functional blindness, functional heart disorders.

Since hypnotic literature is filled with incidents and case studies unsupported by actual medical data, we kept elaborate records of temperature changes, pulse rate, blood pressure, metabolic changes, and other polygraphic records. As a control, and to test the validity and accuracy of regression experiments, we would occasionally repeat a performance at a later time under close observation. In this way we would know whether the patient had given us fantasies, day dreams, projections, wish-fulfillments, or actual events.

One convict checked into the hospital with gastro-intestinal complaints. Laboratory tests indicated that he was not adequately digesting fat. Gordon had reason to believe that the absence of lipase and pancreatic secretions was of psychological origin rather than physical. Under hypnosis the patient was told that he was eating a very fat meal and would be able to digest it without discomfort. We caused him to hallucinate gravy, fat meat, bacon, butter, mayonnaise and he went through the gestures of eating with great relish. The use of a stomach pump later revealed that he had produced secretions to digest this imaginary meal.

In the case of another man we believed that pertinent information was related to a day six months previously when he had had an acute tonsillitis attack. The illness had been complicated by other throat conditions so severe that a trachea tube had to be forced down his windpipe so that he could breathe. When he recovered, a tonsillectomy was performed.

In our therapy we regressed him in time-space and suggested that *today* was the morning of his attack of tonsillitis, that he would go through the day just as he had six months previously. The nurse kept his temperature chart and pulse rate, and Gordon examined his throat at timed intervals. The entire attack was reproduced without benefit of tonsils, and with a development which we had not anticipated. Gordon was called to the patient's bedside in great urgency. The man had turned purple as he had in the original attack, and was gasping for breath. Then we remembered the previous complications, and Gordon quickly inserted a trachea tube. This episode gave us both a profound respect for the reliability and validity of the time-space regression phenomenon of hypnosis.

This case was of more medical significance than the case of Hobson, but perhaps not so dramatic.

Hobson was the victim of severe cardiophobia: fear of dying from heart attack, which produces functional heart symptoms. We were not able to remove this complex about his heart by ordinary psychotherapeutic methods. Drugs and narcosynthesis did not reveal the causative factor. But he proved an excellent subject for hypnosis. After carefully training him in preliminary sessions Gordon and I took a Sunday off to spend with Hobson to see if we could learn from a time-space regression the cause of his phobia.

We took him to the physiotherapy room, placed him in a deep trance, and suggested that it was now the morning of the day he had had his first attack of cardiophobia, whenever that was. He had buried it too deeply to recall consciously. We told him that he would now relive and re-enact that day exactly as it happened. Gordon and I then stepped aside, prepared to wait out the day.

Gordon had put Hobson to sleep on the treatment table. Under hypnosis he now hallucinated this to be his bed on that particular day. Presently he stirred, yawned, got out of bed and began a conversation with what proved to be his cell mate on that day. We could hear only Hobson's side of the conversation, of course, but it was not difficult to supply his cell mate's replies.

"Jake! . . . . You awake?" he asked in a stage whisper. "You still got your nerve with you?" Jake apparently said he had. "Good," said Hobson, "I didn't want you to go yellow on me. Can't have any crawfish on this deal."

Still in trance, Hobson hallucinated a washbowl, bent over it and splashed imaginary water on his face. He walked to a corner, sat down on a toilet which wasn't there, and while continuing to talk he actually defecated and urinated.

As the conversation progressed we knew they were going over plans for a jail break for the last time.

"Now, don't put on too good an act," warned Hobson. To some question from his companion he replied, "Well, I mean, you can writhe on the floor, but don't make it too phony. Now this is the way it's gonna be. You roll on the floor and holler till the jailer comes. Then I'll lay him out." (A pause for Jake's reply.) "That's it," said Hobson. "Then you guard him while I get his keys and we'll make a break for it." (A pause for a question from Jake.) "No—you go ahead," replied Hobson. "You open the outside gate and signal me. I'll cover you till you make the gate, then I'll follow you when I see the coast is clear. If I don't make it, take it on the lam!" Now Hobson spoke threateningly: "But get this straight, kid. Nobody digs up that twenty grand until we both get there. If you touch it, I'll have you killed. You got that?"

Then there followed an interval of silence during which the "seizure" of his companion took place, after which Hobson walked to imaginary cell bars and stood shaking the gate and calling for the jailer. He backed away from the door as the jailer entered the cell.

"Jake's awful sick." The jailer asked a question to which Hobson responded: "I don't know. Maybe a fit?"

And while the jailer was apparently bending over the "sick" Jake, we saw Hobson reach under his pillow, on the treatment table, of course, and his hand closed around an imaginary object. This he raised over what we supposed was the jailer and brought it down with all his might. We saw him give the pipe to Jake. Then Hobson bent down and took the jailer's keys, handed them to Jake, and directed him down the corridor for the escape.

But much to our amazement, Hobson did not follow Jake. He remained in his cell. We saw him pick up the pipe and carefully wipe it. Instead of hiding it under the pillow, he replaced it on the floor. At first we thought he was wiping blood from the pipe, but as the one-sided drama was re-enacted it became evident that Hobson had double-crossed his cell mate. We heard him tell the turnkey who came in response to Hobson's summons that Jake had killed the jailer and made a getaway, and that he, Hobson, had had nothing to do with it, had even argued against it.

"I told him I'd already got one rap," he said to the turnkey, "that I'd be out pretty quick, and I didn't want to queer myself."

After the commotion ceased and the turnkey had left, Hobson staggered to his bed on the treatment table. He lay down with one hand on his head and one over his heart, and gasped for breath.

And that, we felt, was the beginning of his cardiophobia.

We awakened him and found that he had complete amnesia for the hypnotic episode. In deep trance the patient usually does have amnesia upon awakening.

In subsequent treatments it developed that Hobson had turned state's witness and thus caused the execution of his innocent cell mate. The major corroborating evidence to Hobson's testimony was the piece of pipe carrying Jake's bloody fingerprints. What Hobson had wiped off was the end of the pipe which bore his own prints.

"Ratting on a pal" is about as low as a criminal can sink in his own or his confederates' eyes. Hobson's guilt over breaking his codes and ratting on Jake caused him great mental anguish. To steel himself for Jake's trial where he perjured himself, he became addicted to morphine. It was his addiction which led to his penitentiary sentence.

There, deprived of his drugs and locked in a cell to brood over his guilt, he quickly deteriorated, developing night terrors, from which one cannot be wakened as one can from a nightmare. He had somnambulistic interludes during which he screamed about being a rat. His cardiophobia and gastrointestinal symptoms followed these mental terrors. He was approaching psychosis when he came to our attention, about a year after he arrived at the penitentiary. These physical symptoms had now become his whole preoccupation, because in gaining them he had lost the memory of Jake, the break, the murdered jailer, and the electrocution. These physical symptoms were now hysterical effects—substitutes for his guilt. He had complete amnesia for the whole Jake episode, from the morning of the murder to the day following Jake's electrocution. Events immediately preceding and immediately following the Jake episode were somewhat cloudy in his conscious memory, but on the Jake episode itself he drew a complete blank. Except under hypnosis.

The problem of making this buried episode a part of Hobson's conscious memory and integrating it in his personality took considerable time and skill. Whenever the suggestion was made in trance that he would be able to remember the episode, he would resist the suggestion to the point of coming out of his trance instantly. One of the ticklish problems in his hypnotic therapy was that, when he would finally remember having relived the Jake tragedy for us, he must also be able to recall that the confession was entirely voluntary and incident to his heart therapy, not something which we forced out of him. If Hobson believed we had made him talk there would have been no confidence in Gordon and me and no cure, and more important, no further hypnotic therapy in the penitentiary. He would have queered that for us.

He was cured of his heart symptoms in time by the integration of the Jake episode in his conscious stream of memory, where he could control his symptoms. He still had bouts with his guilt. But guilt with a man like Hobson is a relative thing. It wasn't murder that bothered Hobson: it was ratting on a pal. But in a pathological personality like his, remorse for one sin could be wiped out by a subsequent act of charity or mercy: befriending a prostitute, paying for somebody's operation, not killing another possible victim. These are the rationalizations of a criminal.

During one of the periods of dissociation when Hobson was coming in and out of his trance because of resistance to suggestion, he began once to describe where he and Jake had buried "the swag"—the twenty thousand dollars. At that point Gordon frantically urged me to wake him up. I didn't need much urging. I had a healthy curiosity, but the location of that loot was the last thing in the world I wanted to know. If Hobson, upon being released sometime in the future, should find the swag gone from beneath somebody's apple tree somewhere, I didn't want him paying a call on me.

We used other methods than hypnosis in the treatment of the neuroses of the drug addicts. One of these was the polygraph, whose inked record sometimes gave us clues to the source of the subject's psychological instability.

There are a half dozen lie detectors on the market, each of which varies slightly in mechanism and manipulation. In general, however, they all attempt to record changes in the nervous system's responses as indirectly picked up by heart, lung, and galvanic reflexes (the change in electrical potential as measured by skin resistance). These instruments utilize pneumographs, sphygmomanometers and psychogalvanographs.

In the operation of the polygraph a pneumatic tube is passed around the subject's chest to pick up breathing reflexes, another is fastened about the arm for pulse beat and blood pressure, and electrodes are placed on the hands to measure changes in skin resistance. All of these measurements are recorded on a moving chart by means of a series of pens. The subject is instructed to answer Yes or No to each question, whichever is true. The question must be so framed that it can be answered Yes or No without further explanation, because talking disrupts the record.

In uncovering complexes, a simple word association test is often more effective than questions. The patient is directed to respond to a stimulus word such as blue, dog, knife, etc., with the first word that comes into his mind. Indicative words related to his complex are interspersed: death, sex, murder, morphine, etc.

There are many mechanical difficulties in the polygraph. The padded heartbeat of excessively obese subjects, for instance, cannot be sufficiently amplified on the instrument. Also, if the appliances are kept too long on the subject's arm, circulation is interrupted, resulting in pain; and the instrument may have to be removed just when the operator is approaching the important area in his questioning. Frequently it is impossible to re-establish the mood in a subsequent session.

Ross worked with patience, insight and skill in attempting to convert my mechanical instrument into an all-electric one that could be standardized and its impulses amplified.

There is much popular exaggeration and superstition concerning the efficiency of a lie detector. It is still only as valid as the skill and experience of the operator. It does not detect lies; it only gives an index in a record of physiological changes in the responses of a subject when a certain area in his thinking is approached by questioning. In the next twenty years it may be sufficiently standardized to take its place in criminal procedures along with fingerprinting and ballistics. Perhaps it will eliminate some of the third degrees that still disgrace our police procedures.

In the treatment of complexes we also used various forms of narcosynthesis, such as intravenous sodium amytal, a forerunner of sodium pentathol. Narcosynthesis was very new and not too reliable in those early days. Its use in prison presented unique problems. If a criminal talked about unconfessed crimes and the location of loot under one of these serums, fact might easily merge into phantasy. Also the therapist ceased to be a therapist in the criminal's mind and became an inquisitor or an accomplice, which was what we had to avoid in Hobson's hypnotic treatment. In hypnosis, at least a subject could be wakened before the wrong thing was said. We discontinued the use of scopolamine, the so-called "truth serum," because there is no control over the patient's responses. He becomes highly suggestible under its influence and responds uncritically to the intonation of the doctor's voice.

"You murdered the man, didn't you?"

"Sure I did."

"You didn't murder the man, did you?'"

"No, of course not."

Fortunately the wide use of and research in narcosynthesis during and after World War II have considerably increased its efficacy.

Hypnosis gave us more genuine insight into the nature of the criminal and the cause of crime than any other technique. We were frequently able to ascertain the beginnings of his feelings of inadequacy and inferiority, the origins of his defensiveness, and perhaps the episode that caused his initiation into crime. More often than one would believe, it was associated with his having been beaten by a parent, or having been shamed by a teacher before a class; or, being rejected by a sweetheart, the patient visited a brothel where a prostitute belittled him for his impotence. It is hard to believe that often a life of flagrant crime is simply an attempt to compensate for feelings of inadequacy and inferiority, the individual getting ego satisfaction by becoming a troublesome and feared non-conformer. But it can happen, if a man is poorly equipped for life neurologically and psychologically at the outset.

In one case we found the prisoner's life of crime resulted from a series of somnambulistic nightmares in his adolescence accompanying his guilt over nocturnal emissions, the sense of guilt having been supplied by his parents. We learned this much through hypnosis, and were able through ordinary psychotherapy to illuminate the nightmares and their relation to his subsequent life.

At the beginning of our hypnotic work, I had my introduction into prison astrology. A nice Negro boy, Carmichael, one of the convict teachers in the penitentiary school, came to my office one day with a request for a reading list in psychology, and asked that he be allowed to stop in for an hour a week to talk about psychology and to clarify what he was reading.

On the outside Carmichael had been a minister, and he felt that an understanding of psychotherapy would help him in his pastoral work. He had great insight and perspective in some areas, but seemed completely blind to the incongruity of his having been sent up for polygamy, involving four wives. He maintained that, had he known as much about astrology when he was preaching as he did now after having had time to study it in the penitentiary, he would have been able to avoid his sentences—though not his four wives. They, he assured us, were in his horoscope.

Most of the prison population stood in awe of Carmichael, especially after he predicted that a certain guard's wife would be burned to death and implored the guard to keep her away from fire on a certain day. On that day, as she was dry cleaning some clothes, the solution exploded and enveloped her in flames.

The men wanted to know what their horoscopes had to say about whether they were going to be paroled, when they would get out, whether they would get back in, what chance they had of successfully continuing in crime or of going straight, what signs of girls there were in their futures, and other typical problems. I suspect that Carmichael's ministerial conscience affected his horoscopes in answering some of those questions.

Gordon and I felt that Carmichael accomplished a great deal of unofficial good throughout the institution in the influence he had on the sick line and Sick Call alone. As in every institution there were hypochondriacs and malingerers who took a heavy toll on the patience of the doctors, as well as on the stock of placebos (sugar pills) in the pharmacy. We had gastrointestinal cases whose functional disorders didn't get them enough attention, so they developed *anorexia nervosa* and consequently became emaciated. Or they would go into catatonia and have to be force fed through a tube inserted in the nostril, through which predigested liquids were poured. Some of the hypochondriacs were our drug addicts who having "kicked the habit" now

172

transferred their unsolved neuroses to psychosomatic complaints.

Suggestibility was extremely high among these individuals. Instead of being preoccupied with their future after they were released, they were concerned with their health now. In casting their horoscopes Carmichael would sometimes state that he could see that certain malefic influences in the horoscope would clear within a few days or a week. The calendars were watched religiously by these men, and right on schedule their symptomatology would cease. We could not help but feel that, as Carmichael learned more about psychology, his psychosomatic predictions were not so much found in horoscopes as in textbooks.

Though my staff showed lively interest in all therapeutic tools they themselves made no personal use of them. After a year's apprenticeship they now considered themselves psychologists, not patients.

There was one exception.

The day I returned from my vacation at the end of my first year, Ross, the forger-engineer, did not report to work. He was in one of his depressions. On the third day he came to me unexpectedly, requesting hypnosis. He told me then that he had been hearing voices in his periodic depressions for several years.

From the first I had wanted to help Ross, but he was a man who would want to make his own overtures. I knew that I had to wait and that it was possible he might never talk. I was glad therefore when he did.

There was nothing in the first thirty years of the life of Ross to suggest that at forty-five he would be serving his fourth term in a penitentiary. He had come from a family of quality and position. He had been precocious as a child, was given a fine education, distinguished himself in his profession, married happily, and had a son and a daughter. His qualities of mind and heart were surely not acquired in prison; they had always been his. They were what saved him from total ruin in the hands of early twentieth century penology. Ross endeared himself to every one by these qualities. He inspired not only admiration but affection.

His first sentence resulted from his circumstantial involvement in a crooked construction company. He had as a matter of courtesy receipted invoices and orders at the request of a fellow-engineer, using the other engineer's name, not his own. One day that engineer lost his life on the job. During investigations following his death many irregularities in the handling of material and money by the dead engineer were uncovered. Ross could not square himself regarding the diverted materials and "forged" signatures. He found himself in prison, where he encountered hunger, filth, idleness and brutality.

He showed me scars around his wrists. There were holes below his misshapen thumbs. He had attracted the eye of a brutish guard, in the days when guards were chosen without having to meet any requirements whatsoever. For no apparent reason than that the guard was offended by his superiority, education and gentility, Ross was charged with getting out of lockstep, and was strung up by his thumbs. They had to bear the whole of his two-hundred-pound weight. There he hung for hours on three different occasions for equally trivial offenses.

This kind of suspension is more painful than crucifixion. A man can live for three or four days in crucifixion. A day can kill a man suspended by his thumbs. The muscles knot, the ligaments are pulled. The pain is so excruciating that the victim goes into convulsions which jerk the body and pull harder on the torn muscles and ligaments. The intense suffering produces excessive toxins in the body, gangrene sets in and often causes death. The knotted muscles lock, cutting off circulation and creating cyanosis. Intermittent fainting produces circulation changes and enforces relaxation, otherwise more of the victims would die.

The guard stood by, watching. Ross was in a comatose state

when he was cut down. When consciousness returned he found himself in the hands of the prison doctor who was not as depraved as the guard. Ross was still in such pain that the doctor gave him a shot of morphine. The pain quickly eased, and he drifted into the oblivion of morphinic sleep.

But when the drug wore off a few hours later the pain was still with him. The doctor gave him another shot of morphine. Again the pain eased, and again he escaped briefly the nightmare of his life and the mental shock of his physical ordeal. When he finally had to face the nightmare without the release of morphine, his abysmal depressions began.

There were ways of getting morphine and he got it, to escape the depressions. His hypnagogic dreams as he emerged from drugged sleep were psychic wish-fulfillments. He was with his family in these dreams, they were happy, he was successful, there was no nightmare. He talked to them and heard their voices.

But soon he realized that he was becoming addicted, and this brought guilt. Guilt brought more frequent depressions, and now instead of the happy voices of his family they "visited" him in his depressions, scolding and accusing him. These were actual auditory hallucinations. He was now not hearing their voices in his memory, but in his ear. To escape the voices and his guilt, he resorted to morphine. And thus the cycle was perpetuated.

When he was released from prison, he rejoined his family. But despite his wife's cheerful letters to him while he was in prison, he found their lives profoundly changed socially and financially. And they found in him a traumatized man. As a result of his prison experiences and his addiction, his resistance to any pressure was low. He took morphine to buck himself up and to see him through the crises that faced him and his family. When they realized what was happening, the shock was so great that he felt the only decent thing he could do was to drop out of their lives. This he did, which only heightened his guilt and deepened his depressions.

175

He was still a good engineer, and none of his fellow-engineers believed that he had been guilty of the charges made against him. He found work without difficulty, and this took him a long way toward his rehabilitation. His longing for his family was intolerable. He sent them money regularly under an assumed name, and had an occasional indirect word of them. Then he would learn that things were not going well with them and he would be thrown into a depression and would have to live with their accusing voices—until morphine relieved him momentarily.

One day when he was in one of his depressions, and as a throwback from his having been accused of "forging" his fellow-engineer's name, he forged a check under a friend's name so that he could send money home. It was not a large check. They were never large checks—he was convicted the last time on a seventeen-dollar forgery—and the money was always sent home to his family.

He lost his job as a result of this first forgery and was sent up on his second term. This then was the pattern over the years: depression, morphine, forgery. Years intervened between his four imprisonments. Each one left him a little more hopeless about himself. But despite his criminal record he was never long without a job.

I asked him why he had not killed the guard who hung him by his thumbs. He understood that my question was theoretical, not a suggestion.

"I don't know," he replied. "I swore I would at the time. I could have done it with my bare hands, and there was plenty of opportunity. Maybe I'm just not a killer. You'd say it's more my pattern to destroy myself, as I'm doing, than to murder someone else, wouldn't you?"

There was a long, jagged scar across his throat which he never explained. I wondered if it had been a suicide attempt.

The men believed it resulted from an engineering experience in the South American jungle.

He never conducted himself as anything but one of the "cons" in the penitentiary or the office, but the men never considered him one of them. They admired him greatly, and seemed to understand the special tragedy in his face. He was no criminal to them, even in the limited sense in which they felt themselves to be.

This fact was openly acknowledged on one occasion. Twice a year a prison directory was circularized, giving the classification and status of the administrative personnel, with street addresses and phone numbers. A few days after the publication of one of these directories a bulletin board appeared inside our office door, on which was posted a *Staff Directory and Social Register*. My men listed their cell numbers as addresses, gave all their aliases and previous penitentiary numbers, and other ingenious classifications.

Connie, the second-story man, appeared as a House Mover (Piece Work Only). King, the counterfeiter's, business was Engravings and Reproductions (I Can Fool Most of the People Most of the Time). Gibbs, the hot car smuggler, was Interstate Commerce—Cars a Specialty. Punch, the gangster, was an Undertaker and Embalmer. Under Scott's name the boys put Gentleman —Smuggler's Apprentice (For Sale—Make an Offer). Under Ross's name they put only Engineer.

A few days later Ross himself went to the directory and inked in beneath his name, *Dope Fiend, Forger,* while the others looked quietly into their work.

"I can't help wondering," Ross said in our first talk, "how my story would read if I had had this chance in my first stretch, instead of being hung up by my thumbs."

I wondered, too.

"What does this chance mean to you, Ross?" I asked.

He looked at me. "It's too good to be true. . . ." But I could see that wasn't the whole answer. "I don't know—I've lost my family, and fifteen years of my life—I thought I'd lost the desire to live," he said.

We were able through light hypnosis to dispel those accusing voices, and through informal therapy to give him some clues to his disturbed nature. Ideally it would have been simple to attack his depressions and addiction through hypnosis, but this would have necessitated a deeper trance than we were able to induce. Ironically he was not a good subject. He was too anxious—he tried too hard. He had to sweat it out the hard way. The birth of hope in him was a slow and agonizing labor, and for a long time I wondered if he would make it.

9

THE STORY of Ross brings sharply to focus many of the outrages indulged in the history of crime and punishment. One of them is brutality.

The adults of this generation have lived through two world wars. Contemporary memory and literature is full of instances of man's inhumanity to man in time of war. Unfortunately torture and brutality are not the issue of war, uniforms, patriotism, forms of government, flags, ideologies, morals or justice. They are the issue of man himself. They have been espoused by the two most influential forces in human destiny: government and church.

Between the twelfth and twentieth centuries these two forces in Western civilization legally took the lives of human beings, even children, by over forty different tortures, among them:

BOILING	DISMEMBERMENT
STRANGULATION	THROWING TO SERPENTS
IMPALEMENT	HURLING FROM HEIGHTS
DROWNING	POISONING
STONING	FLAILING—SKINNING ALIVE
BURIAL ALIVE	CRUCIFIXION
QUARTERING	PRESSING TO DEATH
DRAWING	BURNING
DECAPITATION	SUFFOCATION
FLOGGING	ORDEALS OF THE CHURCH

Nor was death always the end in view. More often it was simply legal disfigurement: amputation of hands, ears, tongue, eyes.

These were done in the name of human conscience and Divine justice. Perhaps it follows logically in our culture, the conscience of which is inured by a God who burns His erring children in eternal fires.

If punishment is to escape the stigma of sadistic brutality, it must have some end bigger than avenging society and placating gods. Civilization's past five hundred years of legalized sadism have illuminated neither the problem of crime nor the nature of the criminal.

The rule has always been that the greater the number and severity of punishments, the more lawlessness increases. Punishment is no deterrent to crime. As the number and severity of punishments on the statute books of a nation decline, lawlessness also declines. There were 240 offenses punishable by death in England in 1780, among them such trivial offenses as fishing in the wrong stream, pickpocketing, prostitution and stealing bread. There were unprecedented waves of lawlessness. Henry VIII executed 72,000 prisoners during his reign.

In 1820 the capital offenses had shrunk from 240 to 160 and lawlessness had decreased proportionately. In the year 1822 a hundred capital offenses were rescinded. At that time, when the population of the British Isles was 15,000,000 the daily jail population was 50,000. By 1885 the number of capital offenses had shrunk to the present three: treason, piracy and murder. With a population of 27,000,000 in 1885, almost twice that of 1822, England's daily jail load was less than 9,000, one-sixth of the former load. She now has the lightest and shortest sentences and the fewest crimes of any major civilized nation, and uses no third degree. Sanford Bates says, "Sentences in the courts of America are the longest in the world."

There were still fifteen offenses carrying the death penalty

180

within our forty-eight states in 1947: murder (in 40 states), rape (17), treason (13), arson (8), kidnaping (7), burglary (5), train wrecking (5), armed robbery (3), perjury or false witness (3), attempted rape (2), dueling (2), prisoner attacking guard (2), armed highway robbery (1), child molesting (1), train robbery (1).

There have been some improvements and remissions in man's inhumanity to man. There are no longer galley slaves. Death by boiling, burning, branding and mutilation was officially rescinded in 1790 in England, although not until 1810 in the United States. In 1808 the British Parliament rescinded the death penalty for pickpocketing because so many pickpockets picked so many pockets in protest against the execution of pickpockets at the attendant festivities! The death sentence for prostitution was rescinded two years later for the same reason: prostitutes engaged in fornication at the scene of execution festivities, protesting both the sentence and the festivities.

In spite of Federal reforms in 1930, a decade later found corporal punishment (a very gentle word for brutality) still being used in half of our state penitentiaries.

A prison in Philadelphia had four deaths among twenty men crowded into a sweat box in 1938. Throughout the South in this decade from twelve to twenty-five chained men slept and lived in wagon cages 7x14x7. One prison out of five in the United States, including Sing Sing, Joliet and Folsom, was still using the open bucket instead of plumbing at the beginning of the forties. At the Frankfort Reformatory in Kentucky there were only 3½ square feet of ground space per prisoner, including flower beds and sidewalk space. In Virginia they were still stringing up prisoners by the wrists. Colorado still used the ball and chain, Michigan and Ohio the confining cage, and Minnesota enforced silence in 1941. In Georgia, in spite of the film, "I Am a Fugitive From a Chain Gang," men were still dying in sweat boxes: in 1941 twenty-one men were piled into a sweat box

7½ feet square—an oversize closet—with a six-inch aperture in the top. In the same state in 1940 several prisoners broke their own legs to avoid being beaten by the bat (a strap four inches wide, ⅜ inch thick, often studded with rivets and weighing about four pounds, sometimes made with holes in the center which raise blisters as the whip descends and rips them open as the flogger pulls the bat away for the next stroke). During the same decade several Texas prisoners chopped off their legs or arms to avoid floggings, but the Legislature still did not outlaw the bat in that state until 1941. The United States Attorney General reported in 1940 that beatings were still administered in prisons in twenty-six states.

Whenever I hear an intellectual discussion about corporal punishment I think the whole problem could be solved very simply by making the job of using the bat a duty devolving upon each adult citizen in the nation by a rotating system: once a month each adult must wield the bat for twenty strokes upon the back of a shackled man, someone like Ross or Gibbs. How would we stand on corporal punishment when we found ourselves shredding a man's back, perhaps breaking his ribs? Could we satisfy ourselves that it was a fitting way to avenge his crime?

Or suppose we could decline to serve our turn at the bat if we could supply a substitute—for whom would we look? That nice genial Irish cop with a beat in New York's Lower East Side, who stands by smiling when the kids crowd into the streets to cool themselves in the spray of the street cleaner's wagon? No, he's not our man. We would be looking for the most depraved human soul we could find, someone infinitely more depraved than his victim.

It can be nothing but naiveté or stupidity that leads men to write books about the sentimentality of rehabilitating prisoners. Rehabilitation is a hard-headed, economic view to take of criminality. It has become almost axiomatic to say that a man becomes a criminal not by his first offense, but by his first imprisonment. He has become a *jailbird,* and that is how society looks at him, with very rare exceptions, when he is released. If society doesn't want to meet that man again in five or ten or twenty years at the wrong end of a gun, it had better study the needs, fears, drives and pathologies of that man and its own evils that helped create them. It had better give him a real second chance. Society will have to decide whether it wants animalistic revenge or a solution of crime. It can not have both.

Is society to be reduced to the criminal's level of character? Is its conscience to be represented by filth, vermin, disease, hunger and brutality, and in these circumstances is the criminal supposed to become penitent? No greater stupidity can be imagined.

Much has been said in these reminiscences about the antisocial aggressions of a penitentiary populace. One can understand how Ross would feel about society's conscience operating in the guard who strung him up by his thumbs. Since this book is the story of six convicts, let me try to evaluate the load of resentment these men always bore, as they might express it themselves.

There were three specific and violent reasons why most of the convicts I knew in the penitentiary were *not* penitent:

The capriciousness of the written law and its interpretation.

The corruption of law enforcement.

The respectability of the white-collar criminal.

My men illuminated these reasons for me during our frequent round table sessions, when they would take voluble exception to popular concepts of criminology. Some of their reasoning was warped by rationalization and projection. Some of it was devastatingly true and shocking. They quoted the recognized authorities on legal abuses and injustices, and recited volumes of statistics and cases to clinch their arguments. Prison life develops a large corps of "attorneys" and "judges" among the men, who study law with a vengeance in their cells, reversing practically every decision handed down by our courts. Other men, like my encyclopaedic Gibbs, carried long tables of statistics and cases at their finger-tips. When some statement of Gibbs seemed particularly improbable I checked it at the library. He was always correct to a fraction of a percent.

While I remember well the men's attitude toward society, law, crime and criminals, I could not possibly reproduce their statistical tables. In an attempt to bulwark an analysis of their attitude with some of their figures, I scanned several recent texts in criminology and sociology, with particular reference to the decade of the thirties and its background in the twenties. I was interested to find in them many of the identical cases and figures the men used in championing their positions.

The documentary source of most of the material presented in this chapter can be found in *New Horizons in Criminology,* by Barnes and Teeters, and *Crime and the Community,* by Tannenbaum.

The sheer cumbersomeness of the body of written laws is one of its vulnerabilities. Three out of every four men (76%) were in prison in 1931 for crimes which were not on the statute books fifteen years earlier.

Only three percent of all crimes known to police are serious; ninety-seven percent are minor offenses.

There are only a small number of serious crimes in the human catalogue. The rest result from the growing complexity of civilized life. Cultural and social changes alone create criminals. Men were still serving sentences for violation of the Volstead Act five years after the repeal of Prohibition.

Over 375,000 new state laws have been passed in the United States in the last thirty years, and these are in addition to the more than one million then existing state, municipal and Federal laws and ordinances.

Surveys have been made concerning the effect on the ordinary law-abiding citizen of such a mass of unknown statutes. One study estimates that the average citizen in one American city, considering himself entirely law-abiding, would unwittingly break sufficient laws to spend over 1,825 years in prison, and to accumulate fines in excess of $2,085,919.55, within one year of orderly living. While such a citizen does not constitute a crime problem, the fact remains that legally he should be serving time under our existing laws. He is a criminal, if a criminal is anybody who commits a criminal act. Is this a supportable definition?

You work in a garage. Have you never stolen a tool? You're a beautician. Have you always paid for the shampoo or the hair nets you took home? Gibbs asked me in this connection once: "On the level, Doc, ain't you never stole a ream of typin' paper from no college?" One chain drug store became seriously interested in my lie detector at one time because the corporation was losing over a million dollars a year from its shelves and warehouses to trusted employees.

Have you never been overdrawn at the bank? Never postdated a check? Never fudged on your income tax returns? Made personal use of the company car?

Have you never had illicit relations with anyone? Or indulged a fleeting homosexual contact in college? A forthcoming research publication by a well-known writer will state that 68% of our brides these days are not virgins. That certainly implicates at least the same percentage of our bridegrooms. The Kinsey Report states that as high as ninety percent of men in the low income bracket have had premarital relations.

Have you ever been a party to collusion on divorce? Finished a cocktail after hours in a bar? Had an abortion, even

185

though you were married and paternity was unimpeachable? Gone to a smokey show? Entertained a "convention girl?" Visited a prostitute? Somebody visits them.

If you have done any of these things, you have committed a criminal act. You are a criminal, according to the above definition.

Perhaps you have never had an abortion, but your best friend has. Perhaps you have always been absolutely honest about your income tax, but you know someone who hasn't. You have never stolen, but you have witnessed a theft. You should have reported these criminal acts. Not reporting a criminal act is a criminal act.

This definition of a criminal does not imply repeated offenses. One theft, one blackmail, one abortion, one incident of withholding knowledge of a crime, and you are a criminal, according to our definition. It is easy to see that if this definition were adopted as a working concept in our Commonwealth, our business houses, underworlds, universities, homes, farms and churches would be largely without constituents.

Do *you* think a criminal is anyone who commits a criminal act?

Perhaps a criminal is anyone who is convicted of a criminal act by a duly constituted court of law. This is the legal concept of crime. But let us examine its philosophy. You are a criminal only if you get caught. The trick is not to get caught.

This is a convict's concept of society's concept of a criminal. You hear it on every side. "You know the difference between me and the guy on the outside? I got caught!" A man is punished, not for his crime, but for getting himself caught. It implies that crime is not an absolute moral offense, but a legal caprice.

Here is another caprice of law which the prisoners rode hard. Not only does the decade in which you commit an act determine whether you are a criminal, but the place where it is committed as well. A law which appears on the books in one state may not appear on the books of another, so that by an act you become a criminal in one state, but not in another. If the offense appears on the books of both states, the disproportionate sentences of the two states are sometimes staggering. Two men in different states are guilty of arson. The prisoner in Alabama is in for one year, the prisoner in North Carolina for forty years. Perjury carries four years in Connecticut, twenty years in New York, life in Maine, death in Missouri, five hundred dollars and forty lashes in Delaware. West Virginia punishes bigamy sixteen times as severely as incest. Wyoming and Colorado punish incest ten times more severely than bigamy.

Another practice that feeds the convict's belief that crime is not absolute, but relative, is the fine system. "$5,000 or three years, $300 or ninety days."

Although debtor's prisons were theoretically abandoned a century ago, one man out of two (57%) in prisons, jails and penitentiaries is serving a sentence because of debt—he can't pay a fine. Many of the remaining 43% would gladly have paid a fine, but they had the bad luck to be sentenced by a judge who did not levy fines. A judge may or may not levy fines, may or may not impose a sentence, or both a sentence and a fine, at his own discretion.

It would be difficult to persuade a prisoner that a fine represents punishment in the sense that imprisonment does. Why, he would ask, does every man who can, pay? And why, when a fine is imposed, does the money go into public coffers instead of into some form of restitution for the offense committed? One man pays a fine and goes home to his family. Another goes to prison, his and his family's life ruined. Like Ross.

England and Scotland have solved the problem of fines by the simple expedient of installment payment. Imprisonment for non-payment of fines in England exceeded 80,000 in 1913, but dropped to 11,000 in 1933, the latter representing largely unemployed paupers. It seems odd that America, with its mania for installment buying, has not applied this concept to its courts. Nearly a fourth of American imprisonments for inability to pay fines are for amounts less than ten dollars, and sixty percent for less than twenty dollars. This is certainly punishment for poverty.

The fact that laws change in point of time, and have become too cumbersome to be prosecuted, may simply be the toll of civilization and the caprice of the written law. But the matter of fines-versus-sentence is considerably more sinister in its implications. Is a man to pay for his crimes or his poverty? For his crimes, or for getting caught?

These two questions gain momentum in the light of prosecution and conviction records. The famous reports of the Wickersham and Seabury commissions and of the Committee of Fifteen published early in the thirties were avidly read by the literate prisoners then, and probably still are. These reports indicated that in large cities at that time a man had an 85% chance of escaping arrest, a 98% chance of escaping conviction, and a 99% chance of escaping punishment. Of 257 gang murders in Chicago in the regime of Mayor Bill Thompson and Al Capone, *not a single conviction resulted.* Even in smaller cities with the best conviction records of that decade, only 10% of crimes resulted in conviction. Current percentages are not much improved.

Until the establishment of the FBI we had no official clearing house for the gathering and disseminating of statistics regarding the activity of police and crime in the nation. One of the early contributions of the FBI was its Uniform Crime Reports for the United States and its Possessions, which attempted to centralize and standardize the haphazard police records of the nation. Consequently, reports are now available showing police and crime activity in cities, towns, villages and counties representing two-thirds of our population. The Uniform Crime Reports are still the best source of this type of information in the country.

But even with these data at hand we are startled to find the term "estimated" used in a tabulation of "Serious Crimes" in both text and tables. The number of crimes committed each second, minute and hour of the day is also "estimated." The number of "Major Crimes" is "estimated," and preceding this table in the 1949 Report is this disturbing statement: "While the larceny figures include *minor* thefts, a number of serious crimes, such as embezzlement, fraud, arson and the like, are *not* included in the tabulation. Thus the *estimated* total of serious crimes is considered conservative." (Italics mine.)

One wonders why the above mentioned serious crimes are *not* tabulated; why the admitted "minor" offenses such as pilferings of under ten dollars, pickpocketing, shoplifting, etc., are included under "serious" and "major" crimes; why tabulations bearing the insignia and authority of the FBI are "estimated" at all, and what the basis of the estimate is; and why so few of the reports which are sent to the FBI for the Uniform Crime Reports are used in the total tabulations.

One is disappointed also that nowhere in the reports can a reader find a capitulation of the total *recorded* crime picture, or its average, for the nation. With a possible total picture based upon the reports of 5,353 police and sheriffs' agencies submitted in 1949 for the 1948 Report, most of the pictograms are based on only 184 cities (with a total population of nineteen million); 353 cities; 373 cities; and 1,654 cities (with a total population of only fifty million). The most inclusive pictogram is drawn from a population of only sixty-eight million.

The researcher is frustrated to find a great difference in the number of claimed serious crimes and those recorded as "known to police." Nor is there a record of total arrests, but only of those finally held and charged in 1,654 cities (1/3 of the agencies reporting). For releases and false arrests, only 1,126 cities are reported (1/5 of the reporting agencies). "Cleared by arrest" is listed for 1,654 cities, but there is no statement as to how many of these were actually prosecuted. *Convictions are tabulated for only 184 cities of the 5,353* police and sheriffs' agencies reporting. Most of the tables refer to only six crimes, but sometimes eight are tabulated. The few tables that cover all offenses are limited to 184, 1,126, and 1,654 cities respectively.

The pictograms of "percentages" of police and criminal activity give a misleading impression. Perhaps they, like the radio programs, are designed to show that crime does not pay. Of course, crime is more concentrated in cities, and the public has a right to such data. It also has a right to the entire national picture. It is difficult to visualize how the diagrams would appear if the 1,600 sheriffs' reports on thirty-four million rural population (with only 150,000 offenses!) were added to the partial compilations.

Accepting Mr. Hoover's claimed estimate of 1,700,000 major offenses (950,000 if petty theft is excluded), there were nevertheless but 220,000 investigatory fingerprint arrests for "serious" crimes, which, as tabulated, include pilfering, attempts at crime, and charges of rape without force. The number of these cases finally held or actually charged is not reported. The hard fact is that penitentiary sentences, state and Federal combined, still remain at about 78,000 a year.

Also missing in the Uniform Crime Reports is any reference to statistics of state or Federal crimes, or of the activities of the FBI agents, the G-men, T-men, C-men, or other of the eleven Government agencies of secret police, although the Reports purport to give a national picture.

As early as 1943 Barnes and Teeters in *New Horizons in Criminology* analyzed some of the presentations of the Uniform Crime Reports, and showed that less than 3% of crimes and arrests are for "serious" crimes, and that, if arrests for petty theft are excluded, only 1½% of crimes fall in a major category. In the Uniform Crime Report for 1942 over 5 million arrests were reported in the 1,200 largest cities of the United States. But 3,800,000 of them were for parking, traffic and driving violations. Another million covered drunkenness, prostitution, disorderly conduct, non-support, etc.

The 1949 Report covering 1948 shows spectacular increases in police "activity" in 1,654 American cities: there were over 14½ million arrests, of which *12 million were for parking, traffic and highway violations,* and another million and a half for drunkenness, disorderly conduct and prostitution. However, for this large number there were only three-fourths of a million "fingerprint" arrests: those in which the police wanted to check on suspicious characters, or get vagrants, drunks and prostitutes on record, or where the offense seemed serious enough to warrant further data from the FBI fingerprint records.

The most confusing presentation of percentages appears in the Reports under offenses "Cleared By Arrest." The tables and pictograms claim that from 22% to 90% of "serious" crimes are cleared in this way. The text, however, explains that "the term 'cleared by arrest' ordinarily means that one or more offenders have been arrested and made available for prosecution." This does not mean that the suspects are guilty, or that there is an actual trial. They are only held and charged. In American cities, to assemble suspects for eventual "cleared by arrest" charges means inefficient trial-and-error arrests. While criminologists decry this sorry practice, my six men, by turns, scoffed and chortled at the police indiscriminately "running in" suspects. Investigations indicate that about half of all arrests are false and result in discharge. Some cities have reached a peak of ninety percent of arrested suspects being released without charge. Both my men and criminologists labeled this practice as kidnaping. In fact, in the only table of releases listed in the Reports of 1949, based on the population of certain cities totaling 33 million, over one million arrested persons were released. This is quite in contrast to the efficiency of the Postal Department inspectors, who gather evidence first and then unerringly arrest the offender.

The Uniform Crime Reports state that 58% of annual fingerprint arrests are of recidivists. But what does not appear is the kind of recidivist that lies back of such figures. The *Los Angeles Times* for February 20, 1950 ran a feature on the world's largest arraignment court in that city, highlighting the "regular customers," some of whom have been arrested over 250 times and many of whom return to court every few days, depending on the length of their sentence. They are drunks, prostitutes, aments, vagrants, panhandlers—derelicts who obviously are not responding to jail sentences.

It is the belief of Mr. Hoover, director of the FBI, that the volume of arrests throughout the nation indicates the extent of police activity. The statement cannot be challenged in the light of 14½ million arrests in 1,654 of our cities in 1948. But one may perhaps offer his condolences to the hard-working traffic cop.

Other evils affecting the convict are stool pigeons, false arrests, bail bonds and fixed sentences—rackets which go hand-in-hand in most large cities in a sorry parade of justice. While there are not many innocent men in the penitentiary, the prisoner's frequent complaint, "I been framed," cannot be too quickly dismissed. Easy preys to false arrest and casual conviction without trial are convicts like Weary Willie and "I.Q.33" whom Scott turned up in his testing. These are sometimes picked up by the police as a convenient way to close a case lingering on the blotter, and the convict finds himself in prison before he knows what has happened. Sanford Bates, the first superintendent of the Bureau of Prisons formed in 1930, himself reports the case of an ignorant mountain boy whose conviction was railroaded by a Federal marshal after getting the boy to "plead guilty to not doing it" on the day the revenuers raided a still. "Ah jes' pleaded guilty to not bein' dar, but heah ah is." One estimate claims that nearly one-third of a prison population is serving time for offenses they did not technically commit. They are in on false charges. Either the offender agreed to plead guilty to a lesser charge in exchange for a fixed sentence, or he was actually framed by a police stool pigeon; that is, a stool pigeon in the employ of the police.

The procuring of a fixed sentence is called bargaining. If the district attorney's office knows its case is weak, it assures its conviction records by throwing a scare into the offender, urging him to plead guilty to a lesser offense in return for a lighter fixed sentence and thus avoid coming to trial. This sounds good to the uninitiated. The offense may be one that the offender actually did commit in the past, or it may represent an unsolved case on the police blotter. Sometimes it is one which is concocted on the spot. The offense to which the man pleads guilty may not even be in the same category as his actual crime.

This procedure accomplishes several things. It increases the conviction records of the district attorney and those of the police department. The offender gets off with a lighter pre-agreed sentence, and often the fixing attorney and all concerned are the richer. A notorious case of this kind involved a highjacker who looted a truck of $30,000 worth of silk. The charge was armed robbery, subject to a sentence of ten years to life. The highjacker pleaded guilty to petty larceny, was fined one dollar and given one year in prison.

Al Capone, when he was finally apprehended, bargained for an eighteen-month sentence on a rum-running charge and expected never to come to trial. He might never have served the seven of his ten-year sentence, if he had not prematurely and publicly boasted of the fix, thus forcing the judge's hand.

A major stumbling block in the way of a convict's developing a respect for the law is society's approval of the stool pigeon. The use of a stool pigeon in the pay of the police and vice squads in most of our large cities is a common device in effecting false arrests. It is a practice used frequently to apprehend the small-time criminal who otherwise eludes the police. The stool pigeon, in one of his varied capacities, is given marked money or stolen goods to place on the person of a victim, who is then immediately frisked by detectives or police lying in wait. What possible defense can such a victim make?

The stool pigeon is not only paid, but protected in the continuation of his own pickpocketing, dope peddling or pimping racket as long as he is valuable to police in his snitches. Thereafter he is sometimes arrested and sentenced himself. It's a hard life. . . .

England uses no stool pigeons. She convicts 70% of her offenders. In twenty-five years, from 1860 to 1885, England closed 137 of her 193 local prisons through reforms in penal concepts. In another quarter century, from 1910 to 1934, the British Commissioners of Prisons reported that annual prison receptions fell from 181,000 to 56,000. They further reported that these results were attributed to reforms in the criminal law, reduction of long sentences; abolition of solitary confinement (1921), useless labor, and the rule of silence; the introduction of school courses, concerts, constructive work, the installment payment of fines, and the assignment of the feebleminded to hospitals instead of prisons. Thus by avoiding recidivism England closed thirty-one more prisons and has now but twenty-five in the whole island. She reduced imprisonment 81% and crimes 43% by these reforms. Scotland's record is even better. Former Federal Director of Prisons Bates concluded, "Not, apparently, by lengthening sentences, or withdrawing privileges, or denying parole, has Great Britain reduced its crime bill."

The practice of rewarding a stool pigeon is used by our Federal government.

A recent movie depicted the mass of legal and illegal obstacles and intrigue under which a Federal agent must operate in apprehending a big-time criminal. It also depicted the role of the stool pigeon in detail.

The film, "Undercover Man," was based on the reports of a former chief of the United States Secret Service. It showed the activities of a hard-working Treasury man on the trail of a gangster-racketeer who had bossed a large metropolis completely for several years. The Federal government has no legal jurisdiction over state and municipal laws or police, so that in this case it could not prosecute the gangster for any crime more vicious than income tax violation. The gangster had bought out the local police, a fact which the film made unmistakably clear.

One of the gangster's bookkeepers "turned stool" regarding the gangster's tax returns, not because the bookkeeper was going to reform, but for "the usual ten percent" of the amount defrauded, which the Government will pay an informer, and for the immunity the Government would extend him covering his complicity with the gangster. The amount defrauded was $3 million. Three hundred thousand was good pay for a bookkeeper. Who wouldn't turn stool, and why don't more? For the reason we find in the movie. He was "rubbed out" by the gang before he could get his records to the T-man.

Bookkeeper Number Two then peeked out from behind his blond mistress to eye the Government's ten percent. He observed philosophically, "The Government don't want to hurt me, it wants to help me. This [$300,000] is what I been waitin' for!"

Thereupon the T-man had to bargain with Number Two's burlesque moll over a cup of coffee. Number Two was in hiding from the gang. His moll demanded protection, immunity and the usual ten percent for him. "Wherever he goes, whatever he does," she said, "he wants protection."

"He'll get it," replied the T-man.

Immunity meant that he would never be prosecuted for his past complicity with the gangster. The ten percent meant a dreamed-of layout in Mexico for Number Two and his moll. He was even assured by the T-man that his moll could accompany him safely, although he was a family man.

They would have gone, too, if he hadn't also been rubbed out by the gang before he got his records to the T-man.

The next stool pigeon to step out of the gangster's ranks was the personal accountant of the gangster's mouthpiece, with more knowledge of the syndicate's finances than he wished he had when the T-man showed up. The accountant did not squeal for money, at first, but for fear. When the mouthpiece made him turn over his—the mouthpiece's—personal books, the accountant did so, but immediately skipped town. The attorney was also to be prosecuted only for income tax violation.

When the T-man caught up with the accountant, the latter stubbornly declined to shed light on the attorney's or the syndicate's books until the T-man used coercion, blackmail and extortion, all of which were somewhat unconstitutional, if we want to bicker. The fact that gave teeth to the agent's threats in the accountant's mind, however, was not only fear of his life at the hands of the gang, but the prospect of the ten percent— and a pleasant sea voyage with his young wife, under Federal protection. He was sympathetically portrayed as a deluded young man who wasn't really a criminal. Punch Pinero, I am sure, would question that a man could keep books for a gangster's mouthpiece without knowing *exactly* what he was doing! Not for long, he couldn't.

As a result of the deal between the accountant and the agent, the gangster and his attorney were about to be investigated by a grand jury in the gangster's city.

The attorney now recognized a lost cause when he saw it. The day before the hearing he turned over to the T-man the inside set-up of the syndicate and a list of the jurors' names, all of whom he had personally "fixed," presumably with either threats or bribes. In exchange for these two documents the attorney wanted, not money (he had $600,000 cash in a strong box) but immunity. He asked that all Federal charges against him be dropped. Although the agent addressed the bargaining attorney contemptuously, he promptly tore up the attorney's summons. The attorney would never serve time for income tax violation, because at the last moment, with no visible signs of remorse or repentance, he turned stool on his client, who was fast beginning to look like a fall guy anyhow.

The attorney was killed by the gangster's goons a few minutes after his exchange of confidences with the T-man.

The agent hurried to the chamber of the judge before whom the gangster was to appear for indictment. The judge met the fixed jury briefly, and since there was no living proof that they had been fixed, now that the attorney was dead, the judge exchanged the panel for one which was about to sit for a fellow judge in the building, and it was this second panel which subsequently indicted the gangster.

Reviewing the movie in relation to the concept of a criminal's disrespect for law, we find that no indictment or reprimand of the fixed jury was delivered. The members continued to serve in the other judge's chambers. Perhaps it was not possible to show such a reprimand in the time allotted to the film. Perhaps, also, this is why no indictment of the police department was suggested as growing out of the Federal inquiry. The omissions seem regrettable.

It was a decided anticlimax to find the gangster given only twenty years in a Federal penitentiary. Actually, a 20-year sentence for income tax violation is rather novelistic. Even ten years is a rarity. One authority states that the usual sentence is from one to three years. In a society in which theoretically punishment is levied in proportion to the crime, even twenty years seemed mild for this criminal. It was indicated that, like Al Capone, he had murdered, terrorized, intimidated, defrauded, stolen, operated all the usual rackets, and bought out the municipal police. With good behavior those twenty years meant perhaps twelve for Big Fellow; with special privilege, if he was influential enough or had enough on enough people, less than that. Does this mean that our crime detection is geared to nothing more serious than an occasional sensational murder and the Connies and Gibbses in our midst? Big Fellow was not punished for his larger crimes against the human race. Why? Because of a legal fluke which tied the T-man's hands, and because Big Fellow controlled the police officials of his city, the only body who could convict him of those larger crimes. There was little reason for Big Fellow to respect the law.

Again, we find four stool pigeons of criminal character who were each promised money, immunity and protection by a Federal agent in exchange for information leading to conviction. The fact that the three "bad" stools were killed and the "good" one spared is again rather novelistic. The money was equally accessible to the three "bad" men. Would any of them respect the law with which they could make such a deal?

Finally, what about the moll who made the deal for Bookkeeper Number Two? It was a great day, she might have concluded, when complicity with a gangster, followed by betrayal, was rewarded by the Government with three hundred grand.

The police department would be inclined to belittle its own corruption. What was the difference, it might ask, between its protecting the gangster, and the agent protecting the gangster's mouthpiece, leaving him free to enter negotiations with another gangster on another day? The police would probably go industriously back to honest work, running in a few hundred small-time criminals to stimulate their conviction records and waiting for a rival gangster to move in and make things interesting again.

"You can't convict a million dollars," is axiomatic in the minds of the convicts in or out of a penitentiary.

The T-man had a hard, thankless job, and he prosecuted it painstakingly and concluded it successfully. It was not difficult to feel sympathetic toward the earnest young public servant who believed in what he was doing. But it makes one wonder if two wrongs make a right.

This is the kind of movie that is sure to be shown in a penitentiary to teach the penitents respect for law. You can imagine its reception. You can see why it will miss.

The stool pigeon system, however, has many friends among authorities. Most penitentiaries still defend and use it. Certain it is that as long as the system of giving immunity and protection to informers is used, no better system will be devised. That there are better systems should be quite apparent.

The stool pigeon is a common bedfellow for another nefarious practice in some of our big cities: the bail bond racket involving police, bondsman, attorney, and sometimes judge. Texts in criminology explain one type of shakedown in this racket, wherein thousands of innocent nurses, shop girls, wives and landladies are paying vice squad members dearly to avoid the publicity growing out of a threatened or false accusation of prostitution.

The stool pigeon is employed to place marked money in plain view in payment for an alleged immorality, and is allowed to "escape" just as the raiding vice squad detail appears on the scene. The woman is then booked on the false charge and released on bail. A shyster attorney agrees to fix the case and keep it out of the papers for an amount, usually ten percent of her bail bond, which in turn may be based on her savings account book or other collateral. If she pays the fee, which is split between the parties involved in the fix, the false charge may be dropped. But sometimes she is repeatedly "bled", and when she can't continue to pay she is convicted on the original false charge. A prison term will usually shut her up. Men too are paying heavily to avoid publicity on false homosexual charges made by the stool pigeons in the employ of the vice squad. A citizen would have a rough time battling the perjured testimony of the police in such a jury trial.

In England there is no racket in bonds. Charging for bonds is a criminal offense. Bond may be supplied by friends or any freeholder who will hypothecate his property for the defendant, but no fee may be charged, and no reimbursement made. Charging for bonds was not exploited in America until this generation. Now a bondsman has legal protection and is a very busy man. There are, of course, many bondsmen who are simply honest business men. But there are bondsmen who are not. If a bondsman is implicated in a fix, he is either at the police station when the victim arrives, or he is phoned by the policeman making the arrest and arrives in a matter of minutes. He sometimes arranges for the hiring of an attorney for the bewildered victim, and procures a financial statement from him or her, so that the bail bond figure can be arrived at by a judge who is in on the fix. Although a bondsman's fees are now set by law, he can always refuse to write the bond in the absence of a bonus, especially if he is tipped off regarding the amount of valuables taken from the victim for safe keeping by a desk sergeant.

Less than two percent of forfeited bonds are collected by courts, yet the courts still accept millions of dollars in worthless bonds annually. Of more than $10 million in forfeited bonds in Chicago courts alone from 1931-1935, less than one percent was collected. One bondsman, who himself had been arrested twelve times, had forfeited $30,000 in bonds within a year; yet the courts accepted $670,000 more in bonds from him within the same year. He secured them with a $24,000 piece of property on which there was a $31,000 mortgage. This was his only traceable asset, although he netted from $33,000 to $100,000 annually in his bail racket. There is record of one criminal being out on nine bonds at one time.

The bitterness a convict in prison feels for the bail bond racket is not only that it is so clearly a racket from which individuals profit illegally, but also that an injustice is done the man who cannot raise bail. Obviously a man who is out on bail has a better opportunity of preparing for trial than a man in jail. The difference between freedom and conviction may be bail, just as it may be one's ability to pay a fine.

Much has been written and documented about the lawless police in many of our large cities in the use of the third degree, illegal search and seizure, arrest without warrant, holding of persons incommunicado, beating and brutality, and other violations of the Bill of Rights. The offender's first contact with a judicial society is the police. If that contact is constructive and just, the possible salvage of the offender is greatly increased. If that first contact is sadistic and stupid, the hostility of the offender is directed toward all society through the police, because to the offender the police represent society. Strange things happen to some men when a badge of authority is pinned on their chests. First contacts with the police are too often not good these days, undermining the possible rehabilitation of the first offender. He comes to regard the policeman—and behind him, society—as stupid, brutal and corrupt, because of the wholesale, unwarranted arrests that increase in America year by year.

In a study of the annual arrests in the major cities of the United States, 47% of them are shown to be false, unwarranted or illegal, and result in dismissal without charge after interrogation and not infrequently a third degree.

Ruth Shonle Cavan's *Criminology* discusses the third degree:

> Only a confession from the criminal can offer a quick solution to many crimes. The legal impossibility of holding a suspect for any length of time also puts pressure on the police to solve a crime by securing a confession. This situation led to a system of forcing confessions by inflicting physical or mental pain, known as the "third degree."
>
> The third degree is linked with detaining a suspect without booking his arrest and preventing him from communicating

with an attorney. It therefore involves the violation of legal rights . . . . and in addition the suspect's right to protection from assault and battery; his right to the presumption of innocence until convicted by due process of law—that is, before a judge—and his privilege of not giving evidence against himself.

. . . . Persistent questioning by detectives working in relays for hours without permitting the suspect to have food, drink, or sleep is one of the milder methods (of third degree). Sometimes the prisoner is compelled to stand during this ordeal. Eventually physical and mental fatigue may cause him to agree with the police that he committed a crime. The prisoner may be confined in a dark, uncomfortable cell and told that he will be kept there until he confesses; or he may be placed in a "sweat box"—a small cell that can be overheated. He may be forced into a cell so crowded with other prisoners that none of them can sit or lie down. . . . Powerful lights may be switched on and off the prisoner's face, or he may be forced to sit in a chair wired to give slight unpleasant shocks. When the crime is a murder the suspect may be taken to the morgue and forced to hold the hand of the corpse. Beating may be threatened and, if a confession is not forthcoming, may be administered, usually with a rubber hose or sandbag, which leave no marks. The person's arm may be twisted or he may be slapped. During this time, the prisoner is not allowed to communicate with his family or friends, and may be worried about this fact; he is not allowed to see an attorney. . . . He is completely at the mercy of the police. As a result of these methods, even hardened criminals may confess to crimes that they did not commit. . . . Innocent persons have confessed to crimes they did not commit because they could no longer stand the torment and pain of the third degree. . . . They may be afraid to protest, for fear of further brutality. . . . Proof is difficult, since many methods leave no physical trace, and the prisoner's word is pitted again the policeman's. Or the prisoner may have been made to face a wall during a beating and may not know who struck him. Usually physical abuse is administered by someone in a minor capacity on the police force.

Criminals quickly learn to plead guilty to almost anything to avoid the third degree. The fact that the rough stuff is frequently delegated by the police to private detectives, who in most states are not supervised, bonded or inspected, fools nobody—certainly not the convict. A cartoon which hung over Gibbs' desk in our office for months showed an exhausted police sergeant and two patrolmen dragging a much-beaten suspect into the captain's office, stating that the prisoner had finally confessed to murder. "Fine," said the captain, "now hold him until we have a murder."

In his public utterances, J. Edgar Hoover has deplored the use of the third degree. But he is apparently without insight regarding the influence of his printed and spoken word in confirming attitudes on the part of the police which perpetuate the "treat 'em rough" school of penology. *The Journal of Criminal Law and Criminology* culled the following excerpts from speeches of Mr. Hoover:

Criminals are not just criminals. They are: "Scum from the boiling-pot of the underworld," "public rats," "lowest dregs of society," "scuttling rats in the ship of politics," "vermin in human form," "the slimy crew who feed upon crime," "desperadoes," "vermin spewed out of prison cells to continue their slaughter," "the octopus of the underworld." These "post graduates of outlawry" and "professors of crime" thrive "in the great fog of crime," and the "swamp and morasses of suffering," amidst the "appalling scourge of perjury" and the "oleaginous connivings of venal politicians," aided and abetted by "sentimental yammerheads," "moronic adults" of "asinine behavior," "maudlin sentiment," and "inherent criminal worship." Away with these "moo-cow sentimentalities" with their "mealy mouthings" and their "whining pleas for sympathy"; these "hoity-toity professors"—

This mosaic is from the speeches of J. Edgar Hoover of the Federal Bureau of Investigation, Department of Justice. He has announced a hearty contempt for "the cream-puff school of criminology whose daily efforts turn loose upon us the robber, the burglar, the arsonist, the killer, and the sex-degenerate." He condemns "these self-appointed ambassadors of the open cell block." He is horrified by the "ignorant blatherings of either ill-informed or selfishly-motivated persons" with their "blatant outcries."

The inauguration of the FBI as an investigative body was a most salutary move in our national life. If there is one phase of our police work which needed and still needs renovating, it was and is the investigative arm. Mr. Hoover's native equipment in this area is enormous. He is to be commended for his tremendous contribution to the development of police science in America. If the same skills were used in training state and municipal police forces, our national crime picture would change overnight.

But it is to be regretted that in our admiration for Mr. Hoover's police science we have come to look to the Federal Bureau of Investigation for a penal philosophy of crime and criminals. It does not inevitably follow that a man who can successfully track down a bank robber will have the instincts or the temperament to ponder the forces which made the man a criminal or the means by which he might be salvaged. Mr. Hoover commands the respect of the world as Director of the FBI, but there has been little in either his training or his career to suggest that he has anything new to say on the causes and cure of crime. His statement that "the only way to make a law breaker obey the statutes of our country is to make him fear punishment" was precisely the premise of the Church and Government in the Dark Ages when they mutilated men and women and children in the name of God. Treat 'em rough penology isn't new. It is old, threadbare, and, Mr. Hoover's Uniform Crime Reports indicate, ineffectual.

In line with Mr. Hoover's concept of respect for law the policeman himself cannot be overlooked. Evidence seems to be growing that it is impossible for a rookie policeman, in a city large enough to support organized crime and whose politics are dominated by a political machine, to remain honest more than three years. Why, then, would a rookie be expected to respect the law?

The Saturday Evening Post in its issue of April 23, 1949 ran a double-length article, "Why Cops Turn Crooked," which reported realistically the story of the modern cop—the almost insurmountable pressure that is brought to bear on him from the underworld and the upperworld, sometimes operating in league with each other. The wonder is not that there are so many crooked cops, but that there are so many honest ones.

The sincere and honest police officer, attorney and judge, of whom there are certainly many all over the country in cities large and small, merit every respect and compliment in these times. It is significant that in communities where public officials are not corrupted or corruptible, crime does not flourish; in this way the criminal himself pays respect to the integrity of a public servant. In this discussion of crime from the criminal's standpoint, the corrupt official alone is under attack.

In 1949 the Los Angeles Police Department had a sensational nine months' bout with the grand jury regarding accusations of many of the abuses discussed in this chapter: police graft, bribery, protection, shakedowns, framing, police perjury, wire-tapping, blackmail, police brutality, etc. Just before this vice squad episode in Los Angeles, there was scandal throughout California resulting from claims that the attorney general's office was protecting gambling and vice rings. Folsom Prison came in for some unsavory publicity in connection with brutality and food graft, a scandal which dropped out of the news as suddenly as it appeared.

The complacency of the public in these matters is what the criminal—and the corrupt police—count on. *Time* magazine for July 4, 1949 ran a seven-page story on the City of the Angels at a time when the scandals and the grand jury investigation had been in the headlines daily for two months, but *Time* made reference in 22 jocular words to the least serious of the scandals then before the Los Angeles public. It emphasized, rather, the past clean-ups conducted by the present city administration.

Apart from some momentary color supplied by Madam Brenda Allen, who served a sentence on the admitted perjured testimony of a police officer, and haberdasher Mickey Cohen, frisked of his guns while dodging bullets, the charges and counter-charges, the scores of arrests and releases, the appointment of a new Police Chief and the intervention of the FBI resulted in the dismissal of a couple of police officers, a minimal police department shake-up, and *no convictions*. It seems it will take a body with the power and efficacy of the Seabury and Wicker-sham commissions to convert all this local smoke into an open blaze.

That there are unimpeachable police departments, district attorneys and judges throughout the country cannot be disputed. But equally indisputable is the fact that corruption in law enforcement bodies as it has existed in the last thirty years in the United States is a *greater* threat to a citizen's confidence in, and a convict's respect for the law, than the open flagrancy of the underworld which at least is *not* committed by oath and office to law enforcement.

The fate of the jury system in the United States was another subject of attack by the prisoners in the penitentiary, and is one of the sad preoccupations of all our big legal minds.

Although through the Bill of Rights and the Constitution we are committed as a people to the right of trial by a jury of peers, less than ten percent of our cases ever reach a jury. This right is completely and unconstitutionally abrogated by the Army and Navy in the court-martial, and in the operation of the growing corps of secret police in America. In Massachusetts only 1.7% of cases reach the jury; in New York, 4.7%; in Chicago, 3.7%; and in St. Louis, 13%. About half of these fail of conviction.

The reasons for the inoperability of the right of jury trial are several. Few people can afford the cost of a court trial. Those who can afford it face crowded court dockets, which sometimes result in the defendant's serving out his sentence in jail before he can come to trial. A judge cannot try a plea of Not Guilty; it must be tried by a jury. In the light of these obstacles, it is small wonder that most cases are settled by the defendant's bargaining for a fixed sentence—pleading guilty to a lesser charge, and getting the whole thing over with. But suppose the citizenry suddenly began to exercise their right of jury trial. With the intolerable number of laws on our statute books, municipal, state and Federal, there would hardly be citizens enough in our commonwealth to sit as jurors.

As I have said, few of the prisoners complained that they should not have been serving time. If they were not guilty of the crime for which they were convicted, they freely admitted they were guilty of others which were never detected. Their attack was on the cupidity of the law that convicts one man and protects another, and on the immorality of society which, having attached a price to almost everything else in life, has also hung a price on crime.

But the last frontier to yield to rehabilitation in the convict's mind is the knowledge that society has hung a price not only on crime, but on *respectability* as well.

The white-collar criminal.

By this term coined by criminologist Edwin H. Sutherland, is meant antisocial practices which flourish not only with protection, but with society's approval and even veneration. The robber barons of land, railroad and oil grants in the last century; the Kreugers, Whitneys, Insulls, Falls, and Sinclairs of this century. The broad interpretation of bankruptcy laws, corporation and anti-trust laws. The suppressed investigations of cartels in the two World Wars involving ammunition, magnesium, rubber, oil commodities, aluminum and binoculars. The manipulation of finance on Wall Street with resulting cyclical depressions, which in the 1929 market crash raised national suicide rates from 4,779 in 1928 to 18,551 in 1930 and 20,927 in 1931. The rape of the Federal Reserve System and the American banking scandals are other cases in point. It seems incredible that we had over 11,800 bank failures from 1921 to 1932 involving $5 billions. England has not had a single bank failure in modern times. Canada has had but one. Sutherland's book, *White Collar Crime,* published in 1949, is a study of 980 court decisions against seventy large corporations in America who in recent years have engaged in white-collar crime involving billions of dollars.

By white-collar crimes are meant such practices as those of the bond salesman and investment broker in selling worthless or watered bonds and stocks. The adulteration of patent medicines, cosmetics and food, about which Kallett and Schlink wrote in their popular *100,000,000 Guinea Pigs.* The medical profession's fee-splitting, illegal operations, unnecessary prolongation of treatment, falsification of insurance reports, profiteering through the dispensing of drugs. The lawyer who will not allow a case to be settled out of court, thus increasing his fees, who secures clients by "ambulance chasing," who blackmails his clients, and counsels businessmen in the adroit use of sharp practices, who operates through a tie-up with criminals and police.

Cavan's text, *Criminology,* describes the social position of the white-collar criminal:

> E. H. Sutherland, who has made the most nearly complete studies of white-collar crime . . . . lists the following qualifications of the white-collar criminal: he is a person of the upper socioeconomic class who violates the criminal law in the course of his usual occupation. He is therefore a person with prestige in the community and respected by his business associates. He finds his satisfactions in conventional society and does not regard himself as a criminal. . . . When he is brought to account in

court it is often to the civil rather than the criminal court, for the purpose of recovering the property rather than of punishment. For those who have lost money this procedure is valuable, but the white-collar criminal is thereafter free to proceed on his way without suffering imprisonment or the stigma of being an ex-convict, experienced by the criminal of lower class origin. It is not unnatural therefore that the white-collar criminal should come to regard himself as above the law and to place higher values on business success and personal gain than on conformity to law or ethical practices.

We as a people have become supine about graft and politics going hand in hand. Occasional protest meetings are held, but at elections the same gangs are too often put back in power. The graft and fraud in the regimes of Big Bill Thompson and Cermak in Chicago and Jimmy Walker in New York, Penrose and the Vare brothers in Philadelphia, left the prisoners in the penitentiary shaking their heads over all the diligence displayed in rounding up the petty thieves and forgers. And then there was the Prendergast machine operating in nearby Kansas City . . .

The box scores of personal bank deposits of police and prosecuting attorneys during these regimes were common knowledge in the penitentiary. Probably the record was held by an attorney for the Zoning Department in New York City during Walker's mayoralty. The attorney deposited $5¼ million to his own account in five years. A Kings County (N.Y.) sheriff banked $520,000; the sheriff of New York deposited $360,000 and his deputy $662,000 in the same period of time. A minor employee of the New York Bureau of Standards was making $25,000 a month on false weights for twelve years. Current statistics on the standard of living of public officials are more elusive than the above, which date from the devastating reports of the Seabury and Wickersham commissions. Ordinarily the public is not given the opportunity of scrutinizing the bank deposits of its public servants.

Probably the most ludicrous incident of city graft in the thirties was in Philadelphia, where a bid of $3½ million for a museum was finally padded to $25 million under the benign influence of the Vare brothers. Six million went into a subway three blocks long, and six million into a tube under the river. Neither the subway nor the tube were ever used. "Except by rats," said my men.

Our national business philosophy of getting something for nothing; our admiration of the rugged individualists who boast they can do anything as long as they do it cleverly; our crooked practices which are considered "good business" or "sharp business"; and our rationalization that graft and crookedness are all right "if they don't hurt anybody" are criminal concepts, whether they are exercised on Wall street or behind a gunman's mask.

Who are our real criminals? Barnes and Teeters, in *New Horizons in Criminology,* discuss this question.

> Who are the great criminals? The natural answer to this question is to name . . . . desperadoes, such as John Dillinger, "Baby-Face" Nelson, "Pretty Boy" Floyd, and so on. The notion that any of these is "Public Enemy Number One" is absurd. Their reputation has been built up by the newspapers, by the G-men and local police, and by the more sensational writers on crime. Dillinger, at the height of his career, was not even Public Enemy No. 1,000.
>
> The leaders of the underworld today are the master minds and directors of organized crime and racketeering. Since they are almost never even arrested, we cannot specifically know who they are. Al Capone was, perhaps one of them, but, as we have pointed out, he was only a crude and relatively inefficient pioneer in this field. Certain journalists and many politicians know well enough who the leaders of organized crime are, but they have no inclination to tell. They remember all too well the case of Jake Lingle, the Chicago newspaper man who was unceremoniously "bumped off" because he knew too much and might tell some of the things he knew. The files of the secret service committee

of organized crime discourage the politicians from divulging any information they possess, should they wish to do so. The public, then, is in the dark with respect to the identity and the actual character of those who control the great empire of organized crime in our day.

Next below them come such desperadoes as Dillinger. However spectacular their criminal deeds may be, this type is not numerous and their depredations are relatively unimportant viewed from the angle of the financial losses involved. Next in order would probably come the gangsters and gunmen who preserve discipline and maintain the local monopoly in organized crime and racketeering. They are the "yes men" of the higher-ups. Occasionally, one of these is convicted and his name gets into the newspapers, but it is relatively difficult to identify and to convict even a subordinate gangster who is operating thus in connection with one of the major rackets.

Coming down the list, we finally happen upon those criminals who commit the traditional offenses: robbery, burglary, thievery, petty frauds, and the like, and also the crimes of violence which are incidental to the effort to get something for nothing. In this group would also fall those who commit various types of crimes, particularly crimes of violence, as a result of psychopathic compulsions and temporary passion. The convicts in our prisons are usually the least competent, the least fortunate, or the least experienced members even of this group. They are also the least influential.

These are some of the reasons why the population of a penitentiary is *not* penitent.

A discussion of abstract criminal character as a cause of crime would be more supportable if these conditions in our national life did not exist. Whom do we mean when we say criminal? The gangster, the white-collar criminal, the corrupt police, or the small-time criminal who is too often made the scapegoat for his more spectacular brothers?

These four are all equally antisocial in their philosophy

that an honest man is a sucker, that "only saps work." But the attitude of the man in prison, for all its being a rationalization, has more basis in objective fact than that of the others. When he sees society give respectability to the white-collar criminal, and sees law enforcement bodies give protection to big-time criminals, it is not surprising that he looks upon crime not as a moral offense but as a competitive profession, and upon his punishment as a gross partiality on the part of both society and law.

The white-collar criminal has learned to hide his antisocial aggressions behind a facade of charities and public-spiritedness: the endowment of a library, a medical center, a research laboratory, a scholarship, a foundling home, a recreation center in the slums. But his basic disrespect of individual rights is seen in his ruthless manipulation of human life in reaching his own ends and building his dynasty.

The convict in a penitentiary watches the three-ring show of the white-collar criminal and the big-time criminal, with the lawless police wedged between the two, and asks himself why he is more criminal than these? Why he should absorb the most sustained impact of law and justice while the serious offenders are so rarely prosecuted and so frequently escape punishment if, for political expediency, they are occasionally prosecuted? Why, he asks, is the written law so inconstant and unequable?

He is not disposed in prison to contemplate his own sins, but the larger sins that go unpunished in a free society. It is not repentance that occupies him; it is reprisal.

These rationalizations of a convict should have more meaning to you and me than they have to the convict himself. He lacks insight and perspective on them. And, frankly, he is not so much interested in social reform as he is in getting a little of that protection and respectability himself. He just doesn't like discrimination. He is too confirmed in his belief in the relative nature of crime, and in his skepticism regarding human integrity, to understand his own attitudes. He just knows he feels the same emotionality about being punished that a child in a family circle does who is beaten for twisting the cat's tail, when his brother isn't touched for throwing the same cat in the fire. It is an analogy that ought to give us pause, in the interest of our own necks.

Crime is with us always, on many levels, in many forms. The proportion of the problem it poses is not reflected in the number of crimes on our books or convictions on our police blotters or prisoners in our penitentiaries. *It is reflected in the attitude of our people toward what crime is. For what a nation comes to agree upon as being the nature of crime is what determines the nature of her criminals.*

Most of us would heartily agree that respect for law is essential to a nation of peaceful communities. But it is not as simple as Mr. J. Edgar Hoover makes it appear. In order to command respect, the law, both in interpretation and enforcement, must be constant, unimpeachable and equable. It is no news to the American people that we have been undershooting that precept for the last thirty years. How could fear of punishment deter crime in the decade of my men, the era of the gangster not yet closed, when an offender had an 85% chance of escaping arrest, a 99% chance of escaping conviction, and a 99% chance of escaping punishment?

If constancy, integrity and equability are not reflected in law, all that is left to respect is the cop's night stick and his third degree. This kind of respect can quickly turn to contempt, both in the law-abiding and the lawless. It is an affront to human dignity and resourcefulness.

Our most serious problem in crime is not the run-of-the-mill convict in a penitentiary. It is the criminal at large who remains so with the knowledge of the populace. It is not reasonable to expect the reformation of small-time criminals while gangsters operate with political and police protection. The small-time criminal then becomes only a red herring thrown to the public

213

to feed the illusion that justice is being done. Organized crime could not survive without protection. The small-time criminal knows this, so does the big-time criminal, so do his protectors. So do you and I.

It is not reasonable to expect small-time criminals to respect the law, while law enforcement is corrupted by big-time crime. Nor is it reasonable to expect big-time criminals to respect the law when they can buy protection.

It is true that one man's having protection is no moral excuse for another man's committing crime. But in the interest of morality, is this really where the emphasis belongs—that the small-time criminal should not bemoan the big-time criminal's protection? It is rationalization that keeps the emphasis there. We shall begin to have an understanding of crime in our society only when the emphasis is shifted: conviction of one criminal does not excuse protection of another, bigger one.

Quo vadis?

The conscientious judge wants to scrap our bulging statute books and start over. The conscientious sociologist wants to equate the philosophy of crime. The conscientious policeman wants to clean up the department. The conscientious warden wants to start with prison reform. An assault on any of those four fronts will carry over to some degree into the others. Any point is a starting point.

Regarding prison reform, it is surely obvious that even if the regeneration of a criminal while he is in prison takes place, he is still released upon an unregenerated society whose evils and complaisance helped to misshape him in the first place.

Of the six men in my office, two were innocent: Scott's taking the rap for someone else was his own idea; Ross was made "criminal" by the brutality of his first imprisonment. Gibbs and Connie were typical small-time criminals. King and Punch were the big-time criminals; their sentences were not in proportion to their crimes, and were the shortest of the six.

Criminals like Al Capone and Terry Druggan did not pay for their crimes in their farcical sentences, despite all the publicity designed to impress the public with the implacability of the law. Who was *really* responsible for the rise of boys like Punch Pinero or Al Capone? How far would they have got without protection? Without the fix and the shakedown? Put my six men, or any six men with their understanding of society and law enforcement, in prison, and what will they learn from imprisonment? *That the way to make crime pay is to line up with the Big-Time Boys.*

If any reclamation of character took place in my men during the time I worked with them, it resulted from the rehabilitation made possible by the 1930 Federal reforms. Even so, when I came to leave them, the problem seemed to be not so much their release upon an unsuspecting society as their fate in that equivocal society into which they were being sent.

10

THEY PASS the flag in the courtyard. They look up at her.

"Hi, Old Girl," they say softly.

Convicts as a class are hotly patriotic. There's no country like America, no flag like hers! In spite of the fact that the convict breaks her laws, intimidates her officials, scorns her courts, defrauds her government and assaults her citizens, if he's going to be punished or imprisoned he wants it to be in his own country.

One out of every ten convicts has seen the world. Oh, not culturally, of course. These ambassadors without portfolio have traveled by tramp steamer and contracted dysentery. They have been threatened with scimitars in the streets of Arabia for molesting a harem. They have been stabbed in the Apache district in Paris and drugged in China—but, then, so have some of our best young men.

They like American food, bathtubs, roads, skyscrapers, magazines, cars, and people. They even prefer American jails. They deplore foreign sanitation, prostitutes, and economics.

America is not the Government, in their minds. She is not even the people. She is the Statue of Liberty, the Golden Gate Bridge, the National Anthem, and the Grand Old Flag. She is an impersonal motherhood of benignity and justice which has never been reconstituted in any of her laws or courts.

By law they forfeit their citizenship for the duration of their imprisonment, but they never acknowledge their banishment. They are Americans to the death. From their cells they run the country, fight her wars, deride her enemies, accuse her statesmen, and celebrate her holidays. They swear their oaths on George Washington's wig and believe all our history books. They appoint their heroes, revere them passionately, sometimes ignorantly, always with blind sentimentality.

This sentimentality was a common erraticism in convicts. As Dorothy Parker said of someone, they frequently "ran the gamut of emotions from A to B." The same man might be without feeling in one area where emotionality is normally expected, and tearful in another area where it is not expected. Sometimes the more gross the crimes in their past, the more tearful their emotionality on other fronts.

Like Punch and Mr. Lincoln, which is now recorded as accurately as my memory holds it.

On February twelfth of my second year at the penitentiary notice was taken that the flag in the yard was flown at half-mast. This mystified Punch. There were undoubtedly other men in prison who had never heard of Lincoln, but I was surprised that Punch did not know who he was. The phenomenon was easily explained. Punch was born and reared in Italy. He had never been naturalized, and was to be deported as an undesirable alien after serving his sentence. In America he "worked" in one of the largest cities of the South where, of course, Mr. Lincoln was not revered.

Punch was alone among the staff members in this distinctive ignorance, and the others made the most of it that day. Scott was broadminded about Northerners and played along with the other boys. They worried Punch about a big shot like him not knowing a contemporary rival like Lincoln. "Things has sure changed outside since you bin in stir," said Connie. They threw figures and statistics at Punch designed to show the size and strength and conquests of Lincoln's mob.

Punch swallowed everything uncritically for a while, becoming more and more frustrated. But not for long. He soon realized that if the flag was at half-mast, Lincoln must be a national hero, because in his knowledge a flag had never held a gangster in sacred memory.

Furious now with the other men, he stomped into my presence and demanded to know who this Lincoln was. I said he was one of our Presidents.

"One of 'em! How many you got?"

When he learned that Mr. Hoover was the thirtieth, he hooted. "In *It-lee* it ain't like that!" He threw out his chest, clicked his heels and raised his arm in a snapping fascist salute. *"Vivo Il Duce!"*

At ease again, he wanted to know: was this Lincoln a right guy? I said we had every reason to believe he was. Such as? he asked. Well, for one thing, I explained, Lincoln successfully conducted the nation through one of its greatest crises. Punch had never heard of the Civil War, but at least a war sounded exciting. After giving him a brief synopsis I said, "Anyhow, Punch, that war produced two of the greatest generals in history."

Punch and I were not alone now. My doorway was filled with Connie, Scott and Gibbs. When office procedure was interrupted to this extent, it meant that King and Ross, though ostensibly at work, were probably listening too.

Scott told Punch about Lee's being the father of trench warfare, that the War College at the Fort considered Lee the greatest general of all time, that with few men and no money he outgeneraled the North at every turn—until Sherman.

Ross had now become interested, and told Punch about Sherman's march: how he deployed his 60,000 men to cut a swathe sixty miles wide from Atlanta to the sea, fighting ten to thirty miles a day, largely on foot, leveling everything in their path—towns, crops, railroads; burning, pillaging, foraging. And that this was accomplished with no lines of communications or supplies, almost without horses or ammunition. Quite an engineering feat, said Ross.

"My granddad was in Sherman's march," I said.

When he heard that sometimes all they had to eat *en route* was the corn they could scratch out of horse manure, Punch retched. He loved good food.

"Now, how come them to go through all that? What in hell for did they do it, Doc?"

Gibbs sucked in an exasperated breath and glared at Punch.

"Jesus Christ—it ain't no use!" he shouted. "Go on, Doc— just don't pay him no attention."

"This Lincoln character," Punch ignored Gibbs, "he won?"

"He won the war and lost his life."

Connie and Gibbs and Scott stood at respectful attention now, as a convict will, when a "right guy" gets a raw deal or dies even remotely a hero.

"Doc means he got shot," Gibbs said quietly.

"In the war, huh?" asked Punch, sensing that something was wrong.

"Naw—in a the-ater. Five days after the war ended," said Connie.

"He was ass-assinated," said Gibbs.

"Huh?"

"Ex*cuse* me!"said Gibbs sarcastically. "He was murdered, you murderer!"

For once Punch ignored the slur. He was aghast at Lincoln's murder. This was awful.

"You sure this Lincoln was a right guy, huh, Doc?" he asked again.

Connie answered for me. "Just about fifty million people thought he was God Hisself, of who I am but one!"

It was clear from the look on Punch's face that Connie

didn't count with him, even as but one. He turned to Gibbs.

"You can spit on my mother's grave if he wasn't a great man," said Gibbs solemnly.

Punch went from him to Scott and King and Ross. Fortunately Scott was the only Southerner; he was out-voted. Lincoln was exonerated.

"He had the largest funeral in history, Punch," I said.

"Yeah? Bigger'n Tony D'Andrea's?" he asked.

I didn't know D'Andrea, but Gibbs did, along with all the statistics.

"He was a no-good gangster, Doc," he informed me. "He got shot," he said flatly, looking at Punch. "You know how many Chicago judges was honorary pallbearers?" he asked me. "Twenty one. Let's see—they was Judge Sabath, Judge Marchett, Judge Scanlan, Judge Friend, Judge Barasa—"

"Shut up, Grandma!" yelled Punch, adding something about a goddam addin' machine.

"You know how many lawyers was honorary pallbearers?" Gibbs continued undaunted. "Eight. You know who was one of the active pallbearers? The state's attorney. You know how many people went to the funeral? Eight thousand. You know how much the flowers cost? Eight grand. You know how long the funeral procession was? Two and a half miles! For a no-good gangster!" Again he glanced at Punch. "Some justice, huh, Doc?"

"That's very interesting, Gibbs." I thought it was. . . . "But Lincoln's funeral train was seventeen hundred miles long." Gibbs ogled me, while I went on to say that seven million mourners lined the path of the funeral train; that only a million and a half of them were allowed to view the body; that six hundred dignitaries passed the coffin in Washington alone.

They all gaped at that.

I had been reading about Lincoln at the time, so I told them the train took the same route back to Springfield that Lincoln had traveled on his Presidential campaign: Baltimore, Philadelphia, New York, Cleveland, Columbus, Indianapolis, Chicago, Springfield, a trip that took twelve days and twelve nights. How his mourners lined the path of the train for hundreds of miles just to see it pass, with no hope of seeing the body. And how the railroad published the train's schedule, and men and women traveled for days to meet it, standing beside the tracks in the rain, through the night, building campfires and flares to light the countryside for a better view of the lonely train. How they built arches, fired salutes, wrote verses, and wept for Abraham Lincoln.

After a respectful silence Connie muttered, "Tony D'Andrea was a bush league bum!"

Punch stood blinking at the facts, visibly moved. A pall had settled on him as he listened. As I say, he had great respect for a corpse, especially a good one.

"Who was it shot him?" he asked quietly.

"A ham. Name of Booth," said Gibbs.

Imagine a ham taking a pot-shot at *Il Duce!* It was unthinkable! Here was Lincoln, Punch said, a really good guy, living for his country, inspiring his generals, freeing the slaves, pardoning the boy sentry who went to sleep at his post—this last really shattered Punch. And when Lincoln takes time out to go to a show he gets it in the back! Where was the FBI when it happened?

"What'd they do to the son of a bitch who got him?" was his last question.

Gibbs, our encyclopedia of social injustice, gave him the story of Booth and the burning barn. He told Punch about Booth's ironically catching his spur on the draped flag when he jumped to the stage of the Ford Theater, breaking his leg; and about the controversy over whether it was Booth who died in the barn with Shakespeare on his lips.

At this Punch began to shake with rage and cry for blood, and the men in the doorway quietly dispersed. On a pretense of business I walked into their room and began thumbing through the files, feeling a word might be necessary. Punch stomped around for a while, cursing and berating American policing. Then he subsided into a black silence.

In the lull I heard humming. I looked around to see who it was. Scott. What a time to sing, with Punch in a mood for blood!

Punch heard it too and wheeled on him. "God damn you, cut it out!"

Scott stopped. But a moment later Ross spoke up.

"That was Lincoln's song, Punch."

Punch glared at him suspiciously.

"The Battle Hymn of the Republic," said Ross.

"So it is!" said Scott, smiling to himself. "Now where d'you suppose I picked that up?"

"It's been blattin' on the radio all day, Kid," said Connie.

"Awright—so let's have it!" growled Punch.

So Scott and Ross began to sing softly under Punch's intimidating scowl.

Mine eyes have seen the glory of the coming of the Lord,
He is trampling out the vintage where the grapes of
wrath are stored,
He has loosed the fateful light'ning of his terrible
swift sword,
His truth is marching on!

Glory, glory, hallelujah!
Glory, glory, hallelujah!

Connie lifted his whiskey tenor. Gibbs hummed on a scanty bass line. King did not sing, but he paled at his work.

Glory, glory, hallelujah!
His truth is marching on!

222

Suddenly the song caught on. They swung it loud and slow now, keeping time with their feet on the hollow concrete floor. My spine began to tingle. The five sounded like fifty, like half a battalion half a mile away.

Glo-ry, glo-ry, Hal-le-lu-jah!. . . .

They kept their eyes on their work as they sang, trying to look nonchalant. Punch's glance went from face to face. It was hitting him hard. His eyes came back to Ross and stayed there. He winced as he listened, as if he were warding off blows. He wanted to cry. Inside he was crying. Little Punch was breaking up. He looked good that way. Better than when he smiled.

The door opened and Gordon looked in, the men still singing. He looked from them to me.

I was having a little trouble about then. I couldn't seem to swallow. I'd had the same trouble when Connie presented me with the *Regular Grind Coffee* and the *Solid Pack Tomatoes* boxes over a year ago. I was thinking now of the old hunger in men for a right guy, and their veneration of him when they find him—say, on the twelfth of February. I was thinking of Zola and Lincoln and Thomas Mott Osborne, and the warden and the captain, and of all men who acknowledge the need of the human soul to believe in his fellow-man.

Gordon flashed me a look which said, Sorry, wrong day, see you later. And he withdrew.

It was the sight of my emotion, I think, more than Gordon's appearance, that interrupted the *Battle Hymn* and sent the men back to work. But all through the day I heard snatches of it and saw Punch and the others glancing at the flag and at me, and turn quickly, with their own kind of gentility, back to work.

Mr. Lincoln sure has a lot of friends in prison.

11

In the following spring the USPHS dropped a bomb-shell on us. It opened the doors of Federal penitentiaries to its female personnel. We had two weeks' notice of the descent of four nurses and a physiologist.

The former were the first registered nurses to be assigned to a Federal penitentiary. Until then male convicts had been trained for nursing care. The addition of a physiologist was a surprise to me, as I had been to Gordon. She was to work with us, conducting animal experimentation in drug addiction.

The prisoners crept through the first week in a state of in-volutional melancholia over the female invasion. It would mean nothing but trouble. Showers, shaves, haircuts, shoe shines. Watch-your-clothes, watch-your-manners, watch-your-language.

Although they did not openly say so, they dreaded the titil-lating sound of a girl's voice and the swish of her starched skirts. It was one thing to become disturbed by a pin-up girl on your wall, but a girl in the flesh was something else. They dreaded the reawakening of dreams and memories finally licked and laid away. What was the use of going through all that again?

But the melancholia expired of its own frailty, and the sec-ond week crept by with the same men at a wild pitch of excite-ment.

The nurses were expected first. As the day approached, bed-ridden patients put in emergency calls for barbers already swamped with work. The laundry complained about the volume of uniforms and denims suddenly thrown at them. Orderlies who until now had had to be browbeaten to keep their hands clean on duty were found with surgeon's brushes and BD blades, manicuring their nails. The commissary had a run on combs, toothbrushes, razors and shoe polish.

In the hospital, space was at a premium. Chronics became acute. Blood pressures and temperatures soared. Sedatives had to be doubled. Patients were off their feed. Ulcers under observation flared, and were rushed to surgery. Manic-depressives in the psychopathic ward who the first week had been depressive now became manic. The number of responses to daily Sick Call after breakfast soared.

Scott asked one day, "What does the warden think about the advent?"

"He ain't said," replied Gibbs.

"Probably paralyzed his speech centers," Connie suggested.

My boys had it all settled in their minds, before the administration had rallied from the initial shock of the news, that the experimental laboratory and the physiologist would be housed in the space adjoining ours in the half-basement. The space was not being used, and the plumbing which would have to be laid in the utility tunnel directly under the half-basement would very simply terminate there. Connie was verbally planning the whole project one day, with Ross as a fascinated audience.

"For once you're right, Connie," said Ross. "Every time you open your mouth you save the Government five hundred dollars!"

"I'm that good, huh?" said Connie. "Well, you sure as hell oughtta know, Ross."

"Just one thing you forgot, Connie," leered Punch. "You ain't said where you're puttin' the *hot air* vent," he said meaningfully. "The dames don't know it, but there's sure a lot of *hot air* on this floor. . . ."

The nurses arrived at ten o'clock one morning. We watched them from our window crossing the yard to the hospital with a guard. The windows and doorways of the buildings along their route were jammed with what must have looked like hoary faces to the four women. They fell into step with each other as they walked, their scarlet-lined navy blue capes flowing gracefully behind them, their regulation shoes sounding very regulation upon the pavement. The peeping men began applauding rhythmically in time with the girls' gait. If the rascals meant to fluster the strangers, they succeeded. The girls, in spite of the guard's deliberate step, looked as if they might finish the last lap on the run.

I met them later in the hospital dining room, where they had lunch with some of the staff. Two of the girls were plain stolid frames with lots of social service in their eyes: one a painfully shy Mennonite from Kansas, the other an apple-cheeked girl from Washington. Both were in their early thirties. The third was a quiet-mannered spinster of fifty who, though very plain, looked like a sure winner. The fourth looked like trouble.

She was an extremely pretty blonde, round and edible, younger than the others. She was, as the boys say, really stacked. But she robbed us men of the pleasure of making this discovery ourselves, in those few sweeping glances which are so dear to our hearts, by loudly crying her own wares.

"I suppose," she began in a predatory voice, "it has been a long time since these men have seen girls like *us.*"

Gordon choked. "Well—hardly *that* long!" He spoke with perhaps more bite than necessary. I kicked him on the shins, but congratulated him afterward.

I was not surprised at what happened to the girl on the wards, but I was sorry. The men froze her out in a few days—she left at the end of a month or so—and gave their attention and warmth to the sweet scrawny spinster.

Gordon sent our beauty to see me before she left, to "get

straightened out." She was still smarting under the men's rebuff. She said she would always remember this as the year of the great freeze. Everybody seemed to think she deserved what happened, she said, especially that Doctor Gordon. The other nurses proffered only a cool good-bye to her, so what went? she demanded. If these men didn't like a pretty girl, they were the first she'd ever seen who didn't.

She was really a nice kid. It seemed a shame for her to go on making the same mistake over and over, so I tried to tell her about the men. Maybe I was brutal, but we were all anxious that the experiment of female nurses got all the breaks possible. This provocative miss with her full lips and her busy hips was the prisoners' idea of a fraud. She had flirted and teased with no intention of delivering the goods. I was sure that if she had thought she would ever have to deliver, she would have kept her white skirts wrapped tightly around her slim legs. She had not only teased and provoked them, but she had done it superciliously and contemptuously, and they wouldn't buy at that level. Even *they* didn't have to do that. They felt there was a basic honesty about most street-girls, who didn't pose as being anything but what they were; and according to the prisoners' codes, conduct like hers lacked the honesty of a street-girl.

When she heard that, she gasped. I quickly assured her that I wasn't suggesting that she get into bed with the patients, but that she just stop queening.

The criminals' idea of women was an odd combination of reality and illusion. They took their sex on the street-girl level, but they wanted the rest of womankind in ivory towers at very dizzy heights. I told her how the men had looked forward to the arrival of the nurses, not because they were expecting to sleep with them, but because with their illusions about women they were hoping for some nice wholesome girls to keep those illusions alive. And when she let them down, they dummied up.

She took it on the chin. She said she guessed they had picked the *nice* girl, all right, admitting she had never before lost to a fifty-year-old spinster. She thanked me, and left considerably sobered. She certainly was pretty. And well stacked.

The USPHS's revolutionary action in sending female nurses into penitentiaries was completely vindicated in time. Their presence had a most salutary effect on the men. But oddly, it was still the plain ones who had the most appeal. The men were not looking for romance in a nurse, it seemed, but for stability and quality.

The boys had just "aired out" the office after our beauty left, and Connie had resumed his post by the door, saying, "It just goes to show what will come through a door if it ain't locked," when the door opened again.

Connie told me later—I was busy at my desk at the time and didn't look up—that what came in was so tiny, "I leaned over my desk to see if maybe the rest of her was doubled up somewheres out of sight." She was not much taller standing up than Connie was sitting down.

"Hello," the cool voice said, "I'm Laurie Kennedy. Will you announce me to Doctor Wilson, please?" she added, probably in view of Connie's blank face.

I came out to find Connie momentarily beyond speech. When I looked at Laurie Kennedy I wished I had detained our beauty fifteen minutes longer. I could have shown her exactly what I meant by quality. There was a quietness all about Miss Kennedy that was breathtaking. She was tiny and quiet. Tiny, dark, and quiet. Our beauty had it all over her for glamour, but Laurie Kennedy at thirty had a look about her that our beauty should have cried after.

It was a long time before we realized Laurie wasn't beautiful. I don't think Connie and Gibbs ever knew it. She had an open little face, which when we met her was framed by a small blue hat. The set of her shoulders in her coat was proud and straight, her blue eyes were direct and friendly. Her voice was low, and there was this quietness everywhere about her, so that I am sure we all thought she was beautiful.

We saw a lot of Laurie Kennedy in the next few weeks. I came to know her quite well. We had long consultations over my vocational records, trying to find a staff for her. She needed a technician. That wasn't easy. The record of anyone who had had even a smattering of college was immediately pulled out, and if he had been exposed to either chemistry or the natural sciences his record was studied hopefully. No luck.

One day she came to my office with a reproachful look in her eyes.

"Why have you been holding out on me?" she demanded. "Why didn't you tell me you had a lab technician not a hundred feet from your office, on this very floor? He's exactly what I need!"

"That would be Davis," I said.

When I told her he had worked in my office for a short time, she was more exasperated than ever. "Why, he's a college graduate, majored in chemistry, worked in laboratories for six years—Not only that, he's human. He's neat and clean-shaven, and—Well, if I must stay up all hours with my furry little friends, I'd like it to be with someone who is congenial. What's up, D.W.?"

"How'd you get a line on Davis?" I asked.

"He came to me today, asked for the job. What's he in for?" she asked, as if she couldn't imagine why he was there at all.

"Murder, Kennedy."

That stopped her. "What kind of murder, D.W.?" she asked quietly.

"Very bad murder. It was a young woman. A mutilated young woman."

"I see. . . ."

I gave her my experience with Davis in the office, and my

229

impression that he was a dangerous psychopath who ought to be left where he was.

"A clean murder is one thing," I said, "but a sadistic murder is another matter. A sadist cuts up his women instead of sleeping with them. And I doubt that Davis is salvageable. I thought of him at once, but I just don't think he's your man, Kennedy."

"No, I suppose not," she murmured. But *damn*—wasn't he fine for the job? Otherwise, she meant, of course. . . . Oh, damn being a woman anyway—sometimes. . . . "But there's not another man in the place like him, D.W. What am I to *do?*"

"Just wait, Kennedy, somebody'll check in."

She made a face at me. Then she fell to thinking, and when she raised her stubborn chin I knew I had lost.

"I'm going to take him!" Seeing my objections mount, she went on urgently. Davis was a lone wolf, she said, of course he wouldn't work well with my men. They were too chummy. Davis wasn't the Rotarian type, like my Connie. That's why he became a lab technician; it took his kind of temperament and absorption. You can't read tea leaves on a microscope slide, but she had a hunch Davis would do just fine, left to himself. "And I'm the leave-'em-alone type. In a lab," she added smartly.

She took him, but not until Doctor Stevens had warned her about Davis's pathology and extracted her promise that she would let him know of any unusual behavior in Davis. I gave her a brief lecture on the prodromal aura—warning signs—to look for in an epileptoid like Davis. She listened politely.

She was right about his being fine for the job. She began to refer to him as her man Friday, and remarked about his grasp of difficult chemical procedures. He was assuming full responsibility for whole units of the animal research, and kept meticulous records. He seemed to be content and malleable, and Laurie teased me about my anxiety neurosis.

"Well, my hunch was right, wasn't it, D.W.?" she asked after several weeks had passed.

What could I say? That I had a hunch too, and that I hoped to God mine was wrong?

The ivory tower illusions grew up thick and fast around Laurie. The fact that she was working with mice, rats, guinea pigs and rabbits in her endocrine and biochemical tests heightened the intrigue. Her probationary period with the men at large passed quickly and painlessly. She was a part of the medical-psychological unit and was therefore accepted along with us. Since her work was restricted to animals, there was no problem of resistance on the part of the prisoners. A woman scientist dedicated to the cause of the criminal was an awesome thing to them. But the real catalyst was her own winsomeness.

My men loved her from the first day. King, whose face was usually in his work, always lifted it when Laurie came in. His appraisal was frank and proud. She was real. No matter how closely he might look, he knew he would find only goodness. Ross was in her suite a great deal the first few weeks, working on the wiring and plumbing, and the two became good friends. I was glad for Ross; she was his kind of woman. I could not have asked for a finer thing therapeutically than for Ross to have the approbation and warmth of a woman like Laurie Kennedy. The only time I saw any recognition in Scott of his status as a prisoner was in his attitude toward Laurie. It was perhaps the famous Southern chivalry which made him feel that a prisoner, guilty or innocent, should stay away from a "lady."

Gibbs and Connie looked at her as they would at the Virgin Mary. But the first time she walked into our office with a white rat in her large uniform pocket and another chasing around her shoulder, I thought the cause of science was lost forever. Connie and Gibbs were appalled. The connotations of the word "rat" are natively unpleasant to a convict. But when she named the two creatures after the two men, and when they watched their namesakes eating with their two dainty front paws the cheese and oranges she gave them, they softened.

"Anyone a rat can trust, I can trust," said Connie stoutly.

However, when she dropped Connie's namesake on his desk for safekeeping one day while she talked with me in my office, Connie stared at it skitting nervously across his desk, his eyes popped, and his Adam's apple leaped wildly. When the mascot turned his pink near-sighted eyes on Connie and scampered up his shirt front, Connie reared back in his chair so far that he and the rat crashed to the floor. There they sat, looking at each other. When he realized that the rat was as frightened as he, he picked it up and began patting it with a long, gentle finger, looking as foolish as a new father and just as proud.

Punch made a few sportive passes at Laurie, but when she dropped a rat in his straying hand he gave up the chase. The creatures made excellent bodyguards. You can bribe a man and shoot a dog, but what can you do about a rat?

She worked next door to us, turning out an admirable piece of work. She addicted the animals to all the important narcotics. She established the dosage which could be maintained without physical damage to them. She maintained the animals at the maximum tolerance point and looked for physiological damage to heart, stomach, nervous system and brain. She studied successive litters of animals which she specially bred and conditioned for the possible significance of heredity in addiction. She tested all the claimed cures in narcotic literature, along with every new hope that was advanced by medicine.

All my men were disturbed by Davis's presence in her office, but none so deeply as King. They did not hate Davis as King had from the first. King became preoccupied and irritable every few weeks, until I began to correlate his episodes with certain preoccupations in Laurie. Was she having trouble with Davis at these times, and did King have some pathological track to

Davis's mind that told him so? I did not keep my toe in Laurie's door, much as I would like to have observed Davis. When I did go to the laboratory he was polite, but noticeably hostile. There was no point in making Laurie pay for his dislike of me.

I thought a lot about King. There was no official or rumored record of violence against him. But there were signs of pressures in King at these times that I would have expected to find in Davis.

Laurie was full of assurances to Doctor Stevens, Gordon and me, when we inquired every few weeks, that Davis was an ideal assistant who gave her less trouble than ninety percent of the prison population gave their bosses. But she had taken him on her own hunch, and we knew if there were crises it would be hard for her to admit them. She would want to handle them herself, being a proud girl. We watched her as the months passed with good will and concern.

If Punch the Lady Killer had no luck with Laurie Kennedy, he was not entirely without female solace in prison.

The penitentiary was periodically host to sociology and psychology classes from the university near by, and from other colleges in the state. Many of the earnest young women among them, ostensibly bent on scholarship, were acutely aware that the beautiful Baby Face Pinero was on exhibition. We had a lot of trouble with coeds. They were always leaving sorority pins behind, and writing letters that scorched the fingers of the warden's assistants as they censored them. The overtures of an American college girl have all the polish of a streetwalker, and Punch was their consistent target. He had no serious contenders for the title of the-man-they-would-most-like-to-be-left-in-a-prison-cell-with. Their invitations were specific and urgent.

Punch was an egomaniac who could take 'em or leave 'em. He left them. Who wanted to go to all the trouble of getting smuggled out, just for a dame in heat? But he liked to be invited, so he'd know the old charm was still potent. Whenever the grapevine forecast a female visitation, therefore, Punch stayed home with a headache for a half day.

On one occasion he returned to the office after lunch, took out of his pocket a sorority pin and hung it on his chest.

"I couldn't talk her outta givin' it to me," he assured us. "Kinda purty, ain't it?"

Connie and Gibbs thought so.

"What's this sorority racket, Doc?" Punch asked. "This kid says somebody dared her to smuggle me into her sorority house for a night, an' she said if I did there was twenty kids just like her livin' there, an' I could have any or all of 'em for free. When I asked her what they usually got for tricks, she got mad somethin' awful. What goes on? They movin' in on my racket? They cuttin' in on a honest prostitute's livin'?"

"That's what some people think, Punch," I said.

"Maybe I oughtta organize 'em, huh?" he asked.

Then he pushed back the cuff of his denim sleeve and displayed a girl's watch set with diamonds.

"She give you that?" Gibbs asked skeptically.

"Nope. But I figgered she probably just overlooked it, wouldn't you think?"

Punch loved the adulation of women, but he had his finger in too many hot pies to be tripped up by one.

Although Punch's empire on the outside was so organized that it continued to flourish in his absence, his revenue was somewhat curtailed by mismanagement and theft, the cat being away.

Punch had compensated for these losses by moving his men on the outside into the race track racket soon after he began serving time. He pored over dope sheets and racing forms. He called his signals to his men by means of phony ads in the personal columns of the newspapers. He reached out myste-

234

riously from his cell in an occasional punitive expedition to deal with a tout or a jockey who had double-crossed him.

He was elated when he learned to apply the formula of *coefficient of correlation* to his racing racket. As I remember, he was watching King diagram some statistical measurements on our first trial data on the research.

"What's this *coefficient of correlation* again, Doc?" he asked.

"It's the inter-influence of variables, Punch."

"No kiddin'!" he said sarcastically.

Ten minutes later such words as concomitance and paired measures were still Greek to Little Italy. I began again, this time blushingly compromising scientific accuracy by using single measures.

I explained that it is the effect of one activity upon another, like the relationship between a man's entering a room and the act of his removing his hat. If every time he enters he always removes his hat, the *coefficient of correlation* is plus 1; if he always keeps his hat on, the *coefficient of correlation* is minus 1; if fifty percent of the time he removes his hat, and fifty percent of the time he keeps it on, the *coefficient of correlation* is zero. It applies to all kinds of things, like the effect of thyroid on I.Q. Or the effect of a muddy track on horses.

"Track? Horses?" Punch was all attention now. "Say that again, Doc, about muddy tracks and horses!"

"Well, let's see," I said, "if I remember rightly, the concept of *coefficient of correlation* originated in England with some men who wanted to predict and control the results of cock fights."

"Predict and control! Now ain't them the sweet words! Now we're gettin' somewheres, Doc! You got a book I could read on it?"

That's how Punch happened to take over the statistical arm of our research.

My men were interested in my getting rich, one way or

another. Connie wanted to set me up with a penny arcade, which was his own dream. Gibbs assured me there was big money—of which he had none—in "interstate commerce." King had only to tap his own resources of counterfeit money. Punch was jumping to cut me into his race racket.

"Look, Doc—it's a system. All you gotta do is cross the state line and place bets with the bookie, like we tell you, an' you can't miss!"

A couple of weeks later he said very seriously, "Doc, how come you ain't placin' no bets? You want us to prove it's on the level? We'll keep the record right here an' let you see how much you could make in three weeks."

Up on the wall went an odds sheet, the horses to bet on for win, place and show, and how they came out in the actual race. For three weeks the men studied the chart during working hours. I studied it after they left. . . .

"Look, Doc!" wailed Punch, at the end of the period. "A thousand bucks you could have made from nothin'. You could make fifty grand this summer. A cool fifty grand! Made honestly, just on tips from nothin'. The system's unbeatable! They ain't nothin' wrong with it, it's legal!"

"Punch," I said "I notice you play the horses at only one track."

He grinned. "That's the only one the system works at, Doc."

But his ebullience, was, to use a word the men were exploiting at that time, evanescent. Soon after the next racing season opened Scott broke into a working period with an idle question that the men kicked around for the best part of an hour.

"Seems to me," he said, "we're hearing less and less of pari-mutuel these days. No races this year, Punch?"

"Yeah," said Gibbs, since Punch was silent, "the way Doc went through his first million he could use another one, quick!"

A few minutes later Connie added his bit. "Wonder if Doc'll

236

go through his second million like he did his first? Maybe it ain't worth it, huh, Punch?"

Punch flared up. "Doc had his chanc't last year. Can I help it if it's too late?"

"Too late?" asked Ross, "what happened to that foolproof system of yours?"

King the counterfeiter, had the last word. "The *coefficient of correlation*," he said, without looking up from his work, "developed a constant probable error."

Punch huffed, but said nothing. His silence meant, of course, that he had lost control of the races. He regained it later, however, in a dog-eat-dog episode starring T. (Big Skid) Hogan, whom my boys called "nationally infamous."

That American phenomenon, the big-time gangster, who mushroomed in the Prohibition era and still lingers on the national scene, is usually *persona non grata* in a prison population. There were always jokes and puns about the inability of the law to convict a gangster of any crime more serious than income tax violation. But these jokes highlighted the stupidity and cupidity of the police and the courts, not the cleverness of the gangster. Most of the latter were only as clever as their mouthpieces.

When one form of gangster rule was ending in Chicago, the Capones, Guziks and Druggans began checking in at the two Leavenworth penitentiaries before migrating to Atlanta and Alcatraz. When an especially famous character would be processed in our office, my boys would be extraordinarily business-as-usual.

Punch administered Al Capone's I.Q. test. The score was not much, even though Punch became so excited that he could lord it over the Great One that he forgot to operate his stop watch. The I.Q. had to be run a second time, and, when the Great One appeared for retesting, Punch leered triumphantly at him and said, "You didn't do so good last time, Al, so we gotta run it again. I swear to hell I don't see how you get nowhere with a I.Q. like that!" The elder statesman smiled witheringly at Punch. "Now, *wouldn't* you like to know!" That, I thought, took care of both of them nicely.

The rank and file of prisoners felt that living by one's own wits and fighting society alone was *bravura*, but the goon squad shakedown and the gorilla murders were considered un-American. These big-time gangsters were therefore never assimilated by the general prison population. And because of the probable presence of rival gangs among the population these big names were often kept in protective wards. The fewer the murders on the inside, the better the captain and the warden slept.

The gangster's use of his power for special privilege in prison was equally distasteful to the prisoners. They considered it a mark of superiority to have something on mayors, governors, attorney generals and Congressmen, and that it was smart to make these public figures squirm. But to precipitate a gubernatorial or Congressional investigation of a penitentiary for the sole purpose of obtaining a private room, outside privileges, special steak diets, or immunity from hospital routine, smelled rankly of class distinction. Such things are to be obtained by one's own cleverness, not through the intervention of powerful influences on the outside, they reason.

The one whom we have called T. Hogan was high on the list of Public Enemies, and epitomized the worst of all these qualities when he sullenly checked into our happy prison one day to serve a short sentence. It should have been a long one. He had so many things on so many important people on the outside, and he made so many complaints about his personal comfort, that high-ranking investigating committees came from Washington frequently to intercede for the long-suffering Skid. The warden was constantly on the carpet, furious but impotent. The committeemen were belligerent, driven by threats of exposure and the big ride. Hogan won nearly every time. The unwilling warden finally made him his chauffeur, thinking there he could keep his finger on Hogan. Eventually Big Skid had a private room on the courtyard, a special hospital diet, wore civilian clothes, and had outside privileges.

This kind of thing was devastating on prison morale. Punch, the only gangster in the penitentiary who was generally accepted by the rest of the convicts, became increasingly apoplectic at this open-faced discrimination. Or maybe he was only sick with envy. At any rate, Punch and Hogan tangled in the shower room one day. The captain scuttled to his files and frantically separated members of the opposing gangs into different work, dining, and recreation details.

Hogan was definitely a bigger shot than Punch, with more territory, money, men and influence. The aftermath of this shower room fight was what cost Punch his racetrack racket. And me my "second million."

Women, all convicts will tell you, are jinxes. Hogan found opportunity during his chauffeuring duties to set up his favorite moll in an apartment in the City. But that was too far away; he established another girl near by.

One of the molls learned about the other and tipped off the authorities in a fit of jealousy. In striking at her rival the squealing moll unwittingly delivered into the hands of the police fairly comprehensive records of the million-dollar track payoff.

She was killed in an "auto accident" the following week.

The warden gleefully clamped Hogan in solitary, first making sure that it would be very solitary. The committees who had recently championed Hogan were now obliged to approve the change of quarters and diet. Hogan lost his privileges, his influence, his gang and his loves in one day. He was done forever as a big-time operator. His henchmen outside divided his empire, and Punch quickly moved in his men and took back his lost racket.

"It's good weather an' a fast track, Boss!" He was stomping up and down the office one day after this crisis, calling off horses under his breath. "Like I said, Boss, the system's perfect. You can't miss!"

"But you said it was too late," I reminded him.

"The *coefficient of correlation* had developed a constant probable error, remember?" said Ross.

"Ah—" King murmured into his work, "The skewed correlation was attenuated for error. The formula is now valid and reliable."

12

THE GROWTH of prison population was a problem in a thriving institution such as ours. The cell blocks became badly overcrowded, and with our ingenious tenants this meant trouble. A couple of years under the 1930 reforms was not sufficient time to complete their reformation.

The new penitentiaries and hospitals being built in Pennsylvania, Missouri and Kentucky were still in construction, so the warden converted a former shop building and a storeroom into temporary quarters. Only trusties were assigned to the new quarters. (Gibbs was the only trusty in the office.) The future occupants were exuberant about the project, and cheerfully wielded hammers, saws and paint brushes during the heat of that second summer.

Since it was a temporary solution, considerable latitude was allowed in the remodeling. Wooden partitions were thrown up instead of cement cells. We all admired the convict's sound, functional cabinet work. How functional it was we could not know till later. We could not dream, in fact.

Curtains appeared from nowhere on the barred windows. An occasional good painting came from somewhere. Some of the occupants doubled up their sleeping space and built bunks to the ceiling in the larger rooms, leaving the alternate room free as a parlor. The place broke out in discarded hospital beds and army cots, in broken-down rocking chairs and a few overstuffed pieces, all reconditioned at the furniture shop, which also turned out some custom-made cabinets for prison-made radios.

They named the place "The Flats," and a large sign appeared outside: "Apartments—Furnished"—God only knew with what, certainly the warden did not. The machine shop worked out a facsimile of a lamp post with a street sign, "Sutton Square." Every free man in the penitentiary managed on one pretext or another to visit The Flats, and tea was kept brewing constantly as a matter of social courtesy. Nobody drank the stuff.

One day after a search for contraband, an inconspicuous and faultlessly lettered sign appeared on the door: "Open House— During Searches Only."

After several months of pastoral and connubial bliss, disaster fell on Sutton Square.

During a demolition search it was discovered that the cabinet work concealed secret panels and false compartments, and two contraband luxuries were unveiled. One was a Capehart radio and record changer wired to a few strategic headphones. The occupants bawled loudly when their collection of records was given to charity.

But the thing that really caused them anguish was the confiscation of their two electric refrigerators. One of these had been smuggled in ready for use by the simple device of changing an invoice to read *two* instead of *one*, when Laurie Kennedy had requisitioned a Westinghouse. The other one was smuggled in piece by piece over a period of weeks and assembled on the spot. It was not so much the stock of stolen delicacies that the men missed as it was the luxury during the summer of having ice cubes and the half-dozen stolen cans of beer a week.

After Ediphones, refrigerators and Capeharts, I was ready to believe the rumor that a baby elephant had appeared one morning in the courtyard of a brother penitentiary.

There are smugglings, however, that are far from ludicrous and that carry real pathos and tragedy.

One unrehearsed drama centered about a brooding wife who, taking a blind chance of finding her mate inside, climbed into a truck being loaded with groceries and vegetables for the penitentiary. Inside, one of the unloading crew spied her, and while the other men distracted the guard, he hid her in the storeroom until her mate could be reached.

No rendezvous in literature was more chastely guarded. Within an hour she was on her way out again.

In the memory of the oldest timer this had not been done before, and it gave the prisoners ideas. If one lone girl could get in unaided for a single rendezvous, what could be accomplished with selective brains and a little organization? I learned of this intrigue and of the complexity of this departure in engineering four months after it was launched.

More planning was devoted to this venture than a $200,000 bank job outside. There were problems. First, the girl had to be selected carefully. It had to be someone with plenty of nerve, who would not boast or squeal, and someone who was not associated with anyone inside who might get in trouble if she were caught. Someone named Maudie possessed all these stellar qualities.

But there were other problems. What would be the safest time of day or week? Which truckload would pass through the least number of gates? Which warehouse or storeroom represented the least hazards and headaches in the matter of search? These details were not simple to control in a penitentiary so well run as ours.

Boxes and crates were kept available as hiding places for the girl in case of unexpected trouble, or so that she could readily be carried from one building to another. Money arrangements were entered into by which part of her large fees

243

would be credited to the truckdriver who was taking a big chance of discovery in getting her inside.

Everything went smoothly the first few times Maudie was smuggled in, secreted behind boxes in the front of a covered truck. Then a guard became suspicious when he was diverted from his post. Discovery was averted only by the prisoner who was checking the bill of lading shouting, "That's all for the warehouse, the rest of this stuff goes to the storeroom!" The driver took the balance of the load posthaste to the kitchen.

Ingenuity in the face of the unexpected is the boast of all good men in a penitentiary. This sweet cargo was received with aplomb by the storeroom detail, well handled, and returned with gratitude.

Because of this hitch in plans, it was impossible to get Maudie out of the institution that day. She had to spend the night in the storeroom barricaded behind cases of catsup, condensed milk and string beans. One wag capped this pyramid with a can of spice.

The morning breakfast crew gleefully uncovered this cache. It was the most hilarious breakfast the prison had ever known. So many trips were made from the kitchen to the storeroom that, through a pardonable mix-up in count, a couple hundred extra eggs were prepared.

The mechanics of safely getting Maudie into and out of the institution once a week was not the only problem. There were social and moral headaches. There were specific seniorities and special privileges to consider. If the truck and garage details were responsible for transporting her, and the warehouse crew responsible for hiding her, and the kitchen force for feeding her, and the carpenter and metal shops for making a trick box in which to carry her, and a counterfeiting ring accounted for much of the money, then all should share the spoils, they reasoned.

But this was not easy. There was no place in the garage to

hide the girl. As the men said, no place for her to *work*. While there was plenty of working space in the warehouse, the crew was small and her talents would be unemployed. The largest gang was in the kitchen, but its storeroom was packed, and too constantly visited by guards to leave her there safely for long.

In desperation they did try the refrigerator in the kitchen once. But the girl objected, not so much to the sides of beef, whole hogs and chickens hanging around her, as to the temperature. This incident led to an endless play on words, such as, what a difference there was between hot and cold chicken, and how could she be cold when she was so hot?

Even with such well-laid plans and clockwork precision, complications developed. On a couple of occasions dispatch orders were changed and the truck re-routed or delayed. Maudie did not arrive. Twice a new driver was assigned to the truck who did not know of the plot and could not be trusted—because, of course, the whole venture was not public domain throughout the penitentiary. Once in a while the girl failed to connect with the truck coming in. The second time Maudie was unable to get out of the penitentiary at night, the men were apprehensive and sleepless, and the girl frightened. Again the suspicion of the guards was aroused, and under the urgency of a fast getaway the load in the truck shifted and injured Maudie. It took some time before another girl could be found who would take such risks.

In the meantime some of the prisoners lost heart. Others were determined. There must be a better, safer way to smuggle.

There was. A convenient accident to one of the trucks demolished the cab and sent it to the garage and metal shop for reconstruction. A false compartment was made in the new cab, partly behind and partly under the seat, with a trick panel opening. The truck was christened "Baby Bunting." The men were no longer worried about the guards. If it was inconvenient to unload the girl at one platform, the truck could be moved

245

to another place. When the coast was clear the trick door could be sprung and the human cargo released from the supposedly empty truck.

The prisoners were jubilant over their genius. But unforeseen complications developed. The compartment was small. The girl was too large. It took considerable search to find Trinket, a hundred-pound girl who still looked like a girl.

But Trinket made complaints. Compartment travel was cramped and uncomfortable. When she could not be unloaded for a couple of hours after arriving, she was seized with painful muscle cramps, and it was another hour before she could walk—or anything. On one occasion engine fumes overcame her. In summer the compartment was hot and in winter it was cold.

All these factors increased her fees enormously. The men calculated that she was probably the best paid girl in history. When newspapers published the annual income tax lists of the highest paid women in the nation that year, the boys were proud and scornful.

Look what Trinket makes in only one day a week, not counting bonuses!

Yeah, multiply that by fifty-two an' look where she is on the list!

An' no income tax to pay. What a racket!

Talk about worth her weight in gold, let's see: one hundred pounds times sixteen ounces times thirty-five bucks a ounce is fifty-six thousand—wow!

The exorbitant fees didn't concern the prisoners, since it was taken care of through counterfeit money and stolen goods.

Sex was so abstracted in the experience of many of the prisoners that they were more preoccupied with its symbols than with sex itself. They were disappointed that their smuggled sweets were wrapped in denims, and the fact that Trinket cut her hair and wore a cap in order to elude detection by the guards was a great blow to the men. They would almost have rather had free run of a girl's long hair and let it go at that than to pursue more rustic joys with someone sporting close-cropped hair. Security and discretion were therefore discarded.

The convict's swaggering about his sexual exploits actually obscures a pathetic fact. A very large percent of all criminal and psychologically inferior personalities are under par sexually. It's not that they won't—they can't. Being inadequate in this egoistic arena, they convert their sexual drive into flagrant behavior in crime, and sex as such is badly resolved in a preoccupation with its ancient fetishes, French heels, black silk stockings, long hair.

If such a personality can maintain a sufficiently crude and sadistic role in the eyes of his woman, she may never pause to reflect that he is a deplorable sexual partner. If he's loud, he's good. There is also undoubtedly something in the fact that a moll could hardly expect to use the word *impotent* in the presence of her lord without losing her front teeth. And there is definitely something in the fact that most of the Maudies and Trinkets of this world are themselves frigid, so that the wear and tear of life is probably not too great on either side.

Things went smoothly in the Cash-and-Tarry Department, until one raw fall night they could not get Trinket out of the institution. The inherent chivalry of the residents of Sutton Square proclaimed that ladies deserved warm beds. Trinket was smuggled into The Flats and placed in the secret Capehart compartment (this was before that commodity was confiscated), until after the evening count and check. After which she was royally entertained, in a manner of speaking.

The next morning when I arrived at the office Gibbs was impatiently waiting for me and began talking before I had removed my coat.

"Boss, I would like a pass to the upholstery shop." I waited, so he continued with a meekness that ill concealed his excitement and urgency. "I don't wanna give you no phony

247

reason, Doc, but I can't give you the real one now. I just need a pass, bad."

Following the marijuana episode the warden had issued directions tightening up on the pass system and all privileges. Gibbs read my thoughts.

"It's been almost two years, now, Doc, an' I never asked you for a thing."

"That's right, Gibbs. But under the new rulings, they're checking on every pass."

"Well, I'm a trusty and I could probably get by without one, but it's important enough that I don't want to work on a forged pass today. I want it so if they call you, you can say, 'Yes, I give him a pass.'"

I still did not know at this time about Baby Bunting's smuggling activities, and I did not suspect why Gibbs wanted a pass.

"There's a reason," he insisted, "that makes it legit. You give Connie a pass when you was here only four months, Doc."

I remembered, and wondered if this was a squeeze play—if every trust or courtesy I had indulged was going to be used coercively. But I signed the pass.

"You're uncanny, Doc." It was King who came up to me after Gibbs had left. "Some day you'll make a mistake. We all do, it's the law of chance. But you're uncanny. That's one signature you'll never regret."

Ross had a word too. "Let me tell you something, Doctor," he said. "A forger and a check artist has to know his man, or he'll get in trouble. I never cash a phony check anywhere except where there's a sign, 'No Checks Cashed.' If there are other signs, like in a grocery store, 'Our Business is Food, the Bank's Business is Money,' or 'Get Your Food Here, Your Money at the Bank,' I raise the ante. I know that man has been taken before, and I know the reason. It's his own distrust. So I hook him plenty. Don't worry about Gibbs, he won't double-cross you."

It was some weeks before I learned the purpose of Gibbs' request for a pass. He finally related it in detail.

It had to do with Trinket's night at Sutton Square. He didn't participate personally in the festivities—he was a family man, he reminded us—but he wasn't one not to know what went on.

"Poor kid," he said, "she didn't get any sleep all night. After all, how many mugs live at The Flats?"

They planned to get her out of The Flats and let her walk over with the early kitchen crew at dawn and wait for the truck in the warehouse. But a roaming guard watch killed that idea. They had to wait until the morning policing of barracks. It was not the regular laundry day, but all of a sudden the curtains had to be washed. The men packed Trinket into her box and covered her up with lace curtains.

Gibbs helped carry her out, and the entourage fell in with the cell block laundry detail. "It's a kick!" said Gibbs, "here we was in line, carryin' this heavy wooden box, an' everybody else was carryin' laundry baskets." One of the men stumbled under the weight. A wall guard became suspicious and called down. But the laundry gang knew what was going on. They deposited the girl in an idle washing machine. When the guards searched the baskets and the wooden box, they found only clothes and curtains.

The laundry gang developed a case of nerves. They wanted to get rid of the hot cargo. They shipped her as far as they could toward the warehouse. The first stop *en route* was the upholstery shop.

Here there was trouble. A conflict of motives and goals developed. The expediency of getting Trinket out of the penitentiary rapidly and without discovery was momentarily obscured by more immediate prospects. The vivid memory of Maudie's unexpected night in the kitchen storeroom and of the joyful uncovering of the cache by the breakfast crew was only a few weeks old. The shop men spirited her into a back room.

But the circumstances were different in this physical set-up. There was danger here in the cramped and supervised quarters.

Gibbs continued.

"Some of the level-headed guys was worried an' wanted to move her on, quick. But they had trouble with the hot-heads. Trinket was scared an' began to cry. Some of the cons didn't like this, an' told 'em to lay off.

" 'Why the hell should we? Everybody else gets a chanc't— we're not gonna be cheated!' An' pretty soon there was fights, the damn fools! An' somebody yells, 'Hey, Rube!' an' then everybody was off his nut. The guards call the reserves an' run the whole gang in. An' imagine it—this poor kid lyin' there all covered up with kapok an' cushions, an' all alone.

"That's when I badgered you for that pass, Doc. Aw, I know she's a chippie, but she's just a kid," said our family man, "an' the way she handled herself that night at The Flats kinda got under my skin. You know, Doc, this is silly, maybe, but she had a kind of class among all them stir bums. She sure did!

"Well, she would have been discovered for sure. So on my pass I hightailed it over there an' got in with the gang sent to clean up the cotton an' broken furniture after the fight. We got her onto the open truck covered up with the debris. An' then —ain't it always somethin'?—a couple guards hop on the truck just for the ride, and there she is headed for the incinerator! Well, this penitentiary ain't never seen a bunch of drier mouthed candidates than us. There was just no hope now.

"But you know that lout, Brody, who stuck up the same post office four times? Well, I never thought he had a brain in his head. The only thing he can do is ride a garbage truck. But no more. Jeez—is he bright. He's a genius! The truck slows down at the corner of the warehouse, see? Where you cut sharp to go out into the back lot to the dump. An' all the warehouse gang standin' on the platform helpless-like, knowin' what's on that truck, an' they can't do a goddamn thing! Well, Brody ridin' on the side of the truck gets an idea—all them mugs standin' there an' everythin'. So he falls, an' grabs the steering wheel an' cracks the left wheel into the corner of the warehouse, blows the tire an' bends the axle. Then he hollers, 'Hey, you—get some boxes, this cotton is gonna blow all over hell!' An' in nothin' flat there is half a dozen man-sized boxes an' twenty guys cleanin' up that truck. You couldn't see nothin' but men, just a blanket o' jackets an' denims. Anyways the guards is swearin' so at Brody that they ain't lookin'.

"Well, we got the kid inside, an' she was so scared she was shakin'. What she went through!" Kept up all night, dumped out of one box into another, covered up with clothes, hurt, shunted around, fought over, stepped on, left alone with guards, thrown into a truck, covered up with ticks and cotton, headed for the incinerator, mixed up in an auto accident, grabbed by her hair and heels, tossed into another box and covered up with cotton again!

Gibbs sighed. "We finally gets this one box back in the warehouse. But get a load of this, gang. An' Doc, maybe you can explain it, I don't know. Here they finally got Trinket safely hid, an' sent messages out to the garage an' gate crews to get the hell the truck in there, an' for the first time in a day you could take a easy breath. But nobody takes advantage of the situation or of Trinket. Now how d'you figger that? Maybe it was because she'd been such a soldier—maybe that's how martyrs get worshiped. Anyways, somethin' in her made them low-minded cons act decent for once, even when she offered to take a few of 'em on—which they wouldn't do, so help me! Boy, no queen could've had more comfort or respect among them packin' boxes, or more attention. Guys came around whenever they could manage it, just to look at her, to remember what a girl was like. How d'you like that, huh? Well—just before closin'

251

time she was curled up in her secret compartment, an' Baby Buntin' was on its way out. Jesus!"

Followed, I imagine, by the most audible sighs of relief since the dawn of time.

The prisoners were unanimous in their protective feelings about Trinket. They felt her ordeal merited sainthood, and certainly immunity from further risk. Trinket herself aided and abetted their *noblesse oblige* by flatly, emphatically, and irrevocably refusing to return.

The third girl provided a short, uneventful chapter which closed when one of the convicts set her up on the outside as his mistress, pending his release in two months.

There was some delay in making arrangements for the next girl, Emmy Lou, Gibbs told me later. The available stock of qualified girls was running low. But the fever of unrest among the men was alleviated by word that she was coming in with a load of steel on the Baby Bunting.

There was a foray of doubletalk when Baby Bunting's brakes threatened not to hold under the heavy load, and the driver headed the truck gingerly into the foundation to stop it.

"Hey, you goon! Don'tcha know what you're totin'?"

"Yeah—it ain't every day Bethlehem Steel pays us a visit!"

"You should show more respect for your cargo. You want to muss it all up?"

A large crew immediately fell to, unloading with an enthusiasm not provoked by Bethlehem Steel. But as the load shrank the crew became more restrained, and then painfully quiet.

When the Baby Bunting had rammed the foundation the pilings were displaced. They had gone straight through the secret compartment.

And clean through Emmy Lou.

The prisoners were terribly shaken, crazy with grief and guilt. There was no more talk of amatory missions.

No guilt could be conclusively attached to any one man or group of men inside. No penalties were invoked. The captain, watching the men's remorse, felt that the incident itself provided all the punishment the most morally astute could ask. The circuit had been completed: they had paid for their sins.

Father Dowd, the penitentiary priest, found it easy in his heart to pray for the soul of Emmy Lou, and to arrange her burial on the outside. The impression that she was buried in a potter's field was not openly denied on the inside, but we all knew that wasn't how it was. The men made up a purse for Emmy, and gave her more respectability in death than she could ever have had in life.

13

THE LIFE and trials of a penitentiary chaplain is a story that should be told by one of them. The role of religion in a penitentiary is a chaplain's story, too. My generalizations should not be construed as the total picture.

The convicts' use of religion was not much different from that of the ordinary non-churchgoer on the outside. There were few real atheists among them. However, their God was a very vengeful Gentleman indeed. They believed in God as they believed in the law—because they had offended it. But they wanted no traffic with either the law or God, if possible. They believed in hell and the Judgment, too. But they thought of hell in reference to someone they wanted very much to send there, rather than with any thought of going there themselves. They had their own eyes on a deathbed repentance to take care of their personal destinies. Anything ahead of that was definitely premature.

However, in disaster or epidemic or fire in the cell block, or the illness of someone's child, God would be ordered to come running on the double.

There were real conversions in the penitentiary, and the men knew one when they saw it. The real convert was shown respect and left alone. But every little while a Holy Joe was heard among them, the man who was not prudent enough to keep his salvation to himself. Usually there was little joy in his salvation; he was happy only when he was riding the iniquities of his cell-mates. His social status was about that of a leper, and his prognosis that of a potential squealer.

At the other end of the table of averages was the occasional black-hearted atheist who was as erratic as the Holy Joe and just as noisy. His career was even briefer than his shouting brother, but for quite another reason. The men were in a constant sweat about a Holy Joe because of his squealing potential. But the atheist they ignored. Without an audience his atheism paid him no dividends, and he soon learned to nurture his doubts in his own chest.

Between these extremes was the large body of men who insured their eternal glory by singing and weeping a little as they strung popcorn and cranberries for the Christmas trees, and by pouring a few salty confessions into the ears of the chaplains. Otherwise they expected to sit it out until the hour of death, when having been merry at leisure they would repent in haste.

All in all, it was hardly an ideal parish for the churchman with ambitions to realize in this world. The penitentiary chaplaincy was no easy go. The chaplains were men of many conflicting responsibilities and responses. They were given the same admonition regarding immunity that I was, but their religious conscience was much closer to them than immunity. When the two conflicted, what then? My case was much simpler. My job was not to convert, moralize or persuade. It was to listen, observe and record. Actually I did more than that, I hope, but still without impinging upon the ancient prerogatives of religion. My research data would have been prejudiced and weighted to the point of being invalid if I had allowed a churchly conscience to exercise itself. But I can see that it would be a thankless job for a chaplain to keep his responsibility to God, the Church, the Government, society, and the convicts, in ethical or even logical order, and still do a creditable job. I am sure I would have wanted many times to tell each and all of such responsibilities to go to hell under such a setup. Which wouldn't have done at all.

The Protestant and Jewish faiths, lacking the external color and drama of the Catholic Church, conducted their services in a classroom or from the bare stage in the dining room. The adherents of these two faiths were counseled by their chaplains in rather cheerless offices, by men as equally conscientious as Father Dowd, but without the sensuous backdrop supplied by Catholic mysticism.

The Protestant and Catholic chaplains worked differently in reaching the men. The Protestant chaplain met the convicts at other levels than religion. He was known as "the man with the ball" because he headed the athletic and entertainment projects of the men. At Easter, Thanksgiving and Christmas he brought festive touches from the outside world. At Christmas, for instance, he supervised the men in trimming and placing at least twenty-five trees throughout the prison, and brought in groups of carolers.

He and the warden's assistants worked together on the prisoners' weekly movie fare. The prisoners were not allowed either sex or crime movies. They hooted at this sociological order. They would single out some particularly grizzly butcher among them, and facetiously and laboriously explain to him that "nice little boys like you mustn't see such *bad* things! You wanna grow up to be a *bad* man?" Actually the directive prohibiting crime and sex films was not without rationale. If there is any doubt as to whether these movies glorify crime and sex, they should be viewed with the thought in mind of showing them to a group of criminals. The answer would clarify quickly. The men had their point, too. The movies learn from convicts, rather than convicts from the movies.

The Protestant chaplain worked closely with the warden

and the school principal in these duties, in an attempt at rehabilitation a little broader than religion *per se*.

The Catholic Church's concept of evangelism was in sharp contrast to this. It made no pretense of selling religion to the men under any name but its own. Her chaplain was looked upon only as the Voice of Religion, and capitalized on the power and pageantry of the Roman Church for appeal. The priest conducted services in the full dress regalia of his Order. The Catholics had their own chapel, a room in the cell block, where Father Dowd was busy the better part of every day doing battle with a terrifying real Catholic Satan for the souls in his grim parish. The priestly mediation in the Catholic faith appealed strongly to the convicts. It spared them the responsibility of keeping their own spiritual records straight. The confessional was as close as most of them wanted to get to God. After that, they put it up to the Father and the Most High to make those weekly soul searchings redound to God's glory and their good. Father Dowd rapped their knuckles frequently for their laziness, his own spiritual life being vigorous and disciplined.

Although our work kept us busy at different points inside, I had more than a nodding acquaintance with Father Dowd and a lot of admiration for him. He was fifty-odd, small and wiry, with short gray hair and sharp gray eyes. The only clerical mark on him was his contemplative walk. He was a tenacious little man and, I suspected, if necessary, tough. He had a lived-in face, with plenty of smiles around his eyes and worries on his forehead. He was a solid, earthy man, more genteel than gentle. He had a respectful, absorbed way of listening that made one feel he was the kind of man God would be smart to talk to when He had anything special to say. He could be disappointed without being discouraged, and in a penitentiary this was essential equipment.

He was standing at the door of the chapel in the cell block trying to light a stubborn pipe when Gordon and I stopped to greet him one day. I gave him a light, and through a gust of smoke he fixed his eye on me.

"Young man," he said mischievously, "do you know that in spite of my prayers and my graces I have not yet gotten you inside my chapel? You've been here over a year, and you've not even seen it, let alone worship in it."

"I can't be that busy, can I?" I asked Gordon. "But you haven't been to my office either, Father."

"That's true," he said, "but that's different. What would a priest be doing in a psychologist's office?"

Certainly not worshiping, I said.

He chuckled.

"I sometimes think you and I should be able to work out a deal, Doctor. You tell these rascals what's wrong with them and I'll tell them what to do about it. What do you say to that?"

"Sounds great," I said. "I wish it were that simple."

"Yes," he said quietly, "it's not that simple, is it?" But he brightened again. "Now then—how about a look at the chapel? I can promise you, you'll get a real surprise. Or does he know?" he asked Gordon.

"Absolutely unsuspecting," replied Gordon.

"Fine! Come along." He emptied his pipe, slipped it into the pocket of his short black clerical coat, and the three of us went into the chapel.

It was small, seating perhaps two hundred men, and not ornate in the usual Catholic tradition. The walls and floor were concrete like the rest of the cell block, the ceiling no higher than an ordinary room. As we stood just inside the entrance, a shaft of sunlight struck one of the rear windows in such a way as to throw the shadow of the bars across the floor at our feet. In spite of this momentary orientation we were unmistakably in another world, set apart from our environs by the unearthly quiet, the cedarlike smell of incense, and the warmth of candlelight.

The chapel was long and narrow in shape, with two-thirds of its length given up to pews on either side of a center aisle, and the rest to the appointments of the Catholic service: the pulpit, the confessional, the baptismal font, the communion rail, the tiny pump organ, the votive rack, and the altar. Much of the light in the chapel emanated from the sanctuary at the front, where the white and gold altar took the eye, as it was designed to do. It completely dominated the room.

"You're right, that's a surprise," I said. "Marble in a penitentiary. A white marble altar."

The priest glanced at Gordon.

"Come along," he said to us, "it's better seen down front."

My eyes were becoming accustomed to the semi-darkness, and as we moved down the aisle I noticed the paintings which hung on either side of the room, the stations of the cross. I was not a connoisseur of such things, but the reproductions seemed faithful in composition and color. The frames were carved to a depth of almost an inch, well wrought and matched, though no two of them were exactly alike.

"You must have a generous benefactor," I said.

We were in front of the altar now. At the priest's suggestion I stepped into the sanctuary and laid my hand on the altar. It was wood which had been sanded, polished, and painted to resemble marble.

Rejoining Gordon and Father Dowd on the sanctuary steps I asked, "What's the story behind it?"

"The benefactor you mentioned," he replied. "One of my altar boys. Chap named Ward. He made it."

"A prisoner?"

"A prisoner, yes," he said quietly. "He's been with me a long time. You see, I have quite a famous altar boy."

Gordon coughed discreetly. "When we use that word 'famous' around here, Wilson, we usually mean *in*famous."

The priest smiled goodnaturedly. "My altar boy was a

counterfeiter," he explained. "But for the last two years he has used his talents to more constructive ends. He was a rascal when he came to us, I can tell you. But I felt from the first that he had the soul of an artist."

He led us behind the altar where there was a small working space the width of the chapel and not more than nine feet in depth. A partition had been thrown up. On one side of it the priest had his desk and effects. On the other side, surrounded by incense pots and candle snuffers, the counterfeiter, Ward, worked out his salvation.

He was a little nervous sprite of a man with pale eyes and skin, perhaps forty years old, who, when we came in, was patiently carving a piece of statuary. In either self-effacement or insolence he took no notice of us, and Father Dowd went on talking as if Ward were not present.

"Ward's a trusty, and my right-hand man. Besides this work and his service in the chapel, he is my chauffeur when I go to the Cathedral in Kansas City. While I'm attending my affairs there, he sits by the hour in the church, studying the statuary and the appointments of the altar. As you see, he's working on a statue of the Blessed Virgin for us now. It's wood, too, but when it's finished you won't be able to distinguish it from its marble sister in the Cathedral."

The priest looked fondly at his altar boy.

"I'm really very proud of Ward!"

Every once in a while after that Father Dowd and I pooled our impressions of the incongruities, both humorous and tragic, inherent in prison life. One morning several months after my visit to the chapel, he and I met as he was arriving for the day. I could see by his preoccupied air that he was about to turn *raconteur* again. The tone in which he said, "Ah, I was just thinking I must look you up, Doctor!" led me to believe this might be a rather special piece.

We went into the chapel and sat down together in the last row of pews. He was thoughtful for a moment.

"You've already heard, of course," he began. I hadn't, but he continued without waiting for my answer. "These boys just can't take good fortune, can they? They've distrusted everyone too long, I guess. Lord knows, I've been here long enough not to have any illusions about them, but I had really begun to feel sure for once." He shook his head sadly. "The rascal really let me down!"

In a pause I put my question. "Who is it, Father?"

His brows shot up. "You *don't* know?"

He was quiet for a moment, thinking, smiling, scowling, not quite sure which he should be doing. "You know, this story should be told over a second bottle of rare wine somewhere, doctor, instead of in my hard pews. But it makes good telling, even with a clear head. You see, it's really a joke on me. It's Ward."

"Your altar boy? The artist fellow?"

He nodded. "All the while I've been bustling about in my pride, I've been *particeps criminis* with Ward in the making of counterfeit money! Right here, Doctor, behind my altar—behind *his* altar! Isn't that good, really?"

The priestly chuckles came unrestrained now.

"I've been buying him brushes, paints, inks, carving tools, drawing boards, and he has been making his dummies and his plates right under my nose! And those ridiculous processions to the city. He has driven me in, and while I was pursuing my soul's good he has been delivering his plates to the presses just ten blocks from the Cathedral! Quite a direct route, don't you think, from organ loft to printing press?"

I smiled with him.

"He would have been out in four weeks," he continued "Think of it—four weeks! I had even found a job for him, reproducing works of art for a museum. Well, I'll have him on my hands now for many, many years."

"At least *you* won't have to choose how he will do penance," I said.

"No. And I'm sure that in the next ten years the warden will keep him away from drawing boards and pencils and carving tools. I'm afraid those delicate hands may have to do a little road work. The soul of an artist and the heart of a counterfeiter. Well," he sighed, "I won't say I won't miss him. He was a fine artisan and a good altar boy. Then again, I won't say I will miss him, either. It's been quite a strain. . . ."

Again he paused to scowl and smile.

"You haven't a nice rugged fisherman or a farmer for me, have you, doctor? A stevedore, perhaps? Someone with big knuckles and clumsy feet, who will trip over the incense pot? I think in my declining years it would give me considerable peace to have less artistry and more piety behind me at the altar!"

14

At the end of my second year at the penitentiary I had a two months' tour of duty in which I visited hospitals, medical schools and penitentiaries throughout the East, to study the findings and techniques of other institutions in a project such as ours. My own vacation period followed, and I planned to spend the time in and near New York.

The boys were impressed by the return addresses on the communications that came in response to my requests for appointments. It was the nearest they had come to the right side of any famous institution. I became their projected ego and their emissary to the outside. They could not have been more excited if they had been planning to accompany me. I was bombarded with the names of people and places where they assured me I would be expected, and with greetings and messages to deliver. Their *bon voyage* present was their own extra-curricular itinerary for me.

Connie spoke for the group. "Doc, you say one of your jobs is to get the lowdown on the criminal. You can't do that in the pen. You can't tell nothin' about a con when he's shavin' Ediphone cylinders." His memory must have played him tricks at the mention of cylinders, because he added sheepishly, "Well, nothin' much, anyhow— Now, in Chicago, here is the best dive on the North Side. An' on the West Side here is a contact place. An' this is a bookie joint. An' this number just off the Avenue'll

263

take your call orders. You've been learnin' your stuff outta books an' at conventions, an' you're doin' all right, under the circumstances. But here you can learn about real and petty crime right where it lives. An' Doc, you don't need to worry about goin' to any o' those joints. Somebody'll look out for you, you won't get hurt."

Punch was horrified at my modest hotel reservations. I tried to explain that I wouldn't be able to pay my way in his class.

Connie shook his head. "There he goes, talkin' about money again!"

"What about King here," Punch persisted. "He's hopped bells in the best joints in the country. With his connections he could get you in anywhere. And as for skirts, King—"

"Lay off, stupid!" growled King. "You didn't get anywhere with Doc on the ponies, and you won't on this. I'll make my own deal with Doc!"

Ross asked me to salute a park bench at the Battery.

He had sat there once, he said, looking at the Statue of Liberty, hoping she would make some sense out of everything.

"And did she?" I asked.

"No, but maybe she figured I'd come to my *own* senses some day. In a penitentiary, of all places. . . ."

Scott's home town was on my itinerary. I asked him if I could run any errands, see any people. He was polite but brief. "No messages, Doc."

The main meal was served at noon in the penitentiary, and for a man to miss his dinner voluntarily was an event that astounded his fellow-prisoners. One day, as plans for my trip were rounding out, King remained bent over his drawing board one noon when the other men left for the dining room. Although he appeared engrossed in his drawing, he looked like a man with something on his mind who was going to have a bad time getting it out. I walked casually over to his desk.

"I've watched you draw that same girl for two years," I said, "what's the story? Is she real?"

"She's real, all right," he said, without looking up. "You'll see. At least I hope you will."

He laid down his pencil, but he still did not look at me. "You don't know much about me, do you, Doc?"

I replied that at least I knew there was a beautiful girl in his life, and that was something. "From here she looks very special."

"I want you to meet her when you're in New York," he said abruptly.

"Fine," I said. But I wondered why.

"She lives in my suite at the hotel." He tried to sound matter-of-fact.

"Something you want me to do for you, King?"

"No. I just want you to meet her and talk to her."

I must have shown some hesitation, because he burst out "What the hell, Doc! I've been watching *you* for two years too —I know what I'm doing!"

He knew my itinerary, he knew I could arrange the meeting if I wanted to, and that no infraction of rules was involved. I was hoping he would fill in the background a little, but that wouldn't have been like King. He was waiting for my answer.

"Sure, King, I'd like to meet her."

He looked up. "Thanks, Doc."

When I saw his expression of relief I wondered again what was in his mind in arranging the meeting. Back in my office I began to think seriously about it.

King had a disdain and contempt for people. He wanted approbation, like the next man, but only from "quality." He had little access to "quality" with his prison record and his pathological predilection for counterfeit money. Now, perhaps, for once in his life, he had a treasure: this girl; and he wanted to display her to someone. Someone who met his approval. I was going to New York, I was his man. Perhaps my going was making him acutely aware of his loneliness. King was a lonely man, had been all his life, in or out of prison. A counterfeiter can't indulge a lot of friends. It's too great a risk. He has to work alone. Furthermore, King's basic disdain for people made him few friends, and he would have no way of knowing how much he needed them. Now I was going into his old environs, and in what could have been his first overt gesture in many years, perhaps he was asking me to share his loneliness and his life for a brief moment, to see his private "museum." If my conjecture was right, this was quite a step for King, one which I had not anticipated.

A few minutes later he came and stood in my door.

I looked up.

"I'd like to have you stay in my suite while you're in New York," he said.

"I'd like to, King," I said. Was *this* part of the background I had hoped for? "But—"

"Okay, Doc," he said, "I know—rules and regulations."

My inhibitions were considerably more personal than a prison handbook, but I let it go at rules and regulations, since that was the way he had put it.

"Anyway," he continued, "check into the hotel, will you? I'd like to think you were staying there, even for a couple of days."

Before I could remind him of my other commitments he went on.

"Ask for my pal, Tony, the bell captain. He'll get you a room. Talk to him when he's off duty. He's expecting you—" He flushed at the slip, but went on. "And here—" he handed me a marked theater sheet from *The New Yorker*. "Take her to this play for me, will you? She doesn't go out—" I had the impression he had not meant to say that either. He was excited. He went on quickly: he had bought into the play, and he'd have Tony get my tickets if I would tell him when I wanted them.

I thanked him, but said maybe I'd better pay for the tickets, as the book said.

He smiled sardonically. "Okay, Doc, that'll make it legal."

Just before he went back to his desk he spoke again.

"One more thing, Doc." His voice was different now.

"Yes?"

He struggled for a moment. Then, "Her name is Marian."

The act of telling me the girl's name was probably the hardest and the biggest thing King did that day. The rest had been inconsequential enough: the girl in the drawings was real, she lived in his suite, she was never seen in another man's company, she was his. He owned her as he did the play, in the same sense of ownership.

But when he repeated her name, she came alive on his lips. He gave her status and place when he gave her a name. Looking at him, I thought perhaps he was realizing it, too."

"Marian," I said. "I'll remember."

I was not surprised on my trip to be accosted at hotels and penitentiaries by a man with a greeting for me to carry back to someone, or by an anxious girl: "Tell the mug I'm awful worried about him, I heard he got solitary. Won't he never get no sense? When'll he get out?"

When my tour of duty was over and my vacation began, I went to see Tony at King's hotel in New York. He was expecting me, all right. He was anxious to talk about King and asked numberless questions. It was easy to see he was fond and proud of his friend. And as he talked I knew King had sent me to New York for another reason than to see his museum. He wanted me to get his story from his friends.

"Does he still manicure his nails all the time? God, is he fastidious! He always was, even when we were kids in Washington. King hung around the Capitol, used his connections and ended up with a page boy job. After that he was always working

267

odd times at an embassy party, a formal ball or a debut, as a bus boy or waiter. He was always hanging around the best hotels, just watching, y'know?

"Seeing them quality dames and debs did something to him. He was crazy about them. He would do anything to be around those high-powered women. He would come home and draw them all the time. They never knew anything about it.

"After his page boy term was up, we hopped bells. One day, all of a sudden, he took up engraving at school. Then he got his old boss, who was a senator, to get him in the mint. It was just a step from there to counterfeiting. There ain't nobody can make counterfeit like King. It's perfect, like everything he does. He only wanted counterfeit so he could buy the real thing, Doc.

"And, boy, could he pick out the real thing a mile away! For years now he's turned his back on the ordinary guests and made the other boys carry their bags. He'll only work with quality folk.

"You know something, Doc? He's rich. He owns property and businesses. He keeps his suite here all the time he's in stir. Pays rent on it a year in advance. He won't give it up. He held it that way one time before, too. The management thinks he's crazy, but he sure knows how to get along with the guests. They think here he's on a trip to Europe. He lives a double life, got sent up from his "business address" in Cleveland under another name, and the dicks never traced him here, he's that careful and clever. And you know, with all that money he won't give up hopping bells? Says that's his only contact with people of quality. I don't get it. He owns a place in Connecticut, but he cuts the neighbors cold.

"And something else. He bought his businesses and his property with counterfeit, but nothing is counterfeit now. He pays his penthouse bills with real dough. He gives his girls real dough. He never lets them have anything but the best. He never lets them wear costume jewelry. It's got to be the real rock, see? All his girls are beautiful, and if they know what's good for them, they don't doublecross him. One of 'em did once." He glanced at me.

"And?"

He looked away. "She ain't beautiful no more. When he gets moody he don't paint. He carves wood. Beautiful jobs, with those hands of his. Everything's got to be perfect. If his girls or their dresses ain't dainty, all hell's to pay, or else they're gone."

"What do you mean, gone?" I asked.

"Gone? Just gone, that's all. They ain't here no more."

"And what do you mean, girls?"

"Oh. There's always one special girl, Doc. But there's always another one, sometimes two. It's funny, sometimes King and his girls live here together.

"Look, Doc," his face wrinkled with earnestness, "King says I can go the limit with you—trust you, I mean. He's a great guy —tell me, what's wrong with him? He ain't a queer, nothing purple about him. But he never touches those kids. Imagine it! Dames like that, and he just draws and paints 'em, worships their clothes, and never lays a hand on 'em! He all the time arranges call girls for the guests, but he won't take no cut—money, or tricks for himself either. What's wrong with a guy like that? What's wrong with a girl that sticks to him?"

I met Marian that evening in King's suite. Tony arranged the meeting. I still had his question on my mind: *What's wrong with a girl that sticks to him?*

When I looked at her I couldn't see that anything was wrong. She was lovely. Perhaps twenty-three or twenty-four, an auburn-haired, brown-eyed girl with sparkle and hauteur and delicacy. A Broadwayite with a Bar Harbor brow. She wore an extravagantly simple apple green gown with a brooch of emeralds at her throat and a square emerald on her finger. She held out her hand and greeted me warmly.

"I've seen hundreds of drawings of you, Marian," I said, taking her hand, "but I've always thought you were a fantasy. King was right, you're very real."

She shook her head, smiling. "It's King who was wrong, Doctor. I'm afraid I am a fantasy to him."

There's one answer for Tony, I thought. She doesn't like being a fantasy.

When she excused herself to mix a cocktail, I took the opportunity to look around the home of my boy, King. His museum. Like Marian, the suite was simple, elegant, full of light. The colors were soft yellows and tart blues. The blonde modern furniture was obviously custom-made. Its opulent austerity was obviously King.

I walked to a large window and looked down upon the most exciting city in the world just lighting up for the night.

"It's beautiful from up here, isn't it?" She was beside me, with a martini.

Against the early evening sky the city flashed like an open jewel box. I said so.

It was an illusion that cost King a lot of money in rent, she said. He loved it because it spared him the noise of the city below and brought him only its excitement, its fantasy.

Then she asked seriously, "How does he bear it in prison, Doctor? How can he build an illusion in a cell?"

I was about to say that he was living for the day of his release, when I realized that this was only partly true. Instead I said that he was working hard in the office in the daytime, and reading in his cell at night, which didn't leave him much time for illusion.

She gave me an inquiring look. "Do you mean he's no longer *trying* to build an illusion?"

"Is that good news?" I asked.

"Oh, *yes*—the best!" She raised her glass to her lips. I felt she was drinking to King. "But he's my man, you know, right or wrong," she added, in a voice I would have liked King to hear.

We left soon after that for dinner.

Everyone knew Marian. The headwaiter at the very exclusive restaurant, the doorman at the theater, the usher who seated us. They were pleased and surprised to see her. She was cordial and happy. Her brown eyes were as luminous as the jewel box I had seen from her window. She was not the only beautiful girl on Broadway that night, but I would not have exchanged her for anyone I saw. The debutantes seemed either petulant or cold beside the elegant young woman at my side, the young queen with the excited eyes.

King's play was entertaining. But even in her enjoyment of a reprieve from solitude, I knew she would rather have been talking about King. Back in the suite later, she launched directly into the subject.

"I think you know you're the first man King has respected for many years. I'm terribly glad. He needs something I can't give him." She waited for me to speak. I did not want to direct the conversation, so I said nothing. She went on. "I'd like to tell you about him."

She sat tense on the edge of the divan.

"It was wonderful to be in the theater tonight. I was a dancer when I met King. Did you know?"

"I knew only that you were the girl in his sketches, and that your name was Marian," I said. "He told me a few days before I came East."

For one season she had known almost everyone on Broadway. "Dancers, actors, directors, musicians, choreographers, all kinds of people." She paused. "The theater will always be full of happy ghosts for me."

And before that? I asked.

She grinned. "College."

I knew something about college girls. I could not think of her as ever having been a scrubbed and bouncing coed. But still she could have been, until some powerful enlightenment came to her, something that struck her down and sobered her and left her with this haunting air. It would have been more than love, the love of just any young buck. You could rise from the ravages of that kind of love unmarked. Her enlightenment had been King.

She had been the ordinary stage-struck college girl, she said, upper middle class. Her parents had thought the dance drama at college was fine, but the stage was something else. Marian had not thought so. She was given a small spot in a musical comedy. "One of those dances about a dance, full of symbolism."

King began coming to performances. For fourteen nights he sat where she and I had that night, front and center on the aisle. He always came just in time for her spot and left immediately afterward. But he did not try to see her otherwise. He soon became backstage gossip: when would Marian meet her dark and sinister love?

"I wondered, too," she said, "he was a hard man to forget! Then one night, after the performance, he summoned me to his suite in a high-handed note. I wasn't a child. I thought I understood what the note meant. I shouldn't have gone. I almost didn't. I've often wondered why I did." She turned to me, her Bar Harbor brow thoughtful. "Can you tell me, Doctor?"

I shied. "I thought ladies liked high-handed summons."

She laughed. "Not every man can get away with it. King can. The truth is, I couldn't have stayed away. I had to know the man behind that dark, brooding face. I'm still trying." She smiled ruefully. "I didn't make much progress that night. He was brutal to me. Utterly indifferent. For two hours he sat there—" indicating a chair, "watching me, while I sat here, floundering on shop talk. Then he told me to strip. Just like that. There was no sign of emotion. It was almost as if a doctor had said it—but different, too. I couldn't be indignant, it would have been silly. I started for the door.

"Without getting up, he said, 'Take your clothes off. I want to sketch you.'

"Well—I stayed.

"He sketched me in silence for an hour. Then he handed me something. It was money. 'That's all,' he said. 'Good night.' I was furious!"

That's my boy, all right, I thought.

"But he knew what he was doing." She was smiling. "I went home in a stupor." She glanced at me. "You'd say I've never recovered from it. You're probably right. He has this way with him. . . . He gives promise of so much, and you wonder if it is good or evil— And then suddenly it doesn't matter. And even when he doesn't fulfill the promise, it's always there."

After a moment she took another tack.

"I'm a dancer. A dancer has to have an audience. King is a magnificent audience. I would rather dance and pose for King than for any audience in the world. It's a kind of orgy, without his even touching me. When the show closed, it was no hardship to give up a chance to go on the road and so I moved into this suite."

I waited for her next words, because they were coming hard.

"Then I learned I was to be only a fantasy. He says my beauty is unworldly, that that's what he likes about it. He has never touched me. He has never told me he loves me, but I know he worships me, as an idealization. It's thrilling, but frightening sometimes. And lonely." She looked suddenly lost.

"What do you do, now that he isn't here?"

"I've gone back to college. For him. I'll get my Master's degree next year, in drama. His release will be so near commencement that he'll have to fly back."

Then she was full of urgency.

"Will he get out, Doctor? Is everything all right? A degree would be meaningless without him, it's the nearest I'll ever come to a wedding. Don't let him get in trouble—please keep him

273

from losing his temper! He doesn't know what he's doing when he loses his temper. He—"

She checked herself sharply. But a moment later her urgency dissolved. "I'm sorry. I've never talked about him to anyone before. I'd like to tell you everything—that's the way he wants it." And she relaxed for the first time since we had sat down together.

"I'm terribly in love with him. I don't quite know why. It hasn't been easy."

He loved a girl, she said, only when she was whole and beautiful. If she became ill, she could not stay in the suite. She was sent to the hospital, and she must recuperate quickly. He would not see her when she was ill. If she were in an accident, it was all right if she were not marred or disfigured. There had been another girl who had broken an ankle, and when it healed it was larger than the other. She had been sent away. *They're just gone,* Tony had said. King would not have deformity or ugliness or age in his girls.

I asked her about the other girls.

"There can be only one girl in his mind at a time," she said. "He knows that, and I know it, too. At the moment I'm that girl. But there's always another at the edge of the ring, in case I slip, or am wrong, or become ill. I know that in less than ten years I'll be too old for him. I'll never make thirty-five. But I want him as long as I can have him."

In a pause she asked, "Are you feeling sorry for me?"

I was, but not in the sense she meant. "No," I said, "I think you're doing what you want to do. Aren't you?"

If the question surprised her she gave no sign. Finally she said quite simply, "There was a time when I could have left. Now I wouldn't if I could."

It was then that I began to listen even more intently.

In some ways it was a good life, she said. He didn't deny her beauty or her brains. It was only her body that he denied. But he drew what he denied, and she was hoping that some day he would be led from the one to the other.

"It isn't the privation that hurts, it's his denial of me. I don't want just any man, I want King. But I want *him*, not his drawings. I want to be what he sees when he draws me."

She went to a cabinet and returned with a portfolio of drawings and paintings. The models were girls, most of them Marian. They were all beautiful, warm and promising.

Then she brought a sealed package from the cabinet which contained engravings and etchings. No one had seen the collection, she said. He had asked her to show them to me. The subjects here were locomotives, ships, skyscrapers, bridges, as well as nudes, among whom Marian again figured prominently. All of them revealed, in what approached dissociated automatic drawing, the erotic content of King's driven mind. It was a close view of his pathology: his preoccupation with phallic symbols in the face of his celibate life.

"I have been with King for years," she said. "I have posed for weeks and months in this kind of intimacy, and he has never touched me. What is it he feels, Doctor? Is it love, or hate?"

She crossed the room and stood before a picture which hung with its face to the wall. She turned it around. I joined her, and my eyes opened involuntarily. The picture was of a young girl with ugly fresh scars across her face and breasts. Even the horrible mutilation could not efface her beauty. Her eyes were closed; her mouth was hopeless.

I glanced at Marian. She was gazing calmly at the picture.

"He keeps this here as a warning to me."

There was no rebuke in her voice, to my amazement. From her manner I thought she must have looked at the picture so frequently that it had lost its horror for her.

"It happened a long time ago," she went on calmly, "before I knew King. When he first had enough money to buy luxury and quality. When he first began counterfeiting. He didn't finish high school himself, but he wanted a college girl and a lady. She said she was from Randolph-Macon. He told me that, when he learned that she was not Southern and had never gone to college, he tied her to the bed and did *this* to her, day after day, in this apartment. Then he let her go."

Under the shadow of that devastating picture she was saying something like, "He didn't paint or draw for a long time after that. He did these etchings and engravings, and carved figures. It was a healing thing, I guess."

He carved figures! No wonder he hated and feared Davis. Davis carved figures, too.

The probable sequence of events in the puzzle of King's shadowy life had begun falling into place when I had talked to Tony that morning. When Marian turned around the picture on the wall, the last pieces were accounted for. It was the final display King had wanted me to see in his museum.

Only one missing piece had to be supplied: the original childhood incident which had assaulted the unstable ego of a sensitive boy and affected the whole course of his afterlife. It was not a difficult piece to supply, however. The subsequent events were so classic and familiar in their progression that no psychologist of any experience need consult his imagination to determine the nature of the original shock. It was not a wild conjecture that King's childhood trauma had been on a sexual front.

It could have occurred in one of several ways. He may have been shocked to find in his otherwise respectable middle class parents an obscene sense of humor that broke out occasionally in a foul exclamation or a crude joke. Perhaps beneath their respectability they held a lewd concept of sex, an incongruity not at all uncommon, and had tried to pass it on to their children. Or, perhaps, King who was not a large man and no doubt had been a small boy, had suffered from physiological comparisons with larger boys or with his father in the easy nudity of a family situation. Perhaps he was ridiculed because he was "small," and developed an organ inferiority, an incipient castration complex. Any of these could have given a sensitive child negative connotations about sex—even a fullblown trauma—while a more robust ego and nervous system would be unaffected by them.

An analyst would say that in the light of future developments King's childhood trauma could have been caused only by his having witnessed his parents in coitus, that one night when the parents believed the children were asleep they were not. Or at least King was not. It might have been that the parents were not cautious, but I rather think this would not have been the case. King's references to his childhood indicated a formidable moral sense on the part of his parents. In fact, their very uprightness would only deepen the shock of a child witnessing coitus. It is not an act that a child should witness. There is nothing in the emotional equipment of a child that prepares him for it. He might understandably hate his father for what would seem to a child an unspeakable aggression toward and degradation of his mother. The accompanying movements and sounds would be received by a civilized child as those accompanying pain and aggressive attack, perhaps torture, not pleasure.

It is not hard to imagine the shock to a child of such a scene. It has launched more than one upon a sadistic career. He had been taught to respect his parents, he was disposed to love them, and now he found them in this unspeakable rite in the middle of the night. What was he to think? Every moral sense which had grown out of his relationship with his parents had been violated. They were bad. It was wrong. *He would never have anything to do with sex.*

Assuming that this was the nature of his trauma, how would he look upon his own young body when he made his toilet the next morning? How would he look upon his parents at the breakfast table? Life would never seem the same after that night.

A child need not be over-sensitive, impressionable and suggestible to be sexually traumatized by any of the possible routes mentioned above. But King probably was over-sensitive and impressionable. How he would resolve his sexual needs in the future, whether normally or through homosexuality, sadism, or aestheticism, or a combination of these, would indicate the depth of his trauma.

King must have been around fifteen when he received an appointment as page boy on the floor of Congress. This was quite a distinction. It meant that he had been an exemplary youth, with such outstanding qualities that he came to the attention of a man or group of men who sponsored him. It was a competitive and highly selective job. However he was handling his trauma at that time, it was not reflected in antisocial attitudes. He was a good boy, a very good boy. His parents, who had distilled in him the class distinction of "Don't try to play with the rich kids on the next street—don't get any fancy ideas, you're just a poor boy", must have been surprised and proud.

With this class distinction ringing in his ears, he went to work in one of the most glamorous chambers in the nation. It would be easy there for a boy to fall into illusions of grandeur. Perhaps King began to dream.

But he was a bright boy. Soon he began to realize that some of his bosses, some of those fine white-haired gentlemen, some of those earnest young men in the chambers, were reaching their goals not by altruistic dreams, but by not letting their right hand know what their left hand held. He learned about graft, bribery, coercion. Some of those men were phonies, he felt.

There is no reason to believe that King was anything but an altruistic boy. He came to the Capitol full of idealism, and suffered there the second trauma of his life: another disillusionment. His parents were phonies, his bosses were phonies. He had lost his emotional equilibrium as a child, and now, instead of fixing his attention on examples of integrity and honor around him, he allowed himself to be hurt by examples of dishonor. He fell into the second disillusionment more easily than he would have if the pattern had not been established by the first.

To supplement his income when Congress was not in session, the page boy became a bell boy in a famous diplomatic hotel in Washington. In this role he was further exposed to the secret workings of committees and to immorality and promiscuity in high places. He had his first contact with commercialized sex when he found girls being supplied to guests. He learned that respected political figures were sleeping one night with a prostitute and the next with a social equal. Having an eye now for phoniness, he found it easily. This realization came very close to his childhood sexual trauma; he retreated further from normal sex drives, deeper into his revulsion.

At the end of his term as a page boy, according to Tony, he worked full-time at the hotel. It was hopping bells that gave King his first contact with the beautiful high-powered women Tony had mentioned. He served them in their hotel suites, in the dining room, at embassy parties and state functions, where he frequently served as bus boy in order to watch them. They were desirable but inaccessible, and that was just how he wanted it. He could look at them and admire them, but he wanted nothing more to do with them.

He began to draw them. The women never saw the drawings. He had no desire to show them. He did them for himself. He did not court the women, or meet them secretly, although Tony had told me that both debutantes and matrons made open plays for the dark brooding bellboy and waiter. Their overtures repelled him. They hurt his quality concept. Why should *they* want anything to do with *him*? He wanted only to draw them.

This was his first solution of his sexual needs: a sublimation of them in his art. His drawings were never pornographic. However minute his preoccupation with physiological detail, his women were not gross. They were almost spiritual in their sensuousness. They were a reflection of King's own passion for beauty and his own need of love. If King were to be salvaged in time, it would be because of his love of beauty and his ability to express it in his art. But for a while it led him head-on into dark and sinister forces in his nature that no one would have suspected.

His first philosophical misstep was to attach his love of beauty and quality to unfortunate life goals. They were, incidentally, the goals of many of the people among whom he worked, who were power crazy. He came to believe that power meant money. To one man power might mean an important Government appointment, or political eminence; to another it might mean houses, yachts, leisure, women. To King it came to mean the last-named, an expression of his libidinous drive.

As a child he had known frugality. While still an impressionable youth he had been thrown into the unreal world of politics. The longer he stayed in it, the bigger and wilder his dreams became. If he could have money, he would have power. If he had power, he would be able to command his life. He would buy life. He would buy his women, and they would be just as he wanted them. Money. . . . Power. . . . Women.

King practiced his first self-deceit in the choice of these life goals. The condensation of his thirst for beauty and perfection in these goals meant that he had blinded himself to the phoniness of both his goals and his way of reaching them. The rest was easy.

He would say that he only succumbed to his environment, that his desire for money was his desire for beauty and quality. It was the only way he could realize them on the level on which he wanted them—the quality level. He would side-step the fact that he himself was taking the phony way to the real thing: counterfeiting. And yet he was the man who hated phoniness.

One day he probably looked around him in contempt at the white-haired statesmen who had spent a lifetime buying up a few pleasures and a little leisure to indulge when they were old.

Perhaps he decided he did not want to wait until he was fifty to start living. He was still a youngster; it was a good time to start. He stopped hopping bells, and learned to engrave. Then he went to work in the mint. Some day he would have more money than the men whose bags he had carried. That, he thought, would be a good joke on the bastards!

He tended to business in the mint. It was quite an apprenticeship for an ambitious counterfeiter. He came well-recommended, his senator having gone the limit in his reference. The making of currency is not learned in a day or a year. King could not have worked in all the various departments or known all the secret processes, but when he had learned enough he left the mint. He lay low for a long time. A former employee of the mint would be promptly investigated if he broke out too soon or too suddenly with too much money. He worked quietly and lived in celibacy, waiting for the day when he could have the kind of girls he wanted. There was no transient sex for King, such as was provided the guests at the hotel. He wanted the real thing.

King rationalized aloud about counterfeiting only once in the office, and then not in relation to women. His reasoning substantiates what has already been said about the criminal's defense mechanisms. It does not differ, however, from the rationalizations of many "shrewd" business men operating unhindered on the outside. King felt his choice of counterfeiting was ethical. He had hurt no one. He deplored the aggressiveness of politicians who destroyed other people in their greed. He said he had not stolen in the usual sense; he had simply created a commodity that did not exist. He had not lied, swindled, robbed, forced, bribed or betrayed anyone in counterfeiting. He had not even worked with counterfeiting rings—he wanted no contact with men whose ideals were beneath him. He worked alone. He reasoned that counterfeit money passes freely from hand to hand, goes on forever, and no one is the wiser. Like Gibbs' story of the washers and the dollars.

When King felt it was safe, Tony said, he had gone to Europe, "converted" his pile, and returned to New York, where he hopped bells again for "quality," and leased his suite. He established headquarters in Cleveland for his second grand scale "conversion" of his counterfeit. Something went wrong, but he took his first imprisonment philosophically. He had been stupid; he had tried too much too fast. But, he comforted himself, he still had a lot of money. He would invest it more wisely next time. He would secure it in property and bonds, and retire. He would be through with counterfeiting. He would have what he wanted.

When he was released the first time, he went back to hopping bells in New York, and back to his suite. He had more money than the men whose bags he carried. Now he wanted a girl more beautiful than theirs. A girl of quality. A girl who wasn't a phony.

The girl in the picture on the wall, the girl from Randolph-Macon. She was his to draw, to exhibit, to own. That was as close to love as he dared to come. His ego was not involved that way, and his trauma was not disturbed. She was property for which he was paying. He had waited a long time for this.

It is not hard to imagine what happened to the girl. This was not the kind of relationship she had expected. She was apparently a normal girl, more normal and more immediate than Marian with her compulsive attachment for King. The first girl wanted love and respectability. She was not a masochist; she did not like being either a chattel or a fantasy. She wanted equality. From what Tony had said, she consoled herself in another affair, which King discovered.

He did not like that. She was the only quality he had, and he would not have her going around like a cheap slut. She had not needed to double-cross him. In view of his celibacy, she had a choice of epithets to throw at him, any one of which would have shattered him. She could have said, "You're a *phony!*" She probably did.

As the irony of the situation struck her, she confessed her lie: she should have known she'd be taken in sooner or later by a phony because *she was one herself*. And thus in complete incredulity King learned that she was not Southern, and had never gone to any college. She was just a beautiful girl trying to get ahead.

This was a disastrous disillusionment for King, because *it was of his own making*. He was not responsible for his parents' sins, or for the lack of integrity in public life. But this girl represented *his* ability to recognize quality when he saw it, and he had made a gross misjudgment. His plan and work of years collapsed at the hands of a phony girl.

But by now King was so self-duped that it would not occur to him that the girl was only doing what he had been doing for years: trying to get along, moving with her "betters" among quality; and that her disillusionment in him as a lover was just as shattering as his in her as an ideal. (She probably never knew of his deceit: counterfeiting.) Her accusations, whatever they were, brought him much too near the truth about himself for comfort. To spare himself the ordeal of facing his own phoniness, he focused his eye on the girl's. She was made to pay for hers, so that he would not have to think about his own guilt. He rose in blind, judicial rage and struck at her greatest asset, her beauty. It was the symbol of her power over him and, ironically, his own life goal. He did not kill her. That would have been too kind. He tied her to the bed and disfigured her coolly and deliberately, a little at a time, day after day. Then he let her go.

He projected his own deceit into her lie, and thus became symbolically his own executioner, his own penance prescriber. His hate of himself was converted into hate of her.

An analyst would say that, on a deeper level of identification, the girl was also his mother-image, his childhood trauma. This was the first girl he had had anything to do with since his early shock, which had filled him with shame for his mother. This girl was now asking for sex. All the emotionality and revulsion he had felt as a child was revivified by the girl's demands, so that she was made to pay for his mother's sins, as well as for her own and his. She was his whipping boy. All his disillusionments, his aggressions, his guilt, the privations and loneliness by which he had reached his goals, were laid at the door of the unlucky young girl, and it was this accumulated load that led King to violence. He had had a strong moral reaction to the childhood trauma, judging his parents harshly in his young mind. He now undoubtedly believed that in mutilating the girl he was delivering a moral judgment upon her deceit.

There apparently had been no easily recognizable signs of sadism in King until this time. Again a Freudian would say that his impossible idealizations and demands for perfection in other people, his withdrawal from reality in his drawings, his compulsion for fastidiousness and his squeamishness about dirt, messiness, blood and violence, were simply an external denial of the internal existence of those very things in him. These sublimated drives needed only a crisis to break out of bounds and overwhelm him. The girl's deceit was his crisis, and it was custom made.

This third blow to King's ego was such that it might easily have led him to murder and suicide, as well as mutilation. But apparently the breakdown of his personality was not total. All his sadistic purposes were served short of murder in the slow torture of the girl.

Newspapers, police records and therapists' case histories are full of these episodes of what approaches *epileptic furor*. A mild recessive man, who has long borne injustice, either real or imagined, and who has always been self-effacing to the point of martyrdom, suddenly decides he has had his belly full, and strikes out. He may run amuck without forewarning signs, and then subside into his recessive life, never to repeat the violence. However, it cannot be stated unequivocally that the furor will not strike again.

Sometimes the personality is completely unseated by such an outburst, and suicide or insanity, or both, will follow murder. Sometimes the aggressor will wall it off from his conscious memory in amnesia, as Hobson did his murder of the jailer and betrayal of his cell mate. In psychological terminology Hobson *undid* his act by forgetting it, and thereby lost his conscious sense of guilt.

King used another psychological technique, known as *isolation*. He walled off his feelings of guilt, not by amnesia but by arguing the moral culpability of the girl. He then did not look upon himself as a transgressor, but as a judge. By this rationalization he lost all emotional reaction to his act and retained only the judicial sense. This is the deepest kind of sadism in the human family.

This is the sadism of war.

King further salvaged himself, after the banishment of the girl, in the long broodings in which he etched and carved the pieces Marian had shown me that evening. He resolved in wood and metal the furor which he had begun in flesh, and re-gathered his forces for another assault on life. He knew now how it had to be. It had to be *more* money, *more* power, *more* security, and a *better* girl. There would have to be one more counterfeiting effort. He was still buying quality across the counter.

This time the girl was Marian. And that was King's lucky break, for Marian was a girl of quality and integrity.

But what *was* wrong with a girl that stuck to King?

For one thing, Marian was a dancer, an exhibitionist who, as she had said, needed an audience. King was a magnificent audience. She was also extremely feminine, a fact which was expressed in a sublimation to King that was masochistic. She *did* like a high-handed summons. She was not, however, a passive girl. Her hauteur revealed fire and spirit. She had bowed to King, but it had paid her well. She got what she wanted, even if it was on strange terms.

Marian was also a girl who liked to take chances. She had defied her family in going on the stage. She defied her judgment in becoming King's girl. She liked the thrill of taking a chance.

Thrill is produced by the presence of incipient danger coupled with the probability of escape. Terror sets in only when escape is cut off. There is a thrill in riding a roller coaster as long as one believes the car will not jump the track. There is a thrill in being the girl in a knife-thrower's act, as long as she believes in her partner's aim. It was a thrill for Marian to be around a man like King. She lived with the constant internal menace in him and liked it. It was this that had attracted her to him and sent her home in a stupor the night she met him. Somewhere in their relationship, perhaps at the time of his last big counterfeiting effort resulting in his sentence to the penitentiary, he had hung the picture. She had not tried to retreat from it, or him. She did not want to. A masochistic girl is attracted to a sadistic man. She was probably shocked that he had done such a thing, but she could not believe it would ever happen to her. She felt secure in her power over him. She was different. It was a thrill to live in the atmosphere of imminent disaster as long as she believed it would never overtake her. Thus their pathologies complemented each other.

So far she had been right about her power. She had been wise enough not to ask King for love, even though she was secretly yearning for it. She had become what King wanted her to be. She was his expanded ego, his self-respect, his necessary quality, bought over the counter.

But he was repeating his pattern of putting all his eggs in one basket: getting his power in money, using his money to buy quality, and investing all his quality in one girl. He was paving the way for another disillusionment, building himself up for a cataclysmic collapse if she failed, if her compulsive attachment to him was dissipated, if in her loneliness and his absence she looked at another man and lost King's enchantment to some more immediate goal. King was only as secure as Marian was constant in beauty, quality and fidelity. He kept another girl always in the periphery to bulwark his position with Marian. He had to be sure of her. When he went to prison he did not lock her up and station guards at the door of his suite. He hung the picture on the wall.

I did not know how much Marian understood about herself and King. Very little, I guessed. Her narcissism and compulsion were still so strong that she probably was not too interested in the truth. But I wondered how long she could live in this relationship with King without doing what the other girl had done: find solace in another man. I wondered if she would never rebel against the tyranny of the picture on the wall, and what would happen to her if she did rebel. The prognosis was not good.

I did not know, either, how to answer the question she was asking now: "What's the matter with King, Doctor? Is he always going to be like this?" We were still standing under the picture.

"I wish I could assure you he won't be, Marian," I said fervently.

I thought about King's two years in the office. He had lived in a desexualized world, where there had been no external agitation of that internal problem. He had been engaged in a humanitarian work in a compatible environment. For the first time he was not working alone. He was having his first experience of a *we* feeling in a community of work. It was good therapy for him, as it was for Ross. He was developing a respect for the disparate personalities on my staff, too, an enjoyment of the company of men whom he previously would have despised.

He had been exposed to impersonal and analytical thinking.

Although my approach to psychology was eclectic, King probably now knew by memory all of Freud's defense mechanisms, which are standard equipment in any therapist's kit and most of which were needed to understand King's pathology. It was therefore not unreasonable to hope that he was beginning to have some insights about himself, his counterfeiting, and the picture on the wall. Perhaps his omnivorous reading in psychology in those two years had been directed toward himself and his own problem.

I did not fully understand King's motivation in wanting me to see Marian. I doubted that he himself did. It was an arbitrary choice on my part to interpret his gesture as a hopeful sign that he knew something was wrong and that he wanted help.

But I had so little time with Marian that I could not answer her question by exposing her to the shock of a full picture of King's and her pathology and then run, leaving her perhaps to collapse and flee him. It would not help King to lose Marian now.

So under the shadow of the picture I gave her all the assurance I could: the therapeutic value of his work and his probable insights about himself, the significance of his wanting me to hear his story, and the healthy look on his face when he had given me her name.

She was eager to believe it all.

"So go back to school, Marian, and pick up that degree," I said, in leaving. "I have a feeling he'll be on hand when you get it." What then? I asked, after the degree? Were there any plans?

"Oh, yes!" she said, brightening. "He's planned a trip for us. Greece, Italy, France—Then he wants to settle in Connecticut." She smiled. "He says he'll want to hop bells once in a while, just for old times' sake. But no more counterfeiting, and—" She glanced involuntarily at the picture.

I reached out and turned its face to the wall again, and led her away from it.

"You've been a real soldier, Marian," I said, "damned if I wouldn't play my luck a little longer."

"Thank you for that," she said quietly. "Damned if maybe I won't!"

On my first day back in the office King listened politely while I talked impersonally of his paintings and engravings. I knew he didn't care what I thought about them—they pleased him. Neither of us mentioned the picture on the wall.

When I had no more to say of them, he made no attempt to pick up the conversation. But he did not leave. He was doodling on a piece of paper before him, waiting for the real business between us.

"I saw Tony," I began finally. "He's looking forward to your coming back. . . . . So is Marian, King."

He did not look up, but he stopped drawing.

"We talked for a long time."

He looked up then.

"She's beautiful, King. And good. There's nothing phony there. She's always been yours, and she always will be, in any way you want her. The future looks good."

"That the way you see it?" He tried not to sound too eager.

And that was all that was ever said.

After a moment he placed in front of me a sheaf of graphs on which he had been working during my absence, and began to discuss them in a completely natural way.

Although he never mentioned Marian again, I did not feel she was a forbidden subject. I felt rather that he was at rest about her and his future.

15

At the beginning of my last year, following my vacation, we paused to look at our mounting data, for the drug research was shaping up toward completion. The final report was made on 1,500 addicts, but the research was conducted in units of a few hundred at a time, each unit involving several months' study. Very little new work was begun in the final year. The greater part of the time was spent in refining the data we had accumulated in the previous two years, retesting for validity and reliability.

In this growing time sense the men also began to realize that I would leave at the end of the project. They gave this fact more recognition then, when my leaving was still a year off, than at any time afterward.

The Porter Narcotic Farm at Lexington, Kentucky, and the hospital for the criminally insane at Springfield, Missouri, were then under construction, and the men wondered whether my successor would be stationed at Lexington instead of at the penitentiary. I did not know at that time what specific plans were being made for a successor to me, although there would certainly be one. The boys made indirect inquiries about him until I jokingly pointed out that I would probably learn more about him from the grapevine, when the time came, than I would from Washington.

They also made discreet and indirect inquiries about my

plans when I would leave the penitentiary. I told them honestly enough that I didn't know yet. I was thinking about clinical work and about continuing research on the polygraph, being encouraged by Ross's accomplishments. A score of experts had taken cracks at it in the East, but Ross had shown more insight into its problems than they.

It was at this time, too, that they began talking about their own futures, in a very off-hand manner.

Connie's day dreams were about the circus. He was lonesome for the midway and the freaks. He was working out some new routine for barking the sideshows—he hadn't enlarged his vocabulary for nothing, and what a field day the sideshows offered a good endocrinologist! A penny arcade of his own, with time out for the circus—that was the life!

As Gibbs anticipated his parole, he began to discard the idea of cars, even legitimate buying and selling, for his real profession of building and contracting.

King, as Marian had said, wanted to go to Paris to study. Things had worked out just the way he wanted. He had his "quality": his home in the country, his real estate, his girl, his money. Now he was through with phoniness. No more working under cover, no more dodging the law. He did not want to risk losing what he had.

Scott was going home, with no apprehension about entering his old life. One door would close, another would open, it was as simple as that to him. If he had been sent to prison before the 1930 reform, he would not have been going home without a mark on his life. Even he would have deteriorated in idleness, filth, hunger, isolation, and brutality. It was true that he was innocent, but prisons made no such distinction in the treatment of their inmates. Ross, too, had been innocent in his first imprisonment.

Ross had nothing to say about his future, but he was making progress. One sign of this was his handling of his parole application. He had applied for parole early in his sentence, as soon as

he had served enough time to make application possible. However, applying for parole was not always a wholesome step in the
experience of a prisoner. It frequently is not even in these days,
except in superior institutions. Many of the men reach the point
of discouragement about their ever being able to go straight, and
become fatalistic in their belief that they will be serving another
stretch in a few months or years. They apply for parole simply to
gain time that might not otherwise be theirs. It may be largely
rationalization on their part, but they feel that parole offers an
ex-convict a minimum rather than a maximum chance of recovery. Not only are many of the civil rights of an ex-convict lost,
but he must register with the police, which may result in his
being hounded, sometimes blackmailed, by them. Imagine, the
convict argues, hiding the fact that one has served a prison sentence when a social case worker appears on the scene periodically to make inquiries of his boss, his landlady, and his family
about his character and associates. These visits are made to check
on the convict's reports to the parole officer, and they sometimes
result in the ex-convict losing his job and his landlady. Whereupon he is thrown back upon his old resources and with his old
companions. If the full sentence is served without parole, there
are no follow-ups, the break is clean. Society is not yet fulfilling
its responsibilities to the implications of parole. Who wants to
hire a jailbird? Only one-half of the prisoners in a penitentiary
apply for parole, and then often with only the motive of gaining
a little time before they are picked up again.

Ross was at this point of discouragement when he applied
for parole at the time he transferred to my office. Now, two
years later, when the other men were talking about their futures,
I learned that Ross had long since withdrawn his application for
parole. In his case this was healthy action. It meant he was beginning to think hopefully about himself and his future, that he
wanted to break with his past. He wanted no special favors at
the hands of a Parole Board and no social case workers, even

though parole meant time off his sentence. He was becoming independent, feeling superior to his environment. He was discovering his own integrity. He wanted his future in his own hands.

Work is man's oldest therapy, and one of the best. We had tried to keep Ross busy. He was on regular call at the power house. There was often trouble with the movie projector in the dining room because of its abnormally long beam. Ross was their man when the projector acted up. He was still working conscientiously at the polygraph for me. He installed automatic circuits and thermostats and did sporadic carpenter jobs in Laurie's laboratory, a contact which I encouraged. He was learning to relax in Laurie's company, remembering how to tease and laugh. This feminine and cultural equality meant a great deal to Ross. Time passed more quickly for him, because no two days were alike any more. There was less time to think about himself, and when he did it was with more detachment and perspective.

Punch was neither discreet nor indirect about his future or mine, when I began my last year. He had it all worked out. He was going home to Italy. He would never admit he was being deported, he was always "retiring." Things were "too hot" for him over here now. He had made lots of money, and now he wanted to make lots of love in a beautiful Mediterranean villa. I guess Punch was finally succumbing to the first peace and quiet he had had in his stormy life. He had begun to suspect he hadn't done much living in his gangster days. I cannot say I saw any remorse in Punch for his past, but he was dissatisfied. It was time for a change.

He demonstrated his taste for a change, surely, when he asked me to go to Italy with him! He was quite serious. He would set me up in a private villa, where I could work and study till hell froze over. I was amazed at his invitation. I had never felt as close to Punch as I had to some of the boys. I came to the conclusion that his hospitality had something to do with his love of power. He liked to think he could buy anything he wanted. It would have amused him to buy an American professor, set him up in opulence and style in the old country, and let him study and contemplate until he expired at his books. That would have been something different in the way of patronage. It would have been finesse, like Connie's gifts to Higgins and the captain after his trip to the city.

Punch carried his propagandizing to surprising lengths.

One day he met me halfway between the hospital and the cell block as I was returning with another doctor from my daily rounds of the psychopathic ward. He asked to see me, and I excused myself to Doctor Jamison.

"I want you to see a pal of mine, he's in trouble," Punch said, as we started obliquely across the yard.

We were soon intercepted by four men whom I had never seen. One of them touched his cap, and handed me some papers. It was an emergency requisition and pass for a drum of oxygen. I said I thought they had the wrong doctor.

"No, we haven't," he snapped. "We're going to the warehouse, and if a guard stops us, it's all right, see? In fact, it's an emergency."

I looked for Punch, but he was gone. In response to pressure from behind me, I became part of a group walking toward the warehouse with all the nonchalance of a Boy Scout troop stalking a bear.

"Don't look so serious, Doc," one of them warned. "And don't get wise and try any signals. What's wrong about you walkin' across the yard with a bunch of men?"

I didn't know, but I fervently wished I did. . .

There was a brief, nervous delay at the control gate, and once through, the men said, "We've got to go faster. Hurry up, Doc!"

As we neared the warehouse, I noticed the guard leaving his

post at the door in response to a couple of excited, gesticulating prisoners. The guard gone, we entered the warehouse and descended into the basement, into what I felt was extraordinarily dark darkness.

Halfway down I heard distant sirens and alarms, then shots.

"Goodness gracious, such a noise!" said one of my companions. "This ain't Army Day, is it?"

"Must be somebody's boithday," said another, "it ain't *your* boithday, is it Doc? Maybe da boys is celebratin' Doc's boithday, you suppose?"

"It's a break," I murmured.

"Well, whatta you know!" somebody chimed, "he *is* smart, just like the boys say! Tell you what, Doc, we hear you like to get wised up," said the man whose face I never saw again. "We pulled this squeeze for Pinero an' your boys on account they think yer a okay guy. An' also, they don't fergit. Remember Gibbs ast you for a pass onc't an' you took a chanc't? Well, this is a kind of a pay-off."

"But suppose you didn't take no chanc't on Gibbs," said someone else, with more fact and less feeling. "We don't take no chanc't on you. You get took on the break today—they've some guns, an' you get yer belly caved in when the shootin' starts. Like yer old lady always says, Doc, it pays to be a good boy!"

When the shooting terminated I found I was alone in the dark with the packing cases. I felt my way back up the stairs. The guard was standing at his post at the door.

"What's going on?" I asked feebly.

"A break, I guess. Jeez—I'm sure glad I'm not on duty at the front gate. I think they took it with 'em." He looked curiously at me. "What you doing over here, Doc?"

"Oh—I hadn't been over here for a long time, I thought I'd just fall in with some of the boys for a quick tour—"

We glanced quickly at each other and quickly away.

"Well, nothing ever happens over here," remarked the guard over-loudly. "Maybe a little 'snatch' once in a while. . . ."

" . . . Yeah. By the way, I missed you when I came in the door. You left suddenly. What happened?"

"Oh, one of the dopes stumbled over a box and knocked himself out. Or else somebody dropped it on him by mistake, I couldn't make out. He wasn't hurt, came to a minute after I got there. No bumps or bruises or anything. The damnedest things happen to these dopes!"

In a break or riot, all intermediary and control gates were locked, the keys were dropped into a trough in the gate out of reach of both guards and prisoners, and everyone remained in the area in which he found himself at the sound of the siren. It was an hour before the gates were cleared and I could get back to the hospital. My men were hopping with excitement, especially Punch.

"Jeez, Doc—did ya hear about it? A bust-out! They take the deputy an' one of the doctors."

"Jamison!"

"Why, yeah, Doc, they have to have a patsy—the screws in the tower make it a turkey-shoot any other way," Gibbs said uncomfortably.

"I guess we know where they picked up Jamison," I said.

"Yeah," said Punch. "Jeez, Doc, it ain't healthy bein' always at the same place at the same time when they're plannin' a break. You was just lucky! Besides, they wanted you, they figgered the guards wouldn't shoot."

I looked at him. My gratitude was overshadowed by a kind of shame about Jamison.

Connie spoke. "They run at the front gate from all directions, like oranges rollin' out of a crate. The screws don't shoot because the guys has the deputy an' the doctor, everybody sweatin' good—an' who wouldn't be? The screws is millin' around every which way, not knowin' what to do. The deputy yellin' not to open the gate, to go ahead an' shoot, but they don't."

"What was the shooting, then?" I asked.

Gibbs continued. "Well, after the cons get the car started, the guards finally get organized an' let go at the tires. They jump an' fidget and fire every which way. A bouncy slug gets Jamison, Doc," he said quietly. "They throw him out on the road. By God, then they know they've copped it! It ain't just a break now, it's *murder!* They run the car into a culvert an' all pile out, bust up an' run for it."

But they were all back by nightfall.

Punch kept exclaiming, "A real honest-to-God prison break! What a story to tell my grandchildren, huh, Doc? In my reclining years, in It'ly. By the way, Doc, where was you? You missed all the fun."

I had been expecting the question. Punch wanted his due.

"Me an' the boys was havin' a game of craps in the basement," I said in poor humor. I was still thinking about Jamison.

But Punch beamed proudly at me. "Well! It's easy to see who won!"

"I'm not so sure anybody won this game," said Ross.

Punch looked at him. "What you worryin' about? Jamison?" he asked. "Somebody's gotta lose, or nobody's gonna win!"

"Maybe Ross meant the stakes were pretty high," said Scott, and Punch looked at him. And then at me.

"I don't get it!" he said peevishly. "I heard o' bum losers, but I ain't heard of a winner that don't wanna count his take. Aw—what the hell!" And he went to work.

But he soon softened, in deference to a prospective corpse.

"It's like you said, Ross," he began contritely. "Jamison's okay. But hell, I ain't so bad myself. This wasn't my bust, was it? An' Doc's still alive and thinkin', ain't he? An' ain't I offered to take him to It'ly an' set him up like he wants? Whatta *you* say, Doc?"

My thanks were not too convincing, I guess. I had not shaken off my scuff with death yet. But, more than that, I was almost embarrassed at being alive, while Jamison, with every right to life that was mine, lay fighting for his. Punch's move had saved my life, but had jeopardized Jamison's. Glad as I was to be "alive an' thinkin'," I couldn't accept the discrimination with the sang-froid of my men. Apparently I was reacting to the fact of life as coolly as the men were reacting to the fact of death, and neither of us approved the other's point of view.

When Punch realized I was not going to say anything more, he turned off in disgust. I went into my office.

"The hell with it!" I heard Punch mutter. "I always say you can't trust a man you can't bribe. I oughtta have my head examined for lunacy. I'm all the time puttin' myself out for some goddamn—"

"Shut up, Pinero!" It was Friar Gibbs trying to apologize for Punch's bad manners.

"Shut up yerself, Grandma!" Punch flared out, "an' mind yer own business!"

I was sorry Gibbs had said anything. Punch would have sulked until I found something further to say to mollify his vanity, and that would have ended the episode. But when Gibbs spoke up, I felt uneasy.

"You know," Punch began ingratiatingly, addressing nobody and everybody, "I can't honestly remember when it was I saved a man's life before. That ain't exactly my line of business. When I do, I like it to be appreciated!"

Gibbs spoke up again, almost fearfully. "What the hell, Doc said—"

"He ain't said nothin' I wanna remember *yet*," said Punch.

I came back into the room. But before I could speak, Connie did. "He ain't sayin' no more, cry baby," he said ominously. He threw down his pencil and peered at Punch. "Jesus God, what's eatin' you, Pinero, wantin' all this gratitude? Wasn't you

298

breast-fed when you was a baby? Feelin' insecure an' unwanted, like the books say? You know damn well if you hadn't a did it, one of us wouldda!"

Punch's face went black. He thrashed about briefly for a point of attack. Then he grabbed a graph sheet from his desk, and before anyone realized his intent, he tore it in half and threw the pieces on the floor.

King turned on him savagely.

"You dirty bastard! That took me a month to make!"

"A whole month?" asked Punch sweetly, watching King pick up the pieces from the floor. Then he lashed out. "It took me three months to get the figgers for you to make it outta! . . . . Three months? What am I sayin'? I been workin' for thirty months feedin' you figgers! Holy Mother of God, am I a sucker! Thirty months of my life beatin' my brains and strainin' my optics. An' fer what, I ask you? Well, what's did can be undid," he said easily, glancing at the papers on his desk.

That was when cold fear entered my brain and my body. At least a year's work lay under his hand at that moment, and we all saw what was taking shape in his mind. It brought the other five men slowly out of their chairs. They converged on Punch. Connie shoved his chin almost into Punch's face.

"I'm callin' yer bluff, Pinero. You lay your hand on anythin' in this here office, an'—"

Pinero hunched, his eyes flat and mean. "Look, pimp," he said softly, "I talk to you just this one time. I don't say it again. *Nobody* pushes Pinero. Not even a little!"

"I ain't talkin' about pushin'. I ain't even talkin' about shovin'. I'm talkin' about rippin' your guts out! You lay your hand on anythin' in this office, an' you'll be a sad apple! I'll have ten chivs in your dirty wop guts before you make the door. You got that, Pinero?"

Punch glanced around the edges of Connie's face at the other men. Their expressions were frozen. He looked at me.

Even I had a pretty good grip on myself. He looked back at Connie who was still breathing into his face. Then he grabbed a mad breath, and yelled in a desperation that we all caught, "I'll do what I goddam please in this office!"

"That's what I'm tellin' you, Pinero," said Connie, menacingly. "You do what you goddam please an' you'll never live to enjoy your handiwork!"

The fight deteriorated quickly into a dog-eat-dog affair. Punch swore he'd get Connie like Pretty Boy Floyd got Frank Nash on the steps of the station in Kansas City—he'd mow Connie down the day he was released. Connie swore Punch would never live to get out to mow him down.

While Punch and his goons were stronger outside the penitentiary, Connie was stronger inside. Punch was always at a loss without his guns and his goons. Connie, on the other hand, would never have threatened Punch on the outside. One of the terrors that seize a man in a penitentiary is watching the days pass on a calendar, knowing that death waits only for his release, or that it waits in a prison corridor somewhere tomorrow, next week, next month. There was no reason for either Punch or Connie to believe the other's threats were idle.

What was happening before my eyes could completely demoralize the last few months of work, the research, my staff, and me. I must have been a ludicrous figure impotently standing by, opening my mouth to interfere, but not being able to get into the arena. Finally I succeeded.

I admitted to Punch before the other men that he or any of them could destroy the records, that I had always known it, but I had never worried about it. I said that if he did destroy records, it would hurt like hell, but that I wasn't going to play his game. I wasn't going to plead or bargain with him, report or transfer him, lock up the records anywhere else, or carry them home with me at night. If he wanted to get me or Connie or the records, nothing could stop him. He would just have to go ahead and do what he wanted to do. But until and unless he did, everything was going to be business as usual with me.

That was as near as I came to brave little speeches—or tremors, while I was in the penitentiary. If Punch was intimidated by my logic, he did not show it. He looked once around the circle of tight-lipped deadpans, said something about seein' how the cards was stacked, now we'd see who was holdin' the ace, and he stomped out.

Then the real trouble broke. I was quickly disenchanted by the other men regarding any intention of theirs to back up my pacifism. They started laying plans for a pitched battle. There was absolutely no doubt in their minds but that Punch would level the office at the first opportunity and keep his threat about Connie. They were good and scared, especially Connie, because he had turned the quarrel into a feud between him and Punch. Connie usually did not get himself into feuds. He lived by his wits, and here he was, leading with his chin.

I tried to persuade them that their course was unrealistic. The way they were looking at things, I told them, there was nothing for Punch to do but try to wipe out Connie before Connie could wipe out Punch. That way I had excellent prospects of losing both my Number One Boy and my statistician.

"By that time ya won't need neither of 'em, Doc," Gibbs lamented. "Ya won't have no records to keep."

That, I said, was my point—we didn't want that, did we? As it stood, I pointed out faintheartedly, Punch had left the office with a dare on his hands: put up or shut up. Burn the place down or come back to work. Did they think Punch would fight, knowing he wouldn't have any opposition? I asked.

They did! They asked: did I imagine for one moment that he would be reclaimed by light and love in time to call off his dogs and come back to work?

301

I hoped so. They almost fell into the wastebaskets in shock. I did not add that I meant to implement my faith by facing my prayer rug toward Mecca for the next few days.

Connie shook his head sadly.

"Now, this here is what Doc calls usin' yer brains instead of yer biceps. Maybe there has been times when it works. Like in the riot, fer instance. But that it should work with Pinero—" He shook his head. "—that I should have to admit he has a better nature—"

"On the other hand," said Friar Gibbs, the opportunist, "maybe we oughtta give Punch the chanc't God never will. We're all in this up to our necks anyways, whatta we got to lose?"

Scott gasped. "Our necks, maybe," he said plaintively.

"That!" said Gibbs disparagingly.

"Well, I will say," Connie began again, "that's quite a spot you got Punch on, Doc. You pat him on one cheek an' slap him on the other. It'll be real interestin' to watch what happens."

It was not at all interesting. It was awful. We came to work the next morning with the night's rigors still on our faces. Everything was intact in the office except Punch. He did not come. He had kept the whole wing in an uproar half the night singing Italian arias, they said, and flushing the toilet every fifteen minutes. "Nervous bladder," Gibbs said confidentially.

Punch checked in the captain's office that day and made out a work transfer. I signed it without comment, much to the captain's annoyance.

"I thought Pinero was the apple of your eye, Doctor, the boy who makes with the figures?"

"He is the apple of my eye, captain."

"He *is?*" But he was discreet enough not to press further. "Says he wants some sunshine. Maybe he's got a spot on his lung?"

"Maybe."

"Mm. . . . I'll put him back in the machine shop. Let him get a spot on his nose, too!"

So Punch went back to threading pipe, and his work piled higher and higher on his desk in the office. He was moved to the machine shop wing in the cell block, and my men lost touch with him, although I was sure he was under the constant surveillance of Connie's boys everywhere in the penitentiary.

The dreams I had the first few nights following the quarrel, in which all my work went up in smoke, were so vivid that not even finding everything in order the following morning could quite reassure me.

The men were harassed, too. But at the end of the second week I suspected it was not only nerves they had. It was homesickness. Nostalgia. The old gang was busted—things weren't the same. I think they began to feel ashamed of themselves, too, for having allowed a quarrel to develop. They did not say anything, but their faces hung down and their eyes grieved. King took a whirl at statistics, and swore a constant stream of oaths. "Dirty bastard! What a time to get sore!"

Gradually I began to breathe easier. It would be only a matter of time now until, as they say in the ladies' magazines, love would find a way.

I never knew exactly what happened. Maybe Punch couldn't recapture his former kudos in the machine shop. Maybe he missed good food, clean clothes, and a desk of his own. Maybe the men worked out some kind of deal. One morning three weeks after Punch had left the office, the captain phoned me just as I was arriving, before the other men showed up.

"Doc, I got a grease monkey here. Says the sun ain't helping that lung—"

"Send him right over!" I cried.

Punch was at his desk working when the other boys checked in—an hour late, they were so sorry. It looked like a deal, all right. In which everybody had lost and everybody had won, and everybody had learned something about courage.

Gibbs looked at Punch and scolded cheerfully: "Why, you goddam son of a bitch—where in hell you been? You lazy, good-fer-nothin', why, I oughtta bust you—"

"Lay off, Grandma!" Punch said gruffly. "Can't ya see I'm busy?"

Connie caught my eye and winked.

"You heard what the man said!" he cried happily.

The only other event that disturbed Connie as deeply as the quarrel with Punch was the illness of his girl in St. Louis and the problem of getting a reputable doctor for her on the outside. Connie had sufficient background now to know that there were good doctors and poor ones.

Because of their avowed and open defiance of society, convicts distrust, resent and fear the few contacts they are forced to have with it from time to time. Most criminals, in the course of their furtive lives, must have dealings with two professions: medicine and law. They become ill or get wounded, and they tangle with the law: they need doctors and lawyers. Yet they distrust these two men more than any of their confederates.

At one end of the linear continuum representing the distribution of criminal "types" are the small-time criminals who are bred on the wrong side of the tracks and never in their lifetime cross those tracks. They are the psychologically inferior personalities that fill our penitentiaries. They have been raised to a philosophy of hidebound class distinction, have battled with abject poverty, and they conduct their criminal careers in their own environment. They are peripheral people, living at the edges of society and life, scavengers, foragers, housebreakers, petty thieves, beggars. They steal food, clothes, rifle inconspicuous tills, live in flop houses, near the dump, or in a tenement. They never carry a gun, they never fight; they always run. They live on the West or South side of town and never see the North side. If in a jam they must have a doctor or a lawyer, they can't "buy" a good man, they patronize only the quack doctor or the bail bond lawyer, who will frequently take them for a ride.

At the other end of the linear continuum is the criminal who may have been born next door to the psychopathically inferior individual just described, but whose aggressive drive has taken him over the tracks. Instead of foraging for a bare living from vegetable stalls, these criminals raid at a higher level of society. They wrest a fine living at this level, splitting their take with the cops, hobnobbing with stylish cafe society, giving interviews to society reporters.

When they find it necessary to retain a doctor or an attorney, they move and choose with great caution, motivated by much the same fears and resentments that the forager back across the tracks experiences. But these criminals can at least buy their medical and legal counsel, and do so with retainers sufficiently large to insure "loyalty," a fact which makes the criminal immediately contemptuous of his man. It is doubtful that either a doctor or a mouthpiece in the pay of these criminals ever rises above the thoughtful eye of his boss. Each recognizes the ability of the other to betray under due provocation. It is not a restful relationship.

Connie's girl lived in the tenderloin district of the city, and therefore could not hope for a reputable doctor. This worried Connie until he became almost ill. An old ulcer flared, and he was haggard and sleepless. The girl herself did not represent a grand passion in Connie's life, as far as I could tell, because Connie took a very pragmatic view of women and love. But he was a very loyal gent. And in this case his worry was more apprehension than concern.

"Supposing she'd have to have the knife an' talked when she's out! Jeez! . . . . Not that she's got anythin' on me, you understand," he added for his own reassurance.

He urged me to visit her on my next trip to St. Louis, to see what was wrong and to get her a "high-class doctor." I told him we could refer her to a good doctor without my seeing her. But my seeing her became an obsession. I finally agreed that since I was going to a professional meeting the following week, I would see her.

Connie was relieved, and gave me careful instructions about the visit. I was to take a taxi and get off a block and a half from her address.

"Why?" I asked.

"*Why?*" He was flabbergasted.

It may have been Connie's protective instincts that suggested this undercover arrival, but it was more probably that the convict cannot do anything the simple, direct way. So I took a taxi from the station and got off a block and a half from her address. . . .

As I left the taxi in the early winter darkness, I noticed that a man crossed the street and followed me. As I came to the next block, a loiterer moved on down the street ahead of me.

I entered a shabby structure and climbed the stairs. On the second floor a man standing in a doorway turned into the room and closed the door, while a girl remained near the banister. I reached the third floor, where another girl standing in the hall said quietly, "In here, Doctor."

Connie's girl was really ill. The specialist I subsequently sent to see her reported that she had advanced tuberculosis, complicated by recent pneumonia which had left an abscess on the lung.

Conversation was a relief to her. She wanted first-hand news of her man, his possible future, and asked the little things any woman would have asked. She said she knew she was dying. She had no hope of living until Connie was released. She gave me no secret message: there was nothing unusual about the visit once the door was closed behind me and I was alone with her, except its very conventionality.

My departure was like my arrival, except that the second-floor man came out of his room and preceded me down the stairs by a full flight. The girls kept their vigil in the hall, and the loiterer came in from the street and murmured, "It's all right, Doc."

When I was outside again, I noticed a cab waiting a half block down, and that a man was standing beside it. As I approached the man said, "Thanks, Doc," and the driver took me downtown, stating that the ride had already been paid for. He deposited me at the door of the lecture hall. The chairman of the evening met me as I alighted from the cab—I was late— and hurried me into the hall. I read my paper to my colleagues, wondering how they would react if I told them about the past two hours of my life.

Connie had no means by which to aid his girl. But Gibbs had friends and Punch had money, and Gibbs went after it unabashedly, though without Connie's knowledge. This provided the final denouement of the office quarrel. Friar Gibbs saw to it that Punch paid up for his trouble. Within a week "Mrs. James Connie" was on a pullman headed for Arizona. She died there two months later, and I understand her final rites were of a scope and quality befitting a burgomaster's daughter, whether under duress I cannot say.

16

THE EARLY punishment cell was not called "The Hole" for nothing. It was a dark, airless pit into which a prisoner was thrown, and the pit then covered by a rock slab. Perhaps the man lived through the ordeal, perhaps he did not. He may have gone insane, starved to death, or both.

As time went on, punishment cells became a little more humane. There was now a peep hole in the door of the dungeon through which a guard pushed a little food and water daily, a very little.

Punishment cells are still traditionally in the sub-basement of a prison, since their function is to deprive the convict of all sound, deny him light, and prevent his communication with other human beings. The older the penitentiary, the more primitive the provisions for comfort and hygiene, if any provision at all is made. Even in the newer institutions there is no running water in these cells, toilet facilities being provided by an open bucket. The modern cell may measure seven feet high, six feet long and four feet wide. Or it may be the tight-fitting cage mentioned before, which prohibits movement of any kind. The hands and feet of the prisoner are sometimes chained to the floor in such a way that he must remain for hours in a crouched position in awful pain. The insanity rate incident to prolonged solitary confinement is very high. Society's outraged moral sense is thus appeased.

The prisoner in solitary is naked, eats bread and water, and sleeps on a stone floor without heat. Blankets are denied him, both to enhance the punishment value of solitary and to lessen the possibility of suicide from strangulation. In summer the absence of ventilation creates a humidity problem which is as great punishment as freezing in winter. When confinement to punishment cells is from five days to two weeks, these conditions are not much varied. If the sentence exceeds a month, some concessions are made to health and survival: for instance, a blanket may be issued.

Through the peep hole in the door a guard or doctor making daily rounds asks the convict if he needs medical attention and how he is faring on his diet. If the convict makes a complaint he is examined. Otherwise his whole sentence is passed without seeing or touching another person. If he should develop pneumonia or serious debility, and he often develops both, he is removed to the hospital where many days and dollars are spent in an effort to rehabilitate him physically to the point where he can return to solitary to complete his sentence. There is a limit to the extent to which a man can be deprived of heat and light without serious physical involvement. Therefore if a man is sentenced for six months to life in solitary, he may be given a bed, light, and plumbing facilities.

A life sentence to solitary is by no means unheard of. Tannenbaum reports that four men in one western penitentiary alone were serving such sentences at the same time.

Perhaps the most incredible case of this kind in this century was that of a 14-year-old boy sentenced to life in solitary in a Massachusetts prison. In 1929 he was removed from his cell after serving forty years in solitary.

Leavenworth had a man serving the balance of a life sentence in solitary at the time I was at the Annex. He was one of the few such cases ever to have any privileges. Through the aid and encouragement of the chaplain, the prisoner became an authority on canaries, breeding them in his cell. Somebody somewhere, in line with the old philosophy of punishment, construed this situation to be a form of what J. Edgar Hoover calls the "moo-cow sentimentality" of "the cream puff school of criminology." In a sweeping triumph of justice the man lost his canaries, and was sent to Alcatraz as "a menace." Of his forty-two years in prison, he is serving his twenty-eighth year in isolation.

While most state penitentiaries still maintain primitive punishment cells, the Bureau of Prisons in the late thirties provided solitary cells with light and air in all Federal institutions, with the notable exception of Alcatraz, which enjoys the doubtful distinction of subscribing to many of the ancient rigors of penology. Its only accomplishment is that it keeps something like two hundred "incorrigibles" out of circulation at a time, at great expense to the Government. Alcatraz has done nothing to enlighten the cause or cure of crime. It has the approval of Mr. Hoover of the FBI, without which it would probably have been closed long since for being the white elephant it is.

Solitary punishment is one of society's atavistic hangovers from the Dark Ages, reflecting more seriously upon the slim resources of penology than upon the incorrigibility of the prisoner.

Every solitary cell contains endemic drama. I learned this one Friday afternoon as my last year was rounding out. Gordon and I had completed our rounds of the psychopathic wards in the cell block, and went below into The Hole to see one of the prisoners, a Negro called Hadad. Thompson and Red, the guards on solitary row, reported that Hadad was acting up again; there had been nothing in his bucket for a week.

I commented that there could not be much from a piece of bread and a gill of water a day. Gordon agreed. But Thompson, he said, just didn't like a man who wouldn't urinate. "'It ain't regular,' he says."

Gordon had seen him the previous day. "He was in the pink.

When I asked him about the empty bucket, he said in that damned Oxford accent of his that his guidance had been contrariwise. 'But a thousand pardons,' he said, 'if I have inconvenienced you by my spiritual ascendency.'"

The hospital staff was interested in this psychopathic convict. He was a character right out of Sax Rohmer's inkpot. Weird tales surrounded his origin and history, as is always true of these prophets of magic. He claimed to be a Chaldean astrologer with direct lineage reaching back to 400 B.C. He also claimed to have been educated at the universities of Carthage and Oxford, and that by profession he was a Zombi priest from Haiti. Rumor connected him with voodoo rites and devil worship. He fed these rumors by refusing to deny them and offering his own embellishments. His few intimates informed us that he was part Hindu and part Senegalese. He looked like the latter, large and magnificent in bearing. He was strikingly handsome in a statuesque way.

He had an enviable reputation in some of the large penitentiaries in the country for magic, hypnotism and escape artistry. He claimed friendship with Houdini. To the edification of the prisoners and the mystification of the guards, he was able to escape from handcuffs, strait jackets and cells almost at will.

A warden felt it was an ill wind that brought him Hadad. He completely disrupted the morale of prisons and as often as not left the wardens distrusting their own five senses. How could they be sure when he stood before them whether they were in the presence of his corporeal permeability or his spiritual extenuation? to use Hadad's own fine words.

There were no such things as authentic records on Hadad. They were always disappearing or changing, especially when under his frequent sentences he was in transit from one institution to another.

He himself had been known to be lost in transit between penitentiaries. It was never a matter of his eluding capture. He was most cooperative. He simply would not be in the paddy wagon when it arrived. He would turn up anon, knocking on the main gate for admission, explaining that he had "gotten lost" on the way, or had been detained on business. He never announced his departures, but no one missed his arrivals. He had been seen by some of our staff in the foyer of a Kansas City theater at the close of a concert. In explanation he said, "It has been some time since I have been to a concert, and I felt it would be such a shame not to go. After all, I am just a short distance from the city."

The warden shouted that his sentence did not include theater privileges.

"But sir, I came back, as I always do," Hadad reasoned. "I have no intention of avoiding my sentence. Whom did I harm in doing this? No one even knew I was gone."

For this last impertinence the warden slapped him in solitary for fifteen days.

As Gordon and I descended the stairs to solitary row, Thompson, the guard, met us with relief. Hadad was a hot potato for any guard. We went directly to Hadad's cell. There was no response to our queries. Thompson opened the steel door and his flashlight revealed a black body hanging against the bars of the cell gate.

"Cut him down," ordered Gordon, "and get the lights on!"

Thompson summoned Red, the relief guard, to help him, and when the latter joined us Gordon gave him a quick look.

"What's holding up your pants these days, Red?" Gordon asked.

Red's hands flew to his waist. Then he relaxed.

"You had me scared for a minute, Doc," he said. "I'm too old a hand to pass my belt around in solitary."

Thompson stared at Red. "Ain't that your belt around our late friend's neck?" he asked in a kind of croak.

Red looked at the corpse. "What do you mean, belt?" he

demanded of Thompson. "Can't you tell a piece of rope from a belt?"

I looked at Gordon, and Gordon looked at me.

"Anyways, what do you mean, *my* belt?" continued Red. "My belt's right here! Can't you see it?" He tapped his waist.

We all looked. He was hallucinating a belt which definitely was not there. Thompson lost his color, but not his tongue.

"The guy's nuts!" he screeched.

"*I'm* crazy!" Red was losing his patience. "How do you like that, Doc? Who's crazy around here, I ask you?"

"Tell you later," Gordon replied.

We did, when we brought him out of Hadad's post-hypnotic influence. Even then he remembered nothing except Hadad's getting his attention on his first round early that morning. He recognized his belt, of course. He was badly shaken by the fact that he could not remember being hypnotized. Later, when he learned the denouement of the whole affair, Red requested transfer from solitary row, if not from the penitentiary itself.

Upon superficial examination of the corpse Gordon pronounced Hadad dead.

"How long?" I asked.

Only a few hours, he said. He told Thompson to put Hadad on ice, and as we left the basement he observed that the belt was not pulled tight enough to cause strangulation. "We'll see what the autopsy shows," he said.

With his background, Hadad was a psychiatric curiosity. His autopsy would be quite an event. It was delayed until Sunday when a consulting neurologist could be present to assist Doctor Fellows.

Sunday morning Fellows, the visiting neurologist, Gordon and I met in the morgue and gathered around the majestic body for the final disposition. Fellows and the neurologist agreed upon Fellows' making the abdominal incision to excise the lungs and heart, and the neurologist's removing the cap of the skull to

313

get at the brain. The two surgeons put on their gloves, and Fellows was picking up the knife from the instrument table when we heard the soughing sound of a breath. Involuntarily we all looked at the corpse—and saw the ripple of Hadad's gleaming black muscles. He stirred, and slowly rose to a sitting position on the slab, as if he were propelled by invisible gears. He opened his eyes, and in his impeccable Oxford accent said, "Gentlemen, I would rather not, if you don't mind."

Nobody moved. Nobody could.

The knife slipped out of Fellows' limp grasp and clattered upon the concrete floor. Hadad slipped from the slab, stooped down, picked up the knife, laid it on the instrument table, sat on the edge of the slab, and asked for a drink of water.

"Holy Mary, Mother of God!" murmured Fellows, crossing himself quickly.

The neurologist tried to hide his shock, but he choked on a nervous cough. Gordon sucked in a startled breath and swore sharply. I began to breathe again at the sound of Gordon's voice.

There was not a man around the table who had not had some experience, either in his practice or in medical school, with catatonic trances, and who did not have some knowledge of Hadad's corporeal heterodoxy. Nevertheless, in spite of our scientific smugness, none of us were prepared for what had just happened. We had all thought Hadad was respectably dead.

Gordon committed Hadad to an unwilling guard with instructions that he be taken to the psychopathic ward for observation, and we men sat around in the morgue talking among ourselves. We did not feel like going back to Sunday golf. We reviewed our experiences with catalepsy, mysticism, and extrasensory perception. Fellows, the religionist, made it quite plain that Hadad was my boy from that moment. That was how I wanted it; he would be an interesting study.

Catatonic trances lasting several days are not uncommon in institutions for the insane, in psychological and medical records, and in East Indian magic lore, in the latter of which it is always given an occult complexion. The laws of many states demand that the undertaker embalm a corpse to avoid burial alive, and because of the too-frequent spectacle of a corpse reviving in time to climb out of the coffin and disrupt his own funeral service. Literature is full of tales of a corpse being committed to the family burial vault, and of having the grieving cortege find that the bones of the last interred member of the family were no longer in his crypt, but in a pathetic heap at the vault door. These tales all have their counterpart in fact. It was not very long ago that an undertaker found himself in serious trouble when a ten-year-old boy, who had not been embalmed, resuscitated himself during his last rites.

We all agreed that Hadad's three-day trance was not uncommon, but the fact that he had retained consciousness and memory during the trance, so that he could terminate it before Fellows' first incision was made, put him in select psychological company.

On Monday morning Gordon and I had Hadad brought to my office. One would have thought it was he who had summoned us. He addressed us as if we were precocious school boys, saving us the banality of questions.

"You are, of course, interested in the phenomenon of the weekend. It was nothing. I did it only as a means of coming to your learned attention."

He paused to study Gordon's and my expressions.

"I can see," he resumed, "that, being scientists, you are naturally skeptics, that you must have proof. Very well. Gentlemen," he said, "you will concur with me that among the epileptics in the psychopathic ward there are several hopeless cases with severe brain deterioration, who suffer seizures daily?"

315

This was true.

And was it not true, he asked, that even with the use of drugs we still could not delay the seizure of a deteriorated epileptic for as long as three constructive days?

This was true also. Delay for even a few hours was problematical among such cases.

He straightened in his chair and fixed his black eyes on us. His voice was quiet, intense.

"Gentlemen, as a demonstration of the use of mental telepathy in healing at a distance, I will delay all seizures in the psychopathic ward, including these deteriorated cases, from this hour, until the same hour on Thursday. For three days and three nights. As further proof of my control," he continued, "the seizures will resume on Thursday morning, beginning at this hour."

He looked from Gordon to me, and waited.

What he was proposing to do would be spectacular. He was committing himself to two phenomena: the abrupt cessation of seizures at one hour on one day, and the abrupt resuming of them at the same hour on another day.

"What about you, Hadad?" asked the practical Gordon. "Where will you spend the time between now and Thursday afternoon? You have a history of being A.W.O.L on several occasions, you know."

Hadad smiled at the dig. "I will stay wherever you wish, sir. In my solitary cell, perhaps?"

" 'Perhaps' is right," murmured Gordon. "What do you say, Wilson?"

I said I would be willing to let him launch his experiment with the epileptics, that even a three-day respite would be something for them.

Hadad inclined his head in thanks. "It is gratifying to find you two gentlemen accessible to the influence of the stars," he murmured. "I can teach you healing, mental telepathy, and psy-

316

chic control of the body, even at a distance. I can teach you the mysteries of astrology. Not the astrology of the common Hindu and East Indian fakir, but cosmic-somatic astrology."

Neither Gordon nor I spoke, a fact which Hadad may have interpreted as skepticism. I was not interested in hocus-pocus, but if underneath his hocus-pocus the man had integrity and altruism, and could add anything to the existing resources of hypnotic therapy, I would go with him as far as I could.

He soon resumed. "You will ask for proof again. My teaching credentials, if you will," he said, bowing to me. "Very well: in a few moments I shall again return to the astral plane. You learned men will call it a trance, catatonia, or even death. But I shall at all times be completely in possession of all my faculties. Gentlemen, I will cause the signs of the zodiac to appear on my body!"

He rose, removed his hospital robe and stood before us naked.

"You will find Aries appearing on my forehead, Cancer on my breast, Sagittarius on the thighs," he said. "All twelve signs of the Zodiac will appear on my body at the appropriate places."

He moved two desks together, lay down on them, and threw himself into rigidity and convulsions. The whole process took only a few minutes.

We bent over his body. It was difficult to establish erythema (red blotching or flushing of the skin) on a body so black, but unmistakable dermagraphia (raised, hive-like patches) began to appear. The wheals and welts assumed a shade that could, with a little latitude, be called red. Then, while we watched there appeared on forehead, breast and thighs the three signs he had mentioned, and elsewhere on his body the outlines of three others. The remaining six areas, even with generous Gestalt, could not honestly be called the signs of the Zodiac. The phenomenon, however, lay in the fact that without external irritation of the skin, and at will, he had produced localized, controlled dermagraphia.

Gordon checked the quiet black body, and for the second time in three days pronounced him dead by all tests. There was no stethoscopic heart sound, no breath on the mirror, no corneal reflex.

"Let's see if he will bleed." For this test Gordon punctured one of the veins in Hadad's wrist. As in death, there was not sufficient blood pressure to cause a flow of blood.

"There's everything here but putrefaction," Gordon said, without further conjecture about the state of things in Denmark. "What about these other signs, Professor?"

"I can't honestly say they look like signs of the Zodiac," I said.

At that moment Hadad relaxed his convulsive posture and resumed his precise and patient speech. Our untutored eyes, he said, would properly envision the appropriate astral signs in detail, if we would obtain a large magnifying glass.

This was no ordinary trance or simple suspended animation. It was beyond the usual psychotic catatonia or catalepsy. This was the second time Hadad had retained both consciousness and memory while in a trance, and had terminated it at will. It was not a statistical accident.

While Gordon went for the glass Hadad again induced rigidity, which he maintained until the seance was over. The glass brought out two more signs of reasonable credibility.

Later I asked Hadad how he could remain conscious to the extent of knowing what was taking place, and of speaking to us when he was in such deep trance as to be considered medically dead.

"Suspended animation, Doctor; it is simple," he said.

But it wasn't. The best exponents of the occult cannot, or will not, iterate their powers. His explanation trailed off into gibberish and superstition.

We watched the epileptics closely night and day in the next seventy-two hours. It was as Hadad had said it would be. There were no seizures in the ward, even among the cases of deterioration. Hadad was kept in his solitary cell, and paid no detectable visits to the psychopathic ward. On Thursday morning the tragic hell of the epileptic broke upon the ward.

Hadad had called this a demonstration of mental telepathy. But inasmuch as he had spent the twenty-four hours from Sunday morning to Monday morning in the psychopathic ward, it was much more probable that the delay of seizures was the result of post-hypnotic suggestion given by Hadad while he was still with the patients from Sunday to Monday. It would have been simple for a hypnotist of Hadad's skill to hypnotize the patients during those twenty-four hours, giving them post-hypnotic amnesia, so that they would not remember being hypnotized. But it demanded hypnosis of a very superior order.

Gordon and I admitted to ourselves that, though science might explain much of Hadad's magic in terms of psychological phenomenon, science was not reproducing it on Hadad's scale. We might explain what his magic was, but, with all our training and knowledge, we could not yet interrupt a deteriorated epileptic's seizures.

We were struck with the incongruity of the fact that here was modern science epitomized in a research hospital with the last word in equipment, and with the best consultants in the country only five telephone minutes away. But no x-ray machine could penetrate, no microscope reveal, no surgery excise, no cosmic ray illuminate, no test tube break down the rationale of a black man in a dungeon five hundred feet away, quietly working the ancient mysteries of the world outside the body and the senses, quietly reflecting the ancient philosophic victory of mind in the impingement of the unknown and feared upon the known.

We hoped that Hadad might be a man of sufficient character and integrity to work with us in illuminating the unknown and the feared in the No Man's Land of the mind. We listened in the weeks that followed for some sign of integrity while he engaged us in dissertations on hypnosis, yogiism, telekinesthesia, mental telepathy and occultism in general. He knew most of the authentic literature in these fields.

He made quite a point of the symbolism of his three-day death and resurrection, which he repeated at our request. He explicitly pointed out that from his Friday afternoon suicide to the Sunday morning autopsy was, as the Orientals reckon, three days. The implication was clearly that Christ had nothing on him.

We were not learning much, beyond his strong sense of his own destiny. He was greater than Mohammed, greater than Christ. One day when we began to weary of his egoism, I asked him why, with all his powers of escape and healing, he found himself in a penitentiary.

"Thank you, Doctor. I have been waiting for you to ask. You see, gentlemen, I am here on a mission. It is, in fact, a dual mission. Both are good, although one is a mission of death and the other of life."

Here it comes, I thought. Gordon and I offered him only our combined acute silence, so he continued.

"I am destined to wander throughout the world seeking two excessively evil and malign spirits, and to relieve them of their corporeal anatomy."

Gordon glanced at me with raised brows. Hadad smiled amusedly. "No, no, gentlemen, not you. I have, in fact, already found one of those spirits, and he is not."

Murder in the name of God. I was sorry to hear it.

"The other mission is to find two men upon whom I can bestow my mantle of therapy, the like of which has not been known since Christ. It has been revealed to me that you two gentlemen are the worthy successors."

320

That was one time Gordon and I didn't look at each other. We both looked at Hadad.

In addition to our own observations and our conferences with Hadad, we conducted some investigations into his past. Reports from two penitentiaries confirmed his boasts that in each he had committed suicide and that all recognized tests for death had been positive. The doctors, always willing to admit new evidence, had quickly revised their diagnosis to schizophrenic catatonia when on one occasion a watchman in the morgue found the stiff flexing his muscles.

We also found verification of a murder charge, but it was not the murder of which he had told us, or those on which he later elaborated.

One stubborn piece of data stood on record. At one time, perhaps when he was in search of one of the two malign spirits, he had been a member of a famous gang that was terrorizing the Southwest. He was inside the turtleback of a car when the police closed in and riddled it with machine gun bullets. It careened into a cornfield, and Hadad was extracted from the sieve unharmed.

His time was not yet, Hadad explained to us. "I found it expedient to deflect the bullets from the anatomical headquarters of my spirit."

"What do you make of Hadad's anatomical headquarters?" Gordon asked me later.

"I don't know," I said lamely, "I wasn't there."

As the days passed Hadad became increasingly aware that we were more curious than convinced, and he began to press the matter of our succession to The Mantle.

"Since my cosmic mission is almost completed," he said, "and I shall soon depart this sphere, I wish to impart to you these priceless therapeutic secrets in an initiation, a blood rite."

He told us that according to his Order, the rite must take place at astral midnight, which was two o'clock in the morning according to our time, and in the solitary cell which had been the scene of his "death."

Gordon and I wondered between ourselves whose blood would be used for this rite, and exactly how much? and if something beside his mantle would descend on us at astral midnight?

In his last appeal, Hadad assured us that after the initiation we would never be the same again. We would be, among other things, ageless and timeless.

This we could believe.

The prospect of the midnight rite brought to my mind Gordon's words on my first day at the penitentiary. "A little honest fear's a good thing around here."

Hadad was many times a murderer. His activities as the "finger-man" of the terrorizing gang meant that he had used his occult skills nefariously to draw the gang's victims out of hiding, whereupon he liquidated them.

Further, although he was a superior exponent of his profession, he was also a small-time showman. With his lofty sense of personal destiny, it seemed incongruous that he should spend his time turning up missing for the amusement and consternation of credulous prison populations.

Although in his personal relation to Gordon and me he was always cooperative, deferential and charming, he was all these almost to a fault. However charming he was, he lost me when I learned of his murder mission, and when he invited us to a blood rite. I had too much respect for his ability as a hypnotist to put myself under his influence. Hadad was not above seeking added prestige by discrediting medicine and psychology in a practical joke. Had we placed ourselves in his charge, he could have left us hypnotized in the dungeon, to wake at the morning cell count unable to explain our stuporous presence to the guards or the administration. Or, having hypnotized us, he could have incapacitated us physically or crippled us neurologically. He could have left us mentally dissociated. We could have awakened from the trance insane. He could have given us amnesia for our scientific background and training, and left us wild-eyed exponents of the occult. We had no way of knowing what he might do. He might have killed us.

When Gordon and I declined the Mantle, and when there was no further apparent value in studying his case, Hadad went cooperatively back to the psychopathic ward, and was finally absorbed again into the general prison population.

As has been said, Hadad's parapsychology can hardly be posed as rare in the annals of medicine and psychosomatics. However, the following phenomena in his case were unusual:

The uninterrupted function of consciousness and memory during his catatonic and cataleptic trances.

His control of the depth and termination of his trance.

His controlled, autonomous dermagraphia in producing the signs of the Zodiac upon his body.

His post-hypnotic therapy with the deteriorated epileptics of the psychopathic ward, who in our knowledge were beyond hope.

In explanation of Hadad's metapsychics, psychology would say that his catatonic trances were induced by autohypnosis; and that his disappearances from paddy wagons and cells, his presence at the concert, and his getting Red's belt to effect a fake suicide were accomplished by his generous endowment in escape artistry and contortionism, and by hypnotizing whoever stood between him and freedom at any given time: a keeper, a guard, an attendant; giving them amnesia for the incident in post-hypnotic suggestion.

He was a magnificent hypnotist. Gordon and I were only sorry he could not have passed on to us his skills in some other way than in a blood rite at astral midnight in a dungeon.

Regarding his corporeal impermeability when he was fired upon in the turtleback, I have no further light. I don't know, I wasn't there.

I hope it will be something more spectacular than the common cold that finally successfully invades Hadad's charming anatomical headquarters. As I remember, he *did* have a highly susceptible upper respiratory tract. . . .

17

THE HARRISON NARCOTIC ACT outlawing the use
of all narcotic drugs except by medical prescription became
Federal law in 1914, as an outgrowth of the Pure Food and
Drug Act of 1906-09.

When the United States Public Health Service undertook
the study of drug addiction and established the Porter Narcotic
Farms in the thirties, the existing scientific literature in that field
consisted of a half dozen books which were controversial, scanty
and sometimes weird in content. The only organization which
was producing reputable evidence was the Narcotics Commission
of the League of Nations, with which the USPHS was working.

Endogenous with man is his archetypical search for a fountain of youth, a pot of gold at the end of the rainbow, a magic
carpet, an invisible garment, an aphrodisiac. This is a concept
which enjoys enthusiastic social approval from the cradle to the
grave. We teach our children and our youth in fairy tales, nur-
sery rhymes, comic strips and classic mythology to dream of exploits in a world that does not exist. Man has tried to make contact with that unreal world, to escape the pressures of life on
two levels of wish-fulfillment: a depressant which will make him
insensitive to pressure, or a stimulant which will make him
superior to pressure. These two escape mechanisms form the
basis of drug addiction the world over. The inadequate, insecure,

fear-ridden, confused individual—in other words, the neurotic personality of our time—makes up our addicted population. He is the victim not so much of a vicious drug as of a vicious social philosophy of escape, and of a comparatively new and very profitable international traffic in a humane commodity which never before in the history of the world was a moral problem until England launched the opium wars in China in the nineteenth century, and until the United States passed Federal narcotic laws in 1914.

From earliest times alcohol served these archetypical needs of man. Later, but still in antiquity, the poppy of India came into use, then hemp. Ancient and mediaeval literature refer to magic formulae, love and hate potions, and drugs which dissociated personality. As early alchemists refined their techniques, opium and hashish powder emerged as an improved concentrate supplanting the old process of chewing or soaking the leaves.

When Europeans first came to South America in the early sixteenth century, they found that the natives since time immemorial had been chewing coca leaves for solace from fatigue and pain.

Opium was smoked for the first time about 1800 A.D. Morphine, an alkaloid stronger than opium, was isolated in 1803-05. Within ten years the Indian opium traffic became of commercial importance to England as illicit barter to China in exchange for silks and tea. China, who had been free of opium and had prohibited its import, took militant action against the black-market smuggling traffic. Through commercial and political squeezes, opium from India continued to be smuggled into China. However, Chinese resistance so crippled British trade that England launched the first of the infamous opium wars against China about 1840, seizing and retaining several coastal cities as "indemnity" and to enforce "free trade." Chinese officials continued to destroy occasional shipments in protest. The second opium war of 1856 was concluded shamefully in 1858, when the American Minister to China negotiated a trade agreement between China and Britain demanding free entry and protection of two incongruous commodities: opium and missionaries.

The hypodermic syringe was invented in 1845, and cocaine was isolated and refined between 1855-77. During the Civil War the use of drugs to deaden pain became so prevalent that the addiction which resulted was called *the Army disease.*

Morphine was found to be more stable than opium, more concentrated, more transportable. England launched it on the world market, and in the eighties, from the royal courts of Europe to New York's Fifth Avenue, solid gold and silver hypodermic syringes set with jewels and diamonds were flashed, to the envy of the less fortunate. Soon doctors were giving patients syringes indiscriminately, for morphine, the wonder drug, was prematurely reported by doctors to cure many ills, such as cancer, asthma, tuberculosis, and heart disease.

By the end of the century morphinism had become a problem. It was not living up to its claims as a cure-all, and it caused addiction in some cases. Doctors again prematurely hailed the discovery of heroin in 1898 as a cure for morphinism. This also proved not to be so. Heroin was only a substitute for morphine. The doctors therefore gradually withdrew the hypos from circulation, as a result of which less demand was made on druggists for narcotics.

The patent medicine business absorbed most of these hypochondriacal addicts. The patent wine tonics and pain killers were generously loaded with laudanum, heroin and cocaine. A well-known beverage advertised: *The more you drink, the more you want.* The Pure Food and Drug Act curtailed the narcotic content of patent medicine and beverages by legislation beginning as early as 1909.

The hysteria was over. Even after twenty-five years of epidemic use, addicts were very few and declining steadily, until there was less than one addict per thousand of population in

327

1914, when the Narcotic Act was passed. Treasury Department figures and other estimates at this time ranged from 60,000 to 100,000 users in the United States. About half of these were using it under medical supervision. The user was still able to buy his supply openly at the corner pharmacy, he was known in the neighborhood, the cost of the drug was low, and there was no association between the use of drugs and criminality, either in professional literature or police reports.

But upon the passage of the Harrison Narcotic Act, the use of drugs acquired a social stigma. All drug users not under medical supervision became criminals overnight, not only nominally by the Narcotic Act, but in many instances actually. Instead of going to the neighborhood pharmacy for his supply, the user now had to consort with the underworld to get it, for the underworld immediately grabbed and stimulated the drug traffic, as it later did the liquor traffic.

Now, instead of the former few pennies per grain, the bootleg price shot up toward fifty cents a grain and higher. In that era, on a salary of $2 or $3 a day, and a 5-grain daily dose of morphine costing nearly as much as he earned, the user became a petty thief to support his habit. The stable personality who took his morphine in moderation, as he drinks his daily cocktail, gave up its use. But the unstable personality, the neurotic who used his morphine as an escape from life and pressure, and who comprises the addicted population of this country, became desperate for means to support his habit. Unscrupulous doctors and quack sanitaria bled the user financially, and then by blackmail built a pitiful traffic in human life.

When the underworld takes over a traffic, it becomes profitable, because gangsters set in motion a formidable propagandizing and proselyting campaign. They are not interested in the medicinal use of drugs—the doctors still take care of that— but in its enslaving properties. The traffic must therefore expand. This means smugglers, peddlers, and more and heavier users.

One of the most enigmatic basic truths regarding human nature is that forbidden things have a secret charm. The Treasury Department estimated that by 1918, four years after the enactment of the Narcotic Act, there were 1½ million users of drugs, an increase of 1,500 percent.

There have always been sporadic outlaws in American history. But organized gangsters and racketeers, who took over certain areas of American life and controlled them for three decades, were a formidable innovation. In five short years the Capones of our cities took over the billion-dollar rackets growing out of four specific prohibitions:

> The Harrison Narcotic Act
> The Volstead Act
> Legislation outlawing Prostitution
> Legislation outlawing Gambling

Since morphine and heroin had become prohibitively expensive, marijuana was introduced in the United States following the first World War. Although it is easily and cheaply made from hemp, one of the oldest sources of narcotics, for a decade its use was not so large as to become a national problem. But in 1929-31 narcotic agents began bearing down on the morphine and cocaine traffic, and as a result the use of marijuana became widespread. The first Federal law outlawing marijuana was passed in 1937, and instantly its use became epidemic.

A new evil attended this development. For the first time drug usage became a children's problem. High school students as well as juvenile delinquents were solicited by the underground peddler. The cigarettes cost from five cents to one dollar apiece.

A little known fact regarding both the Harrison Narcotic Act of 1914 and the Marijuana Tax Act of 1937 is that they are in reality only revenue measures with provisions for the prosecution of nonpayment of tax, according to a decision of the Supreme Court of the United States. The use of drugs is still not a felony in the United States. The implications of felony in the violation of these two Drug Acts is the result not of the Acts themselves, but of an interpretation, a *ruling* of the Narcotics Division of the old Prohibition Unit of the Treasury Department, as sustained by the Department of Justice.

The total number of drug users in the United States at the present time is unknown. Estimates of legitimate users ranged from 77,000 to 1,600,000 in 1927. Various present-day estimates of illicit users range from 100,000 to 4 million, depending on which concept the compiler is championing: control by legislation, or control by self-limitation. Less than one million might be a closer guess. Statistics on drug addiction, like statistics on crime, are highly unreliable because they are based only on the offender who is apprehended—*less than one percent of all users*. This does not mean simply that law enforcement is inefficient. It means that most illicit users are men and women who do not develop symptoms which get them into trouble.

As a quiet rebuke to sensational propaganda, the FBI Uniform Crime Reports list for 1942 but 1,383 narcotic arrests in the 1,100 largest American cities; in 1948 there were but 3,125 narcotic arrests in the 1,654 largest cities—less than two per city.

We are always cutting off the snake's head at the wrong end. The heroic conferences at The Hague and at Geneva have been made ludicrous by the legalization of the world drug traffic through international trade agreements. The prosecution of the traffic in the United States by valiant T-men, as reported in the newspapers and movies, also would have more point but for these agreements. Nations, like gangsters, are opportunists.

It is no secret that the yearly quota of drugs needed for

medicinal purposes is exceeded ten times by the amount of drugs imported into the United States as a result of these agreements. It then requires only an under-the-table transaction to get the 90% surplus of legally imported drugs to a profitable illegal market. *This* is the point at which to control drug addiction, rather than by legislation making criminals of users, a traffic created by "honorable" trade agreements. This would be morality. We have the brazen example of England, for instance, who sent, as her representative to the first several conferences at The Hague and at Geneva studying the international control of narcotics, her government official charged with the responsibility of *increasing* the acreage and output of opium in India!

The exaggerated derelictions and crimes of the "dope fiend" in news reports, movies and novels are well-known. There is an appalling misconception and warp, even in scientific literature and among professional men, as to the effects of the drugs and the nature of the crimes committed by the user. Part of the confusion lies in the failure to recognize the two kinds of drugs: depressants and stimulants. Part results from quoting authorities out of context, or championing only one side of a theory. Much of the misconception comes from not differentiating the symptoms of denarcotization from the actual effects of the drug on the body, two distinctly separate problems in addiction.

Part of the error in thinking lies in the physician's generalizations drawn from the occasional case in a private hospital. These observations differ radically from findings when large numbers of addicts are studied and denarcotized. The clientele, procedure, methods of control and perspective or frame of reference of the operators differ, and consequently so do the results.

A prolific source of popular misconception regarding the "fiend" arises from propaganda designed to discourage addiction. Addiction should certainly be discouraged. But the ancient and impotent philosophy of fear and punishment and the pointing up of horrible examples are abysmally ineffectual. The extreme cases chosen and the inclusion of non-related or non-scientific data have violently boomeranged. The unstable, neurotic personality who is the incipient addict in our midst is not repelled but attracted by prohibitions and lurid tales.

In the search for facts among the fiction surrounding drug addiction, our research project at the penitentiary hospital attacked the drug problem from many angles: biochemical, physiological, psychological. Every claimed cure was retried and retested. Existing theories were investigated. These results were studied and evaluations made concerning the discrepancies which appeared.

In spite of this research and other more recent projects, superstitions regarding addiction still persist. Professional journal articles carrying such titles as "Exploding the Dope Fiend Myths" have only a small influence on yellow journalism, propaganda, and careless professional literature.

The following example regarding contrasting methods of denarcotization alone will illustrate how conflicting statements arise:

The USPHS found immediate and total withdrawal of drugs the best method of denarcotization. Several thousand cases were so conducted without serious complications, and the patients recovered weight and health more quickly than by any other method studied.

However, private hospitals and sanitaria report delirium, shock, and even death accompanying immediate withdrawal. The addict knows that, if he creates a scene and disturbs other patients and hospital routine, he will be given a relief shot. The sanitaria cannot afford the disturbance and publicity attending such scenes. As a result the drug is withdrawn gradually in such institutions, the patient's addiction continues longer, which incidentally means more revenue for the sanitarium.

There is no such hysteria in a Government hospital because

no relief shots are given. The addicts know this, and "kick the habit cold turkey" with a minimum of symptoms and beefing. The patient is discharged in four to eight days, instead of in as many weeks in private institutions.

Another common source of misinformation regarding addiction and denarcotization is the police authority, who usually makes his observations while the addict is in jail without drugs, or during a police third degree designed to force a confession. At this time the addict's threshold is lowered, his resistance is poor, and he may easily become erratic and hysterical at being beaten, manhandled, grilled, threatened; or merely at the sight of a hypodermic needle kept out of reach until he confesses. If the same addict were denarcotized in a Government hospital, there would be no hysteria, because there would be no promise of a hypodermic. What the police observe in these circumstances is not a fiend, but a neurotic individual under pressure.

In the same way, the police relate the addict's emaciation to the use of morphine, forgetting that they do not meet the large proportion of addicts who eat regularly and maintain a relatively normal set of vocational and social habits. What the police observe is an end result of an incapacitating neurosis, rather than the specific influence of a drug.

The user of opium, morphine, heroin and the barbituates wishes to sleep, and often does. His wish to escape from life and responsibility is aided by these drugs which inhibit the higher cortical centers and allow the vegetative nervous system to take over. All the addict to morphine, opium and heroin wants is to be left alone.

The medical dosage of morphine sulphate is ¼ grain or less. One grain can be lethal to the non-user, because it inhibits the respiratory centers. The body gradually achieves a tolerance for the drug, and dosage can be increased enormously. It is this ratio of increase that determines whether the individual remains

333

merely an upper-class user, becomes an average addict, or degenerates into a "dope fiend." The necessity of increasing the dosage is psychological, not physical. This classification of addicts is arbitrary. It is made only to emphasize that there are thousands of users who have none of the characteristics or symptoms assigned to the fictional fiend. The man who can hold his dosage of any narcotic at a minimum for months or years, regardless of the vicissitudes of life, is of no more worry to the psychologist than the citizen who must have his daily highball or evening cocktail, or the toper who is unlivable until she has had her morning cup of coffee.

An analogy can be made between addicts and drinkers. The psychologist is concerned about three kinds of drinkers: the man who drinks to forget or escape; the one who drinks to buoy himself up before he can approach a sales prospect, a problem, or his wife; and the solitary drinker who ends up with delirium tremens. Social and holiday drinkers represent no serious psychological problem, because they are not drinking to avoid life. This latter kind of drinking remains a festive event.

It is significant that some research studies find 70% of drug addicts were once serious drinkers, having given up alcohol for drugs because they found drugs paid more dividends in escape and also provided a better substitute for an involved and maladjusted sex life.

A moderate dose of morphine need not put a man to sleep, but it does make him less sensitive to the assaults of life. The more inadequate and psychologically inferior the individual—that is, the more neurotic, the greater his sensitivity to the pressures and competitions of life, the greater his fears, the more bitter his memories, the more hopeless his failures—the greater the increase in his dosage. As rapidly as the body tolerates the drug, so that guilt, shame, failure, and memories become vivid again, the more morphine must be taken to inhibit the cortical centers and provide escape in lethargy and sleep. This is the *construct* of an addict.

The addict, for financial reasons, would like to keep his dose low, to perhaps three grains a day; but his neurosis, rather than the drug, almost invariably gets out of hand. The extreme addict, when he reaches the outer boundaries of escape and apathy, becomes careless about his person, health and appetite, and manifests many of the characteristics of the *real* dope fiend: a completely beaten piece of protoplasm, not a sex-crazed maniac.

Our research unit at the penitentiary was composed of 1,500 addicts. Opium, morphine, heroin and barbituate users accounted for ninety-five percent of our addicted population. These drugs are depressants. The users of cocaine and marijuana accounted for the other five percent.

Our research cases gave a range of from three to sixty grains a day, with an average dosage of 12 grains a day of morphine, 20 of heroin and 10 units of opium. Those who used both cocaine and morphine averaged 23 grains of cocaine to elate themselves and 18 grains of morphine to quiet themselves. This dual drug use is analogous to the neurosis of many people who use coffee and other stimulants to get through the day and sleeping tablets to get through the night.

We found that pathological lying was common among our addicts. They boasted of their dosages and conquests, obviously tall tales spun for the investigator, who too often believed them. In our research ward we kept a few incoming addicts under drugs for experimentation in dosage, tolerance levels and effects. One of our prize cases claiming a dosage of 55 grains daily of morphine was able to tolerate only 35 grains. And one small-town yokel, struggling to keep his prestige among so many big-city toughs, claimed single intravenous injections of 12 grains of morphine four times a day. He fainted and fell off his stool on four grains. Since most of their supply of drugs was underworld bootleg, not USP strength, it is probable their dosage was diluted from 25% to 40%.

Our addicts at the penitentiary had been using drugs for from four months to fifty years, the average duration of addiction being fourteen years. The ages of our addicts ranged from seventeen to seventy-five years, the average being thirty-five years. The average age at the time of addiction was twenty-three years. Their average educational level was at the fifth grade. Their I.Q.s ranged from 34 to 120, with an average of 74, the same as that of non-addicted prison populations.

Seventy percent of our addicts used morphine, 20% heroin, 5% opium, and 5% the various other drugs: cocaine, hashish, marijuana. Sixty-five percent of the men had had from two to more than twenty previous "cures." The ordeal of denarcotization or "kicking the habit" was no deterrent to addiction, just as punishment was no deterrent to crime. About 90% of them came from unskilled walks of life: laborers, personal servants, door-to-door salesmen, and derelicts without jobs. Addicts in a penitentiary represent those who get caught—the lower one percent of drug users. The upper and middle-class users in medicine, business, law, engineering, teaching, and the theater use discretion, watch their health, show none of the symptoms of addiction, and are almost never detected or apprehended. Statements regarding this high class user are based on individual observation, while researches made on masses are heavily weighted with people from the wrong side of the tracks who are maladjusted, maladroit and inadequate in the face of life and pressure.

The opium smoker commits no crimes. He is either asleep or stuporous. His colored dreams and visions are fictional. He is practically anaesthetized by large doses, and all his sense cues, especially color, are reduced. He has no sexual dreams either, for he is impotent and without sexual desire under the drug. The drug is a passive substitute for active sex. The much sung sing-

336

song girls are kept in an opium den to serve only the smokers' opium needs.

The morphine addict, whether he takes the drug by mouth or by intramuscular or intravenous injection, is not a hollow-cheeked fiend. He may well be hollow-cheeked, because morphine reduces appetites of all kinds, so that he may eat very little. But he is not a fiend in any sense, especially sexually. He is not an aggressive criminal or a rapist. The latter is a mechanical impossibility, because he is impotent under the drug. Avoidance of sex is one of the psychological drives to addiction.

The morphine addict may become a masochist, a fact which is inherent in his neurosis rather than in the drug. When oral administration or intramuscular injection no longer provide a "jag," he becomes a "main line shooter," who takes the drug intravenously. Since addicts are solitary people, they must, in giving their own injections, do with one hand what a skilled nurse or doctor needs two hands to perform. In his nervousness and inexperience an addict frequently damages the vein of his arm, and if he is deeply masochistic he irritates the wound, even forcing foreign matter into it to create an abscess. Many addicts have lines of scars along the veins of both arms or legs, caused by infection following their unskilled injections, or by their deliberately prodding the wound.

Men ordinarily inject their arms; women are more prone to use the thighs. Women are seldom "main line shooters" unless they accidentally hit a vein. Then they become converts to intravenous injection, because this method produces a sudden thrill, and may on occasion induce a substitute sexual climax in which they experience the physical and psychic manifestations of a violent male-like orgasm. There is no pharmaceutical aphrodisiac. This reaction is subjective, due entirely to the individual's psychological set and warp, and is dependent upon the contagious expectancy and day dreaming mustered for the occasion.

The reactions of men to intravenous injection are less violent, the thrill merging into a passive feminine type of orgasm, often not recognized as sexual at all by the user. The Freudians explain this by a concept of passive sexuality and latent homosexuality. A male addict will sometimes addict his wife, and thus they both escape sexual responsibility.

While morphine, heroin and opium are depressants, cocaine and marijuana are temporary stimulants, although depression follows elation. The psychological effects accompanying the use of drugs are as various as those accompanying the use of alcohol. Most people handle alcohol quite well, but there are those who react wildly to it. Their reaction is inherent in their personality disorganization, not in the alcohol. This is especially true in reference to cocaine and marijuana. The more intact the core and organization of the personality, the less erratic the effect of the drug. It is related to the internal consistency of the person. People have been known to use drugs moderately for years without appreciable effect. However, if the personality is already unstable and pre-psychotic, the effect of either of these two drugs is unpredictable, except that its course will exaggerate the specific neurotic drives already threatening the personality. This is why generalizations regarding the effects attending the use of cocaine and marijuana are misleading.

Cocaine is usually sniffed through the nostrils. The powder is called "snow" and the user a "snow bird." In average doses exhilaration and euphoria are experienced. In overdoses, restlessness, irritability, sporadic aggression and over-stimulation of all the senses are characteristic; there is exaggerated sensitivity to sound, touch, movement, taste and sight. There is a constant flight of ideas, with attendant silliness and hysteria. Reaction time is so speeded up that few autocritical faculties remain. In extreme dosage, illusions and hallucinations occur, especially skin paresthesia, wherein the patient feels a sensation as of bugs

338

crawling on and beneath the skin. Suspicion, fear and a compulsion to hide are aroused with little provocation.

While morphine and opium are solitary, seclusive pursuits, the users of cocaine and marijuana prefer company, because of the talking jags which accompany the use of these drugs.

Lurid literature depicts "snow parties" which degenerate into sexual orgies. Actually a snow party is very rare. When it does occur, it is the result of orgiastic dosage and its progress is constantly interrupted by watchers posted at doors, lookouts at windows, terrorized and hallucinated people hiding behind doors and trying to climb into dresser drawers. Attention and responses are so scattered, and suspicion, fear and paranoia so dominant, that sustained sexual activity would be very difficult to achieve. Consider what kind of orgy would be possible in delirium tremens, or with a patient suffering delirium with 107° temperature.

Marijuana is made from hemp, which is ordinarily used in the manufacture of rope, hats, paper, soap, linoleum, food for animals, fertilizer and bird seed. Canaries, for instance, sing lustily on it. The physiological reactions to marijuana are similar to those of cocaine. The effects are similar also to those of benzedrine sulphate. In moderate use there is stimulation and exhilaration, and marked increase in reaction time. This is one reason why creative people use the drug over a period of years without negative symptoms, and why news reports of arrests seem so frequently to concern actors, artists and musicians.

In overdoses of marijuana there are tremors, spasms, ringing in the ears, and phantasmagoria. In extreme usage it is the most unpredictable of the drugs. Its exposés are more spectacular, because its users are frequently youthful gangs of delinquents who themselves are immature, unstable, antisocial and violent, before the added irritation of marijuana cigarettes. Its effects not only vary from person to person, but from time to time in the same person.

Another disturbing drug virtually unknown in pure form in this country is hashish, also made from hemp, and a cousin of marijuana. When Turks and Arabs run amuck, it is sometimes under the influence of hashish, hence the name *assassin*. They also, however, run amuck under the influence of alcohol, like the American Indian and the American debutante and the legionnaire. The furor already existing in the psycopath is released under the dissociation resulting from hashish, which stimulates any incipient violence in an individual who is already potentially dangerous.

Marijuana, hashish and cocaine do not have withdrawal and denarcotization symptoms in the usual sense. Hangovers may result from either occasional use, or from overdoses. Morphine, opium and heroin, the depressants, are the drugs which bring specific denarcotization symptoms and require a denarcotization period of from several days to several weeks, depending on the method used in withdrawing the drug.

The popular concept of physical damage done to the body and brain by prolonged morphine and opium use is not borne out by research. There seems to be no damage to the structure and function of the brain, mind or nervous system. A normal individual can be addicted to large doses of morphine for years without damage to either personality or body. By normal, it is meant that he is not neurotic—is not attempting to run away from life and its pressure. He takes morphine as his neighbor takes his cocktail. That is why, when a normal man volunteers for experimentation in addiction, no symptoms develop from his use of drugs. But when a neurotic individual volunteers, there is an accompanying shift in personality and certain physiological signs.

Morphine, for instance, inhibits the appetite, the addict becomes careless about eating, and develops malnutrition. Malnutrition means vitamin and mineral deficiencies, which are frequently evidenced by the dental problems of the addict. But in spite of emaciation and its accompanying deformities, the pathological addict maintains a remarkable constitutional stability, no one knows why. Many amusing conjectures have been advanced, such as: the addict lives in isolation and so does not encounter contagion; he is so unhygienic as to immunize himself by constant exposure to germs of every kind; he sleeps so much that his resistance is kept high in spite of malnutrition; his vegetative processes are so low that he does not incubate germs; his toxins from chronic constipation keep his basic defense armamentarium aroused and at a high pitch; his lethargy keeps him from all extremes, even illness.

Morphine does constipate, and the careless addict, avoiding life in general, avoids even the responsibility of evacuating regularly. After long conditioning, an addict may defecate only three or four times a month. Consequently he develops fistulae, hemorrhoids, and a grotesquely distended colon. This is the extent of the physical and mental damage of morphine and opium addiction, regardless of the duration of the habit.

Neither is there organic damage from cocaine or marijuana. Personality impairment is in proportion to the existing neurosis, and the dividends of escape from reality. After denarcotization the individual gains weight, his normal reaction time is established, and physical symptomatology disappears. But unless the neurosis which led to addiction in the first place is treated, a relapse is almost certain. Prison life is hardly the cure for neurosis or addiction.

There are always exceptions to every rule of human personality, and even of human physiology. Such personal idiosyncrasies are seen in response to drugs. Some people are allergic to morphine, so that it becomes a stimulant instead of a depressant. There are clinical records of a person's taking morphine to stay awake in order to finish a protracted piece of work. On the other hand, occasionally an individual will respond to cocaine with toxemia and depression.

There is no relation between morphine or opium addiction and serious crime. The addict of these two drugs is not aggressive by nature. He is an escapist. He is recessive, passive, and masochistic. His absence of drive makes it impossible for him to plan a crime skillfully, and he would be inept and maladroit in carrying it out. This leaves him only pilfering, pickpocketing and shoplifting merchandise that can be disposed of through a "fence" as a means of supporting his habit. Even in this connection he does not plan for the future. He steals only enough for today's needs. He doesn't break into a place at night and clean it out. He works in the daytime for the reason that he sees very poorly at night. His pin-point pupils which result from his use of a depressant do not adapt themselves to darkness.

The relation between serious crime, cocaine and marijuana is sporadic. The users' aggressive-defensive crimes must be committed during the short period of elation, before the depression or hangover sets in.

Generally speaking, gangsters and organized crime rings will have absolutely nothing to do with an addict because the latter is unstable and undependable. In the use of cocaine or marijuana he may become overbold, careless, and trigger-happy; or he may become jittery and lose his nerve altogether. The addict of morphine, opium or heroin may become lethargic and forgetful. He would quickly "sing" to either the police or a rival gang in exchange for a "shot." He cracks easily under a third degree after two days' privation.

Less than one-fourth of all convicts in prison for drug offenses have any charge against them other than possession of narcotics—not even petty theft. Peddlers, who are usually themselves non-users, account for many of the petty larcenies of the drug offenders. Former Federal Investigator Fishman in his study of 1,200 addict-convicts also found that *there was not a single serious crime charged against any of them.* The popular statement, "An addict will do anything to get his shot," is not borne out in fact. The dangerous dope fiend myths grow out of police, reporters, and even doctors watching the "show" of denarcotization and its apparent mania. The extent to which police are concerned with this problem is evidenced by this fact: last year, the entire United States, including its possessions, made only 4,846 fingerprint arrests of suspects in connection with all variations of the narcotic laws—tax evasion and peddling as well as addiction.

There being no biochemical or physiological habit in addiction, in the popular sense, there is no pharmaceutical cure. Thousands of amputees, surgical cases, patients injured in accidents or suffering protracted illnesses, are given morphine daily and do not become addicted. Other individuals become addicted after a brief illness, an inconsequential surgery, or one hypodermic injection, because of their basic personality instability.

Physicians sometimes use morphine to sober a drunk or to hasten his recovery from a hangover. Seventy percent of our research addicts at the penitentiary gave this as the cause of their original addiction. However, our research indicated that the addict's neurosis was in control of the personality before either drunkenness or addiction developed.

The use of phenobarbital compounds is becoming a serious problem in the nation. A generous number of the 20,000 annual suicides are due to overdoses of sleeping tablets. The so-called dangerous drugs do not figure in suicides. The constant user of sleeping potions and sedatives develops complications of nervousness, irritability, barbiturate rashes, gastritis, tremors and more insomnia. The physical damage done by phenobarbital compounds is more insidious and extensive than that of the dangerous drugs under discussion. Several states are currently instituting legislation to curtail the careless and generous prescriptions of physicians accommodating the insistent demands of their neurotic and insomniac patients.

Drug addiction is a medical and psychological problem, and the addict belongs in a hospital, not a penitentiary. Wherever

343

research in addiction has been undertaken, the answer is the same: addiction is a neurosis, the nature of which is the individual's inability to cope with the pressures inherent in his environment. The Government no longer regards the addict as a criminal. There are no concrete walls and no gun turrets at the Porter Narcotic Farms. The procedure at these hospitals is immediate withdrawal of the drug, the restoration of health through good and regular eating habits, dental care, opportunity for work, vocational rehabilitation, and psychotherapy provided by resident psychiatrists and psychologists.

The Farms accommodate from 600 to 1,500 patients. The turnover is rapid and "sentences" are short. It is too early to comment on recidivism under this regime, but it is sure to be lower than if the addict were sent to prison, where the nature of his abnormal existence would attack and confirm every inadequacy in his already faulty psychological structure.

18

One day about six months before I left the penitentiary, Gordon, Laurie Kennedy and I were studying the yards of statistical tables and diagrams from which the foregoing impressions were drawn. Taped to the walls of my office, they completed a circle of the room in a four-foot belt; there were about two hundred and fifty of them. Punch and I had tabulated the statistics; King, with sporadic help from Ross and Scott, had drawn the diagrams.

By this time the main body of data was in. The indices we saw that day were not materially affected by any additional figures which came in during the next three months. My last three months were given to final compilation and interpretation of data.

Laurie was usually spirited and voluble in such a meeting. But she sat in deep abstraction that day, speaking only when she was spoken to. The second time she missed a question addressed to her, Gordon asked quietly, "Something wrong, Kennedy?"

"No," she said quickly. "Nothing's wrong. What would be wrong?"

"Davis could be wrong," he said.

She smiled. "Still worrying about Davis? He's just fine. Gentle as a lamb!"

But her smile was brittle. Gordon walked over to her.

"Look, Kennedy. Will you forgive me if I remind you that

you've promised to report any odd behavior of Davis to Stevens?"

"I remember!" she said shortly, and abruptly excused herself.

The next morning when I arrived at the office, none of my boys were in sight. This meant something was up. Somebody's visit was being covered. In a few minutes a man appeared whom I did not remember having seen before, and, like the cook who had once interceded for Doctor Fellows, he began to talk urgently.

"It's about Miss Kennedy," he said. "An' Davis. It ain't safe, Doc. She don't understand about that con. He's dangerous. We know things about him none o' you civvies do. About women, an' kids. I ain't sayin' no more, but you're a psycho, see? We figger you oughtta know. There's things not on his record, see? an' he's gettin' that way again. That's all."

This was not a fidgety squealer talking for revenge. By now I had a high regard for my men's evaluation of fellow prisoners. This appeal was on the level and urgent, or my men would not have covered for him.

I considered talking with Laurie again, but it would not work, I knew. Gordon and I had both tried that. There seemed to be nothing left to do but go to Doctor Stevens, a course of action I did not relish professionally, philosophically, ethically or personally.

Disturbed, Doctor Stevens called Laurie, asking me to remain through the interview. She was respectful and quiet, but adamant, even defensive. There was nothing wrong with Davis, she said, adding that it should be understandable that a thirty-year-old man might become depressed once in a while at the thought that his life was behind him, that he might live for fifty years in prison. But she assured us there was no aggression toward her personally.

She discounted my impressions of his inherent sadism, saying that on the contrary he was unusually gentle. He wouldn't even kill the experimental animals; she had had to ask another man to do that. When I suggested that Davis might be afraid to kill the animals for fear it would unhinge him and start him on a path of violence, she said, "I think his violence is all behind him, D.W."

Doctor Stevens was of the impression that Davis should be locked up at once, at least until his brooding passed. But Laurie pleaded so eloquently that her work not be interrupted at that moment, especially the series they were running on a group of specially bred rats, that Stevens capitulated to her. Not at all reassured, I walked back to her office with her. At her door she turned to me.

"You know what I think, D.W.?" she said. "I think you're a stinky little tattletale, running to Stevens with some hysterical con's babblings. I thought you psychologists minded your own business!"

I assured her that this was my business, that Davis was a psychopathic killer and she was his kind of victim. "You're proud, Kennedy. I know you want to handle this yourself. But it may be too big for you."

"Thank you, Stinky. But I don't think so," she replied, and turned on her heel.

The rest of the day my men were nervous and preoccupied. Little work was done except the routine testing. Every half hour one of them would leave the office for a few minutes. So many trips to the men's room were hardly defensible.

When Laurie stormed into my office I knew what had been taking place. Her eyes were snapping.

"Are you sending your men down to spy on me?" she demanded. "They're coming in relays, looking like bereaved relatives expecting to view the remains! I'm really *quite* annoyed, D.W. We can't get any work done. Will you *please* call off the bloodhounds!" She left, looking small, proud and pathetic.

The men kept away from the laboratory, but they worried

347

through the rest of the day. Although King had not participated in the relay, he was more disturbed than those who had. He was brooding and irritable, and drew furiously on a constant chain of his elegant oval cigarettes.

The next morning the unrest among the men was sharper. I was coming out of the vault during the morning when King wheeled suddenly on his stool. His face was twisted with anguish and fear.

"Why the *hell* doesn't somebody do something—"

Connie's face popped out of the testing room, Scott's and Gibbs' from their cubicles. They stared at King. I thought of the picture in Marian's room in New York, and I had a feeling King was thinking about it, too. Our faces brought him to himself. He looked at us self-consciously for a moment, then turned and went morosely back to work.

The other three were looking uncertainly at each other.

"You'd better go back to your work, men," I said quietly.

They obeyed with great reluctance.

It was some time before my men and their testees settled down to the point where I could leave the office. Because of the almost telepathic sensitivity that seemed to exist between King and Davis, I didn't feel it was melodramatic to look in on Laurie. When I walked into the laboratory I found her bandaging her throat.

"Morning, Tattletale," she said, attempting gayety. "Are you going to run to Stevens about my throat?" She was full of nerves, on which she was keeping a tight hand. "If you do," she continued in the same voice, "be sure to tell him Davis tried to choke me!"

When I asked her what did happen she said a test tube had blown up in her face, but that it was nothing serious.

"When was this?" I asked stubbornly.

"Just a little while ago."

When King had wheeled around on his stool and screamed? I wondered.

"Where's Davis?" I asked.

She looked steadily at me for a moment. "Outside," she said finally. "In the vivarium."

I started for the outside door. "Mind if I take a look at the animals?"

"Yes—I do."

I paused and looked back at her.

"I mind very much, D.W.," she said quietly. She was not looking at me now.

"Kennedy—"

When she finally raised her eyes, I saw she was pretty badly shaken.

"You're being a damn fool, Kennedy," I said as gently as I could.

For an intsant she wavered, and I thought she was going to break down and talk. But she went back to her work, and I left.

When she left the hospital that afternoon, she stopped at my office on the way out. King looked at her sharply. She wore her coat collar high around her throat, so that the men did not see the bandage; but I was sure King questioned the upturned collar. She seemed more relaxed than she had been for many days. She stayed just long enough to leave some records in my vault. She would pick them up in the morning, she said. There was a little more work to do on them before she gave them to Stevens. Then she looked straight at me and said, "I'm seeing him in the morning."

I dropped by the laboratory when I left the office later. Davis was still there, apparently working on an all-night pass, as he frequently did. He and I exchanged no words. He met me with malevolence in his eyes. I was glad Laurie was gone.

I arrived early the next morning, firmly resolved to insist on Davis' isolation. As I walked down the hall one of the floor guards rushed out of Laurie's laboratory, almost knocking me down in his haste.

"Jeez, Doc—" he breathed. "Take a look! Gotta get the cap'n." He rushed on, calling over his shoulder, "Don't let Miss Kennedy in when she comes!"

At least she was all right.

I stopped in the doorway of the laboratory—and surveyed the maniacal devastation Davis had created. He had mutilated, disemboweled and beheaded every animal in the room. In his frenzy he had dismembered the creatures and thrown them everywhere. The ceiling and walls were spattered with entrails, fur and blood. All that remained of the data covering the special series they were then running was a heap of black ashes in the sink. I thought of my own scare over Punch, and the thin sheaf of records Laurie had brought to the vault yesterday. A handful of records and a few animals in the vivarium outside was all that was left of several months work.

I did not hear Laurie approach. But I caught her gasp at my shoulder, and found her looking into what she could see of the room. She was too stunned to move or cry.

"So sorry. . . ." she said, over and over. "So *sorry*. . . ."

I knew what she meant. It was not her losses she was lamenting. It is the way one feels in the presence of madness. Disarmed, helpless—sorry.

Almost at once the guard was back with the captain and another guard, and a stretcher. The captain patted Laurie's arm. "Sorry this had to happen, Miss Kennedy," he said gently.

Her mind cleared a little then. "Davis?" she asked. "Where's Davis?"

"He's in your office, Ma'am," said the guard. "He's . . . . we think he's dead."

Laurie closed her eyes. She was not really surprised.

The captain took charge then, sent for the surgeon, and asked me to take Laurie to my office. She watched the captain and the two guards with the stretcher pass in front of us and go into the laboratory as if she were in a dream.

"Come on, Kennedy," I said. "Do you want to go home?"

"No, D.W. Just let me sit down somewhere."

She sat in my office most of the morning, not talking, still not crying, wanting to be left alone. She spoke only once.

"I wanted so much to help Davis," she said, and lapsed back into her silence.

Gordon drove her home before noon.

When my men came to work that morning, their indifference to the incident was all the admission I needed that they already knew what had happened. Ross, however, asked if he might go in and help the orderlies clean up the debris.

I was surprised to find King rise and follow him. In the hall door he paused indecisively, then turned around.

"I'd like to go, too, Doc."

There was nothing unusual in his manner, no sign of yesterday's disequilibrium. But this was King with the compulsion for fastidiousness asking to mop up after Davis's slaughter. He saw me hesitate.

"It's all right, Doc. Honest."

I took the chance because of what I hoped was happening to him. It could be a wholesome thing for him to get his hands dirty. His fastidiousness was an inverse symbolism. It was important for him to break his compulsion for cleanliness, because it was an external denial of internal violence. If he could go to the laboratory and clean up Davis's mess, it might mean that the volcano inside of him had been dispelled.

Later I glanced in on the laboratory and on King. He was working without frenzy, with a quiet air of satisfaction. His clothes were spattered with blood and gore. When he noticed

351

me, he stopped working long enough to show me his hands. "Look, Doc—cleanest dirt in the world, huh?"

Ross heard him, and in a flash of insight understood that something important was happening to King. He straightened, gave King a fraternal salute, and they both went back to work.

When Laurie wanted to talk the next day, she admitted that the test tube had not broken, that Davis had tried to choke her.

"I thought he was all right when I left in the afternoon," she said. "I thought the mood had passed. He seemed quieted." She looked appealingly at me. "I really meant to tell Doctor Stevens yesterday, D.W."

"Sure you did. Want to tell me how it happened?"

"I guess so." She closed her eyes wearily for a moment. Then she spoke quietly and dispassionately. Davis had been under great mental pressure for several days, she said. Spells of depression had occurred before, but they had always passed. But when my men began checking in every hour that day, Davis became distracted. He wanted to know what she knew about his past, and what I had told her about him. Did she know he was a killer?

She told him that she had known that, when he came to work for her. But who had told her, he had demanded. He seemed to have forgotten that those things were a matter of record. Even when she reminded him of this fact, he still insisted that my boys and I were plotting to frame him, to get even for the trouble he had made in my office. He asked Laurie if she thought that because he had killed before he would always be a killer. She had answered, certainly not—hadn't she proved that by working with him for almost two years?

Then he asked why she hadn't made him kill his own animals instead of having the other technician do it. Did she think he was afraid to kill them? She said she was sure he wasn't afraid of anything.

352

"Never say that to a killer, D.W.!" she said wryly. "He said he'd show me he wasn't afraid. He grabbed one of the animals and wrung its neck with his bare hands. Heaven knows I've killed hundreds of animals myself, and have seen hundreds more killed, but never in a frenzy like that! Then he turned on me.

" 'You'll never believe I'm not afraid of anything until I show you I'm not afraid of you, will you?'

"And he started for me. Believe me, D.W., I tried to tell him I'd be ever so glad to take him at his word. I don't like being choked! It was some disturbance in the hall, or in your office that distracted him." I didn't tell her about King's outburst. I let her think it was a commotion in the hall. "Whatever it was, it saved me," she said.

She slipped out of his grasp and began to talk to him, as much to quiet herself as him, she said. I had come in a few minutes later when she was bandaging her throat.

"I was very rude to you, wasn't I?"

"You were scared," I replied. "Why didn't you let us help you, Kennedy?"

"That's hard to understand, isn't it?" she said. "I was the only friend he had, and he seemed to need someone. With all this talk of rehabilitation I thought he should have his chance, too. I thought I could handle him. I did, you know, for months. Then, after I had stuck my neck out so far with you and Stevens, I was too proud to pull it in again. As you say D.W., I'm a prize damn fool!"

"Me too," I said promptly. "I should have backed up Stevens' impulse to lock him up. So, as one damn fool to another—" I held out my hand, "it's nice to have you with us."

"*Still*, you mean," she said drily. "Well, it's very, very mutual." Then she sobered. "Will I have to leave, D.W.? I've caused so much trouble."

"You mean you'd stay?" I asked.

Her eyes widened, and I felt the old quiet and the old strength in her.

"Why not? If Stevens will let me. I'm not afraid, if that's what you mean. I've never been safer than I am now."

"You're right about that, you've got 2,000 men watching out for you," I said. "Make that 2,001."

"That's nice, D.W." After a minute she added thoughtfully, "I guess I'm a scientist, all right, right down to my subconscious. Why else would I come to you to put my records to bed that day? I guess I knew I'd need them to start over again."

It was not hard to reconstruct the events of the last two days. Davis knew the cons were "on to him," and that the administration was "wised up." With his mounting madness and his suspicion of me and my men, knowing that Laurie had been called into the CMO's office and that I had seen the bandage on her throat, he realized he was a marked man.

In such circumstances the ordinary criminal would have sought the protection of immediate isolation through the warden or the captain. The other course open to him would have been to fight out the first assault against him, or take his own life before the prisoners could get him.

The prisoners ordinarily will take justice into their own hands without giving the authorities a chance to prevent disaster. In this case they had not, perhaps out of respect for Laurie's work. But Davis knew they would not delay long. He realized that if he went out into the yard or back into the cell block that night, he would be killed.

The thought of suicide undoubtedly went through his mind, in view of the hopelessness of the situation. But psychologically it is more probable that the obsessions and compulsions released in him when he decapitated the animal in the presence of Laurie earlier in the day had mounted until he was no longer capable of cool thought, but only of madness and frenzy. Once the killing orgy started, it could not terminate until the last living thing was destroyed—himself.

Somehow he held himself in check until the guards made the last night count at ten o'clock. There would be no further check for eight hours. It was after this that he began the slaughter which cost him his own life at his own hand. The autopsy placed the time of his suicide at about eleven o'clock.

However, when his body was found, there was not only evidence of self-destruction but also of a beating which had been administered several hours after his death. It is probable that the kitchen crew, reporting to work at five o'clock in the morning, and having their bead on Davis anyway, found his body in the laboratory and administered the posthumous clubbing. He was barely recognizable. But no one among the orderlies, the convict nurses, or the kitchen crew, the only ones who would have had access to the corridor, knew "nothin' about nothin'."

Connie illuminated this *coup* for me.

"He killed hisself, all right," he said. "Maybe it was the only good thing he ever did. They beat him up as a lesson to the rest of the cons. They couldn't let them think he got off as easy as suicide."

The death of Davis marked the end of much of King's antagonism toward life. From then until I left the penitentiary he was more mild and positive-thinking than I had ever seen him. I thought of Laurie's wishful words about Davis, "I think his violence is all behind him."

I sometimes had that feeling now about King. But it was only a feeling, and not one that could be assured by any of my professional tools. It was possible that King had "lived out" his own violence in watching and suffering over Davis, whose pathology was so like his own that he identified himself with it. He hated Davis because the latter represented his own pathology. In hating Davis, he had come to hate his own pathology. His catharsis was completed, perhaps, when he got his hands dirty cleaning up the laboratory.

King would have reasoned that his violence was always in the nature of a judgment on an unworthy or guilty person, while Davis struck out blindly and attacked indiscriminately. King would have said, "He just blows his top and kills for pleasure. I have reasons." This distinction is indefensible and pathological, of course, but it represents a difference between the two men that gave King a much better prognosis for the future than Davis ever had.

King had many release valves for his aggressions. He had goals, even though his method of reaching them was not admirable. Those goals were beauty, quality, wealth, independence. Davis had no goals, except self-destructive ones. King had internal means of reaching his goals: his ambition and his creativeness. His art was a means of skilled functioning and one that gave him pride and satisfaction. Davis's work only deepened his preoccupation with destruction, for it was more than coincidental that he had chosen as a profession a study of disease, decay, and death in a laboratory. King had no preoccupation with death, just a painful idealism about life and a passion for perfection. He ran amuck only on the forces in life and people which "counterfeited" perfection.

Though the two men committed the same crimes, it was not for the same reason. They exemplify strikingly, if pathologically, Freud's concept of *Eros* and *Thanatos* complexes, *Eros* being the will to live and function, which was strong though confused in King, and *Thanatos* being the will to destroy and to die, which was strong and clear in Davis to the end.

19

THE NEARER the time of my leaving came, the less my men talked about it. It was not only the press of last minute work that occupied them. Inherently, the deeper their feelings ran, the less they were inclined to show them.

Punch plugged my Italian villa again.

"You always talk about doin' a study in genius, how about writin' somethin' real sharp about *Il Duce* on the spot, huh?"

"How would you like to read what I wrote about *Il Duce*, Punch?" I asked.

"Yeah," he said resignedly. "You *Americanos* ain't got no sense o' proportion. You better think it over, Doc. It's the chanc't of a lifetime."

Gibbs ribbed me goodnaturedly about the money to be made in cars. "You'd find out, Doc, if you ever bought a new one." I could run his books, he said, and he'd take care of the sales. That way everything would be legit.

The Friar verbalized his intention of going straight one day.

"If you'd a told me I could be honest for three years an' like it," he said, "I'd a laughed right in your face. No, sir, I just ain't got no taste for prisons no more. This one cured me. I don't mean because it's so bad, Doc," he protested quickly. "It's because it's so good. I wouldn't never get a easy go like this again. It's too much for a man to expect." He looked wistful. "I've had the best an' the worst in stir," he said. "I got my back beat off in

one, and my head went soft in another. . . . An' somethin' else,"
he went on, "the way I figger now, even if I make big dough in
hot cars, what with doin' a stretch every few years, durin' which
I make at most thirty cents a day, it kinda works out that I ain't
been so prosperous, after all. I could do better pittin' peaches an'
keepin' my health."

Beneath these good reasons for going straight was a better
one. Gibbs' young son had asked him to go into the contracting
business with him when Gibbs came up for parole. Gibbs
proudly showed me his boy's letter, but he would not talk about
it. He was superstitiously afraid of talking a good thing to death.

Scott, King and Connie said nothing about my going. Connie
worked harder as the last days sped by, he moved more promptly
to follow my instructions, and was a little less boisterous, but that
was all.

I talked to Ross in the last month. I had something on my
mind regarding him, and so did he. I let him speak first.

"You're leaving soon," he began. "I'll be out in six months.
I want you to know how things are with me."

For a moment he studied how to put it.

"I haven't anything sensational to say, Doctor," he said.
"Maybe I'm over-cautious, but I can't truthfully shout about a
miracle. But I can say I have hope now, for the first time in
years. The future begins to make sense. Or rather, I feel I can
make sense out of it."

His face would never lose the lines of shock that the freak
turn of his life had left. But the despair had lifted gradually.

"What did the trick?" I asked.

"Work," he said at once. "The chance to use my head and
hands in this place, instead of being strung up by my wrists." He
smiled. "Like I said, you may tell the Department of Justice I
thank them."

"I'll do that, Ross."

"Engineering is an exact science," he went on without

prompting. "It's mathematical, logical, predictable. Maybe I'm learning to do the same kind of thinking about myself. You know—lay out the problem on paper, think it out, study the obstacles, draw a map, so when the damn thing hits you, you have a plan."

This technique is inherent in *topological psychology,* borrowed from Ross's own field of mathematics and chemistry: valences and vectors—knowing one's weaknesses, computing one's compensatory strengths, establishing one's thresholds of resistance, making one's compromises realistically, and living honestly in the present life space, within one's own knowledge of oneself.

We talked about his family. He had reached a clear decision on that. He would relinquish his family emotionally, instead of carrying them like dead bodies strapped to his back. It was too late to put in an Enoch Arden appearance now, he felt. Too many years had passed. His children were married; his wife had a small business of her own. He could not undo the past. He might endanger the future. It was a wrong that could never be righted in this world, like his first sentence to prison. He would continue to send money, and would never forget them, but it was no good being decimated by their memory.

I felt there was strength and sense in what he said, and that there was health in the tissue and marrow of the man. I had seen it coming. So I spoke what was on my mind.

"Where'll you go when you're released?" I asked.

South America, he said at once. His first successes had been there, and there he would always find a job. When I asked him if he had committed himself to a job yet, he said he had not.

"Then I'd like first chance at you," I said.

He looked at me quizzically.

I told him he had done the best work yet on the polygraph, and that I would like to see him finish cleaning up the bugs. I had some men who wanted to put up the money, if I could find the engineer.

His body became quiet, but all his senses came painfully alive.

"The way I see it, I've got my engineer," I said. "How about coming East when you get out, Ross, and working with me for a year or two?"

He had almost stopped breathing as I spoke, never taking his eyes off me. But when I paused, he glanced away, and I could see how it was with him. He was totally unprepared for my offer. He had hope and determination, but confidence—faith in himself or in another's faith in him—still lagged. But if faith was not there yet, gratitude was, inarticulate and overwhelming. His face masked an agony of wishing that made me momentarily sorry I had tempted him. But the agony passed, and he said quietly, "Thank you, Doctor—I'd like to sleep on it."

"Sure, Ross. There's no hurry."

The next day he came to see me. It was all worked out on paper now, he said, where he could look at it. But however clear his decision, it had not been an easy one. He spoke haltingly.

There had been other men in his life who had believed in him, had helped him, been exceedingly kind, taken the long chance, he said. Some of them had been badly paid for their trouble. He had not wanted to hurt them, but when the depressions came, and then dope, the last name on his tongue was sometimes the first name on a forged check.

"Believe me, Doctor, if I thought just a little less highly of your offer, I'd jump at it," he said. "But you're one man in my life I want to stay as far away from as possible, sir. I can't very well betray you in South America."

"Aren't you anticipating failure, Ross?" I asked.

"Perhaps. But I've got to be realistic about myself this time," he replied. "I don't think I'm allowing for failure, though," he came back. "It's more this transference you've talked to us about. I feel a certain dependence on you, and I think I'd feel it